Sci-Fi

Genre Fiction and Film Companions

Volumes

The Gothic
Edited by Simon Bacon

Cli-Fi
Edited by Axel Goodbody and Adeline Johns-Putra

Horror
Edited by Simon Bacon

Sci-Fi
Edited by Jack Fennell

Forthcoming

Monsters
Edited by Simon Bacon

Transmedia
Edited by Simon Bacon

SCI-FI

A Companion

Edited by Jack Fennell

PETER LANG
Oxford • Bern • Berlin • Bruxelles • New York • Wien

Bibliographic information published by Die Deutsche Nationalbibliothek. Die Deutsche
Nationalbibliothek lists this publication in the Deutsche Nationalbibliografie; detailed
bibliographic data is available on the Internet at http://dnb.d-nb.de.

A catalogue record for this book is available from the British Library.

Library of Congress Cataloging-in-Publication Data:
Names: Fennell, Jack, 1983- editor.
Title: Sci-Fi : a reader / Jack Fennell.
Description: Oxford ; New York : Peter Lang, [2019] | Includes
    bibliographical references and index.
Identifiers: LCCN 2019003119 | ISBN 9781788743495 (alk. paper)
Subjects: LCSH: Science fiction--History and criticism.
Classification: LCC PN3433.5 .S28 2019 | DDC 809.3/8762--dc23 LC record available at
https://lccn.loc.gov/2019003119

Cover design by Peter Lang Ltd.

ISSN 2631-8725
ISBN 978-1-78874-349-5 (print) • ISBN 978-1-78874-350-1 (ePDF)
ISBN 978-1-78874-351-8 (ePub) • ISBN 978-1-78874-352-5 (mobi)

© Peter Lang AG 2019
Published by Peter Lang Ltd, International Academic Publishers,
52 St Giles, Oxford, OX1 3LU, United Kingdom
oxford@peterlang.com, www.peterlang.com

Jack Fennell has asserted his right under the Copyright, Designs and Patents Act, 1988, to
be identified as Editor of this Work.

All rights reserved.
All parts of this publication are protected by copyright.
Any utilisation outside the strict limits of the copyright law, without
the permission of the publisher, is forbidden and liable to prosecution.
This applies in particular to reproductions, translations, microfilming,
and storage and processing in electronic retrieval systems.

This publication has been peer reviewed.

Contents

Jack Fennell
Introduction: The Fetish of Origin — 1

PART I   Antecedents and History — 7

José Manuel Correoso-Rodenas
Science Fiction and the Gothic (1770–1912) — 9

Juan L. Pérez-de-Luque
H. P. Lovecraft's 'The Shadow Over Innsmouth' (1936) – Weird Fiction — 17

Val Nolan
Starships and Space Opera (1928–present) — 25

Tom Dillon
New Worlds and Jerry Cornelius (1964–1976) – The New Wave — 33

PART II   Figures, Tropes and Themes — 41

Sara Martín
Iain M. Banks's *Culture* Series (1987–2012) – Aliens — 43

Nathan Emmerich
Isaac Asimov's *Robot* Series (1939–1985) and Ted Chiang's *The Lifecycle of Software Objects* (2010) – Robots — 49

Matteo Barbagallo
Jonathan Nolan and Lisa Joy's *Westworld* (2016–present) – Virtual Life — 59

Lars Schmeink
Square Enix's *Deus Ex: Human Revolution* (2011) – Posthumanism — 67

Marta María Gutiérrez Rodríguez
Joreid McFate's *The Demon Plague* (2004) – Time Travel — 75

Jack Fennell
Alternate Histories — 81

Simon Bacon
Alex Garland's *Ex Machina* (2014) – Science Fiction Vampires — 89

PART III   Issues and Critical Perspectives

Isiah Lavender III — 95
Jordan Peele's *Get Out* (2017) and Ryan Coogler's *Black Panther* (2018) – Afrofuturism — 97

Amy H. Sturgis
Indigenous Futurisms — 107

Christopher B. Menadue
George Miller's *Mad Max* (1979–2015) and Ryan Griffen's *Cleverman* (2016–2017) – Australian Science Fiction — 117

Raffaella Baccolini
Margaret Atwood's *The Handmaid's Tale* (2017–present) – Women's Dystopian Science Fiction — 125

Alec Charles
The Thirteenth Doctor, *Doctor Who* (2017–present) – Gender
Roles and Sexism   133

Thomas Connolly
Disability in Science Fiction   143

Andrew Milner
Science Fiction and Climate Change   149

Mark Bould
Science Fiction and the Anthropocene   155

Chris Pak
Animals in Science Fiction   161

Jeremy Brett
Science Fiction Archives   167

PART IV   Science Fiction Media   173

Dan Byrne-Smith
Science Fiction Comics   175

Mariano Martín Rodríguez
Science Fiction Metafiction   185

Ian Farnell
Alistair McDowall's *X* (2016) – Science Fiction Theatre   193

Bibliography 201

Notes on Contributors 225

Index 231

Jack Fennell

Introduction
The Fetish of Origin

To the newcomer, science fiction (SF) and genre criticism can be confusing and even somewhat off-putting. The differences from mainstream fiction are numerous: the reader must figure out a narrative world that the characters take for granted; background detail sometimes seems more important than foreground action, and the language involved – often consisting of neologisms with no real-life referent – can seem like re-purposed verbiage at best, or meaningless gibberish at worst. One recurring criticism I hear from non-fan students when I teach SF is that the texts seem to demand that the reader do two different things at the same time: follow a narrative, and solve an interconnected series of logic problems. This is not to be misunderstood as a complaint about the workload, for it is rather a response to what they see as a category violation – to them, SF seems like a mish-mash of contradictory things that they could not respond to as 'literature'. With this in mind, my intention is for this companion to serve as a 'way in' for interested non-initiates, as well as more experienced SF scholars; the aim is to combine informative writing with a somewhat informal tone, the better to provide a warm welcome. Some contributors have elected to give overviews of their topics, while others have focused their work through particular texts to give a 'keyhole' analysis.

Popular culture is becoming ever more science fictional. Beyond prose literature, SF permeates all kinds of media: in this book, for example, Dan Smith focuses on SF in comics, Ian Farnell accounts for SF theatre, and almost every chapter makes reference to SF films and TV series; in fact, SF very often draws attention to its medium by masquerading as factual reportage, as outlined by Mariano Martín Rodríguez in his examination of 'fictional non-fiction' in the genre. Self-aware and apparently unconstrained by form, difficult to grapple with as prose but almost omnipresent in its visual incarnations, SF can seem contradictory and difficult; this difficulty is also apparent in the debates concerning its history and definition.

Much can be inferred about the genre from the sometimes-strained arguments regarding its origins. First, how old is it? Is it ancient or modern? There is Lucian's *A True Story* (second century CE), which tells of a fantastic voyage to the moon, followed by an interstellar war; another suggestive text is 'The City of Brass' from the *One Thousand and One Nights* (ninth/tenth century CE), which features robots and other kinds of automata, and serves as the basis for a novel of the same name by S. A. Chakraborty (2017). Another very notable 'progenitor text' favoured by SF critics is Mary Shelley's *Frankenstein* (1818), in which the titular character is a physician making use of science to achieve something that would previously have been depicted as the result of dark magic. More recent again is the work of Edgar Allan Poe, who incorporated new technologies into his stories and wrote a number of science fictional pastiches, such as 'The Unparalleled Adventure of One Hans Pfaall' (1835) and 'Some Words With a Mummy' (1845). Others might point to the *Voyages extraordinaires* of Jules Verne (1863–1905), or classic H. G. Wells novels such as *The Time Machine* (1895), *The Island of Doctor Moreau* (1896), *The Invisible Man* (1897) or *War of the Worlds* (1898).

Others still would credit the pulp-fiction editor Hugo Gernsback (1884–1967) with the creation of the genre – because, after all, he was the one who came up with the term 'science fiction' in the first place, and the majority of the genre's most identifiable tropes acquired their cultural currency through pulp magazines. The breezy, exciting 'space opera' subgenre – think *Star Trek* and *Star Wars* – originated during this time, and several chapters of this book deal directly with that pulp-fostered legacy: for example, Sara Martín examines the multiplicity of sapient alien races in space opera, while Val Nolan focuses on 'starship stories.'

All these standpoints are convincing and justified in their own right; thus, it seems that despite vexed differences of opinion, there is 'no wrong answer' to this particular question – which, of course, inevitably leads to further differences of opinion. This is the main reason why this companion eschews a 'comprehensive' history of the genre in favour of a thematic look at some key stages in its development, with relevant historical detail woven into the individual chapters as needed.

The second bone of contention in the definition debate relates to the term itself: is it about the 'science' or the 'fiction'?

There is a perceived division between 'hard' and 'soft' SF, with the former relying more heavily than the latter on currently accepted physics, chemistry and biology, striving for scientific plausibility and prioritizing problem-solving. Over the latter half of the twentieth century and the early decades of the twenty-first, this kind of exacting scientific detail acquired a moral dimension as humanity's destructive impact on terrestrial ecosystems became horrifyingly apparent. In this book, Mark Bould looks at SF dealing with the 'Anthropocene' and Andrew Milner provides a succinct introduction to climate change fiction; on a related theme, Chris Pak approaches SF from an animal-studies perspective and highlights fiction dealing with extant non-human intelligences here on Earth.

Soft SF tends to focus more on characterization, but the 'soft' appellation is also applied to SF that centres on social research or philosophy rather than the material sciences. As is the case with most genre subdivisions, the boundaries are porous and the continued relevance of the distinction between 'hard' and 'soft' SF is debatable. However, it is useful insofar as it highlights differences of opinion as to how the genre should be defined. Alternate histories, for example, are understood to be intrinsically science fictional by some SF readers, but not by others. In this book, my own chapter on alternate histories is placed side-by-side with Marta María Gutiérrez Rodríguez's contribution on the intersections between time-travel stories, historical fiction and fantasy; the comparisons and contrasts between the two will hopefully illustrate one of the genre's many blurry edges.

Even in works that strive for scientific verisimilitude, there is a threshold beyond which exposition ceases to be useful. Faster-than-light travel, for example, is impossible according to our current understanding of the laws of nature, but most SF texts that feature it operate on the assumption that some kind of unseen 'work-around' has been developed or discovered prior to the story's setting; once the author demonstrates that he or she is conscientiously thorough when it comes to accepted science, more exotic or implausible inclusions can be hand-waved away (usually by invoking technologically advanced aliens). A large portion of recent SF foregrounds the limits of human cognition and makes them a central theme of the story, rather than a handy means to avoid exposition: for example, there is no guarantee that an alien being would be intelligible to us at all, and a number of SF classics tackle this problem of inter-species contact. As human scientific and medical knowledge develops, we are also increasingly faced with the prospect that future generations of humans will be equally unintelligible to us; Lars Schmeink addresses this unnerving possibility in his chapter on posthumanism, while Nathan Emmerich's chapter on robots considers depictions of a humanity placed in a difficult philosophical position by the emergence of artificial intelligences.

The hard/soft divide is not a dichotomy, however, for there are other strands that privilege the fictive aspect over scientific detail or strictly defined genre boundaries: Weird fiction, discussed in the present volume by Juan L. Pérez-de-Luque, foregrounds the unfathomable immensity of deep time and astronomical distance to prompt a sense of existential unease. 'Slipstream' fiction, meanwhile, consciously mixes and matches SF elements with fantasy, horror and other genres in order to capitalize on their shared literary heritage, demonstrated here in Simon Bacon's chapter on science fictional vampires.

Even if we take scientific faithfulness as a defining aspect of the genre, an intrinsic subjectivity remains when it comes to the author's cultural perspective. If the author regards their belief-system as having an empirical real-world existence, it will necessarily inform their understanding of the universe, and thus, their writing. Few critics would advocate that C. S. Lewis's *Perelandra* trilogy be disqualified from the genre on the grounds of its Christian mysticism, and the conflict between science and religion informs several well-regarded SF works. There are also a great many SF texts in which entirely new realities with divergent natural laws are created or accessed, be it through virtual reality, scientific expedition or even drug use.

Such considerations bring us to the issue of non-Western, postcolonial or 'subaltern' SF. In postcolonial cultures, where the reclamation of indigenous traditions and worldviews is a vital part of the decolonization process, SF is remade with distinctive textures and capabilities that do not conform to the Euro-American, techno-scientific worldview that is often taken for granted in the genre. Moreover, indigenous SF literatures reveal the unconscious biases embedded in the supposedly neutral assumptions and values of Western scientism. Old-fashioned adventure tales of heroic Anglo-Saxon spacemen are increasingly comparable to software that proves unable to detect dark skin or recognize black faces – fundamentally flawed in their blinkered focus on the creators' own social bubbles.[1]

Thus, an important aspect of this companion is the emphasis it places on non-white, non-Western, and marginalized SF literatures: Isiah Lavender III gives an edifying and comprehensive outline of Afrofuturism, complemented by Amy H. Sturgis's similarly thorough overview of North American Indigenous futurisms, and Christopher B. Menadue sheds light on Australian Aboriginal SF, contrasting it with the works of white Australian creators. More broadly, this focus on SF from minority perspectives dovetails into several enlightening contributions regarding groups who have traditionally been excluded from, or marginalized within, mainstream SF: Raffaella Baccolini's chapter concerns women's dystopian SF, while Alec Charles looks at the treatment of gender in popular SF TV franchises, with a particular focus on the attitudes of SF fandom communities.

The number of different arguments and hypotheses regarding SF, its origins and its definition speak to the fact that it is most likely the expression of an imaginative instinct common to all human beings. I personally am of the opinion that nobody 'invented' it or has a proprietary claim on it, but mine is just one opinion among thousands; this plurality of viewpoints is, in fact, vital to the genre's health and continued survival. One of the main aims of this companion is to show how SF criticism has likewise expanded in numerous different directions, and to indicate how an interested researcher can approach the genre from a variety of different critical perspectives. In addition to providing an introductory overview to SF and its numerous manifestations, the present volume will, I believe, give the reader an insight into its breadth and depth.

---

1   To take just two examples, see Babatunde (2017) and Townsend (2017) for further details on electronic appliances (such as soap dispensers) that fail to detect black skin.

Part I
Antecedents and History

José Manuel Correoso-Rodenas

Science Fiction and the Gothic (1770–1912)[1]

In 2009, Carol Margaret Davison argued that in H. G. Wells' *The War of the Worlds* (1898), 'the Gothic is [...] distilled at the end of the century into the burgeoning domain of Science Fiction' (223). That same year, Jarlath Killeen showed that Gothic literature had been interested in the development of SF-ish or futuristic topics throughout the nineteenth century (Killeen 2009). It is true that the *fin de siècle* witnessed a blooming of both genres, marking a period in which the conventions concerning both became interchangeable, as Patrick Brantlinger (1980) has argued. Not in vain, Edith Wharton, in the Preface of her ghost stories, highlights the disturbing nature of the turn of *every* century: the Enlightenment at the end of the eighteenth century provoked the appearance of Gothic novel, and the second industrial revolution at the end of the nineteenth motivated a revival of the genre, along with the first golden age of SF.[2] However, the Gothic had been paving the way for the awakening of SF since at least 1818, with the publication of Mary Shelley's *Frankenstein*. This chapter will explore the interrelations between the two genres and show how the so-called classic Gothic (those works produced in the eighteenth and nineteenth centuries)[3] contributed to shaping the twentieth and twenty-first centuries' Gothic SF.

---

1   This study was possible thanks in part to the post-doctoral scholarship provided by the Universidad de Castilla-La Mancha.
2   It can be added to this that the second Gothic revival that took place in literature at the end of the twentieth century. Once again, a period characterized by technological and scientific progress (i.e. computing, genetics ...) led authors to explore the limits of reality.
3   It could be argued that the 'classic Gothic' ended in 1820 with the publication of Charles Robert Maturin's (1782–1824) *Melmoth the Wanderer*. However, in this case I have decided to expand those limits to the end of the nineteenth century, because those were the central decades in which SF awakened within the margins of Gothic.

Since its appearance in the second half of the eighteenth century,[4] Gothic fiction has been narrowly linked to a multiplicity of other sub-genres that have, afterwards, become independent and strong on their own. Probably, the best-known case is that of detective (or crime) fiction. The theme of a mystery that needs to be solved led authors to switch from the fictional and unreal events of Gothic novel to representations of 'real' cases, which Edgar Allan Poe would later transform into crime fiction; a similar process would be followed by SF. The inclusion of fantastic elements in literature was nothing new when the genre was first labelled and developed – it had in fact been a common practice since at least the Renaissance, when Utopian voyages became a popular form of didactic and philosophical literature. With the advent of the eighteenth century, several authors of the Enlightenment recovered this tradition, but used actual science of the time to compose storylines and essays. This marked the beginning of the differentiation between fantastic literature and SF, as Adam Roberts argues:

> One commonsense way of distinguishing science fiction from fantasy might be to connect the former specifically to discourses of 'science' as we now understand the term – to suggest that SF emerges as a distinct cultural phenomenon at the time that modern science (as both a set of specific disciplines and a broader ideological approach to the world) emerges. That is to say, during the 'Enlightenment'. (2014: 451)

Some noteworthy examples of Enlightenment SF are Voltaire's (1694–1778) 'Micromégas' (1730 [1750]) and Hugh Henry Brackenridge's (1748–1816) *Modern Chivalry* (1792). Both of these works include space exploration and contact with aliens, but with very different purposes. The former attempts to make a travel narrative pastiche of Montesquieu's *Lettres persanes* (1721), substituting extra-terrestrial visitors for Montesquieu's Persian noblemen as ironic outside commentators on European society, while the latter only includes a fictional voyage to the moon as part of Brackenridge's homage to Miguel de Cervantes's (1547–1616) *Don Quixote* (1605 [1615]).[5]

---

4 Usually traced to the publication of Horace Walpole's *The Castle of Otranto* in 1764. Nevertheless, in recent years several scholars (Jarlath Killeen, 2013; Christina Morin, 2018) have argued that identifiably Gothic works can be found preceding Walpole's novel.

5 For more information about the 'Prehistory' of science fiction see, for instance, Brian Stableford's 'Science Fiction before the Genre' (2007).

Figure 1. Theodor Von Holst's iconic frontispiece for the 1831 edition of Mary Shelley's *Frankenstein*.

Today, most would consider that the first major milestone in the joint development of Gothic and SF is Mary Shelley's *Frankenstein* (see Figure 1). Even though this is generally accepted, a few objections and some previous examples are worth mentioning. Among the objections, that of Judith Wilt, who argues that: '[o]ut of the basic Gothic motions and machines, William Godwin began the fashioning of the detective story, Mary Shelley the science fiction tale (in *The Last Man*, that is, not *Frankenstein* which is pure Gothic), and Walter Scott the historical romance' (1980: 124). Among the precedents, it must be noted that a year before, the Prussian author E. T. A. Hoffmann published a collection of short stories entitled *Die Nachtstücke* (1817), in which the tale 'Der Sandmann' [The Sandman] was included. The inclusion of the automaton Olimpia and the Frankenstein-like characters of Spallanzani and Coppola paved the way for the later completion of Shelley's novel.[6] This story also poses a question that has been further explored in recent SF: What is the responsibility of the creator towards his 'creature'? Even before that, the so-called first Gothic novel, Horace Walpole's *The Castle of Otranto* (1764) had already depicted what could be considered the first examples of an 'automaton' in the genre: a giant statue that crushes one main character with a discarded helmet, and then frightens another with an enormous gauntlet that seems to act as if

---

6   However, it must be borne in mind that Olimpia was not the first automaton. In ancient times, the Latin author Gaius Julius Hyginus (c. 64 BC–17), in his *oeuvre De Astronomica* describes King Alkinous of the Phaiakians's gold and silver watchdogs. In the Early Modern Period, probably one of the best-known examples is the 'Hombre de Palo' designed by Juanelo Turriano (c. 1500–1585), which used to frighten the citizens of sixteenth-century Toledo.

it were alive. However, as mentioned above, the innovation introduced with *Frankenstein* was the usage of actual scientific methods to develop the plot. For its part, *The Last Man* (1826) opens the door for the future development of Post-Apocalyptic SF. With a plot focusing on a mysterious plague that has annihilated humanity, this (much less studied) novel is truly a precedent for the fearful narratives produced in the twentieth century at the height of the nuclear era – for instance, Richard Matheson's *I am Legend* (1954) or George A. Romero's movie *Night of the Living Dead* (1968).

The years (and decades) after the publication of *Frankenstein* witnessed a notable increase in the interactions between the Gothic and the emerging new genre.[7] America was increasingly involved in these interactions, since many works by key American authors opened the door for the future development of the genre. Among these, probably the most relevant ones are Nathaniel Hawthorne (1804–1864) and Edgar Allan Poe (1809–1849). Hawthorne's novels and stories are famous for the mixture of Gothic and the religious (Puritan) heritage of New England (i.e. 1850's *The Scarlet Letter*), but some of them are good examples of what can be called proto-SF. The three stories that deserve more attention are, perhaps, 'Dr. Heidegger's Experiment' (1837), which anticipates Robert Louis Stevenson's *Strange Case of Dr. Jekyll and Mr. Hyde* (1886) with youth-restoring water that also causes impulsive behaviour, while 'The Birth-Mark' (1843) and 'Rappaccini's Daughter' (1844) explore the limits of science and human nature: in the former, a scientist's attempt to remove his wife's birthmark causes her death; in the latter, the daughter of an apothecary becomes poisonous herself after a life surrounded by her father's experiments with toxic plants.

Poe's contributions to SF have been extensively explored, with some of his works having been labelled as the first examples of 'modern science fiction', as John Tresch (2002) claims.[8] Even if the Gothic facet of Poe's story has been much more widely accounted for, some of them also constitute good examples

---

7   Among the minor examples that were produced during these years, there is one that, in spite of usually going unnoticed, is interesting for what it adds to the aforementioned debate about automata, and also about the limits of medicine. This unnoticed work is José de Espronceda's (1808–1842) 'La pata de palo' [The Wooden Leg] (1835) in which the pursuit of perfection leads the main character to death and madness.

8   Other interesting contributions to this discussion have been made by María Isabel Jiménez González, Margarita Rigal Aragón and Ricardo Marín Ruiz.

of Gothic SF.⁹ Two interesting pieces are 'The Facts in the Case of M. Valdemar' (1845; see Figure 2) and *The Narrative of Arthur Gordon Pym* (1838). The first deals with the limits of life and death, a theme that SF would explore repeatedly decades later, and it is also a good example of how actual science (or what was understood to be science in 1845) can be used to compose a horrific atmosphere and inform the story's descriptive aspects.

Meanwhile, *Pym* is a good example of SF's revision of the 'fantastic voyage' stories of old. As the world grew wider and wider during the nineteenth century, different expeditions tried to find the natural causes of the 'strange' phenomena Euro-Americans were witnessing for the first time. Interestingly enough, this novel links the genre to *Frankenstein* again, for it is the aim of Captain Walton and the crew of the *Jane Guy* to find the North Pole.¹⁰ Finally, Poe's poems and essays deserve a special mention. Beyond 'The Raven' (1845), pieces like 'Ulalume' (1847) and *Eureka* (1848) also contributed to the cosmologic vision of literature, opening the door for later authors, such as H. P. Lovecraft or, more recently, Stephen King.

The last stage of this essay is the Victorian period, when the interrelations of Gothic and science fiction expanded to levels never previously reached, and when former traditions gathered to conceive SF as we understand

Figure 2. Harry Clarke's 1919 illustration for 'The Facts in the Case of M. Valdemar', in which the titular character is kept alive beyond the point of death, through mesmerism. At the time the story was first published, it was widely believed to be an account of an actual case.

---

9   Many other works by Poe belong to the genre of science fiction, such as 'The Unparalleled Adventure of One Hans Pfaall' (1835), 'Maelzel's Chess Player' (1836, on the theme of automata), 'The Man That Was Used Up' (1839) among others.
10 As Jules Verne's Captain Hatteras would do in *Voyages et aventures du capitaine Hatteras* (1864–1865) or Sir John Franklin (1786–1847) in real life between 1819 and 1827, and from 1845 to his disappearance in the Canadian North-West, narrowly linking these stories (and histories) with the myth of *Ultima Thule*, another good example of Classic precedent for science fiction.

Figure 3. H. G. Wells' most famous works.

it today.[11] Names like the already mentioned Robert Louis Stevenson or H. G. Wells make this moment a first golden age of Gothic SF, which will resurge towards the second half of the twentieth century. The importance of the Scottish author to the relations between Gothic and science fiction comes from his novel *The Strange Case of Dr. Jekyll and Mr. Hyde*. The potion Dr Jekyll develops makes him a valuable inheritor of Dr Frankenstein. Both scholars use science to unleash deeply secreted facets of human nature: the urges toward the creation of life and the release of the impulses. On the other hand, Wells opened the door for the future development of many SF subgenres, with works like *The Time Machine* (1895), *The War of the Worlds* (1897), *The Invisible Man* (1897, clearly an inheritor of Stevenson's *Dr. Jekyll and Mr. Hyde*), or the aforementioned *The Island of Doctor Moreau* (see Figure 3).

These novels dealt, in innovative new ways, with topics that had been explored in one fashion or another by previous authors, now including the unprecedented improvement of science and technology at the *fin de siècle*. Time travelling (with the mysterious and dreadful Morlock civilization), the possibility of threats from outer space, and the intersection of ethics and science are some of the key elements of these works. H. G. Wells' contributions to Gothic SF included not only the incorporation of a great deal of scientific knowledge, but also the open debate about how far science should go.

---

11   As works like Darko Suvin's *Victorian Science Fiction in the UK: The Discourses of Knowledge and of Power* (1983) prove.

Lesser explored examples produced during the Victorian Age are those of Oscar Wilde's *The Picture of Dorian Gray* (1890), H. Rider Haggard's novels, or Bram Stoker's *Dracula* (1897). Neither *The Picture of Dorian Gray* nor *Dracula* are usually included within the category of SF,[12] and it is true that science does not constitute the central feature of their plots. However, in some key scenes, such as when Alan Campbell vanishes Basil Hallward's corpse with acid in the former, or when Dr Van Helsing uses a mixture of modern medicine and superstition to explain the mystery of the vampire in the latter, its importance arises. The novels of Rider Haggard, on the other hand, with examples like *King Solomon's Mines* (1885) or *She* (1886–1887), started a new subgenre: the 'lost world' narrative. This new literary mode would have a great influence on twentieth-century SF, from the jungles of Sir Arthur Conan Doyle's *The Lost World* (1912) to the depiction of outer space in the *Alien* franchise (1979–2017).

All this tradition would contribute to the further development of the genre in the twentieth century. All the ingredients shaped the Gothic SF of the previous century had already been explored before the end of the Victorian Age: space exploration, post-apocalyptic disaster, the limits of science, the actual usage of real science to conceive literary horrors, and so on. Probably, the most interesting contribution (beyond the particular scenarios and circumstances) would be that of H. P. Lovecraft and his inclusion of a new wave of cosmic-primordial horror (see Juan L. Pérez-de-Luque's chapter in the present volume). This final mention marks the end of the long way that the Gothic and SF had travelled together since, at least, the eighteenth century.

In conclusion, it can be said that the Gothic and SF, even though they diverged significantly from their common origins, were destined to merge again, creating one of richest hybrids ever found in the history of literature. The mysteries Gothic fiction first brought to the reader were richly adapted by SF authors, who also incorporated their own visions to make of Gothic a greater genre. Together, both Gothic and SF have also contributed to the reshaping of the human mind over the last two centuries, asking questions that not only concern literary scholarship, but all humankind.

---

12 Indeed, the only work by Oscar Wilde that could perhaps be considered SF is *The Soul of Man Under Socialism* (1891).

Juan L. Pérez-de-Luque

H. P. Lovecraft's 'The Shadow Over Innsmouth' (1936)[1]

It is not a new discovery that secrets are an essential part of horror and Weird literature, and H. P. Lovecraft's narrative is not an exception: there are monsters hidden in a farm attic in Dunwich; there are secret ancient cities that hide the origins of humanity in the South Pole; there are characters that hide awful truths, such as Pickman's models or the Old Man that owns a terrible picture at home. However, secrecy and mystery are also integral to SF, a genre that is nominally all about investigation and discovery, and Lovecraft's work – with its unknowable alien gods and unfathomable scales of time and space – is ideal for demonstrating the kinship of these genres. This chapter will explore how the secrets present in Lovecraft's 'The Shadow Over Innsmouth' configure a complex communitarian development that can be read from different perspectives, fulfilling several of the criteria proposed by Jean-Luc Nancy, Matei Calinescu and Maurice Blanchot (see Figure 4).

In the particular case of 'The Shadow Over Innsmouth', there are two key secrets, interconnected but of a different nature, that completely shape the plot and the narration. The first one is the secret held in the seaport of Innsmouth. The interbreeding between humans and the fishlike 'deep ones', brought about by the town patriarch and cult leader Obed Marsh, is the cause of the town's isolation; this is the big social secret that the narrator Robert Olmstead discovers, and it permeates the communitarian relationships shown the text. There is also a second secret, that of Olmstead himself having Innsmouth blood, which will trigger the final twist of the story.

---

1 This chapter is part of a research project funded by the Spanish Ministry of Economy, Industry and Competitiveness (ref. FFI2016–75589-P), whose support is gratefully acknowledged.

Figure 4. *Weird Tales* (January 1942). The magazine had previously rejected 'The Shadow Over Innsmouth' on account of its length; the version printed posthumously in this issue was an unauthorized abridgement.

According to Matei Calinescu, a secret is an 'intentional concealment of information'. The occurrence of secrecy involves:

> A manipulation of the usual coding of communicational messages. A frequent case is that of double coding: a message is coded 'esoterically' for disclosure of privileged information to 'insiders' (the members of a formal or informal 'secret society', the 'cognoscenti', the gifted who can read between the lines or the attentive, passionate rereaders), while at the same time being coded 'exoterically' for consumption by ignorant 'outsiders'. (1994: 444)

Lovecraft develops a mystery narrative in which the existence of a secret is made clear from the beginning of the text, and it is the narrator's investigation that produces the desire to keep on reading. All the references the narrator finds about the seaport are obscure: inhabitants of the neighbouring villages avoid the town and its people; 'people don't like it' (Lovecraft 1936: 270); 'Animals hate 'em' (273), and whenever the protagonist finds someone who is not reluctant to talk about Innsmouth, the information given does not unravel the mystery but complicates it further. In the opening lines, it is explained that the US government and the police launched a massive operation against the seaport, dynamiting many buildings and arresting several citizens. The presence of a hidden truth is evident, because no clear explanation of what the government was doing in Innsmouth is given. Lovecraft develops a controlled information release that plays to the reader's curiosity, what Calinescu calls the 'exploratory' faculty of the reader that makes him or her 'want to learn what comes next' (1994: 448). This resonates with the 'world building' of SF, whereby the reader comes to know the fictional world gradually, through the eyes of a protagonist.

The protagonist's encounter with old Zadok exposes the Innsmouth secret. The old drunk reveals the terrible history of Innsmouth and the pact Obed Marsh made with the deep ones, disclosing what has been kept in silence for decades:

> Everything cleaned up in the mornin' – but they was traces ... Obed he kinder takes charge an' says things is goin' to be changed ... others'll worship with us at meetin'-time, an' sarten haouses hez got to entertain guests ... they wanted to mix like they done with the Kanakys. (Lovecraft 1936: 303)

From this moment onwards Robert Olmstead, an outsider who gained access to the communitarian secret, becomes the prey of an unknown hunter who tries to sneak into his room in the Gilman House.

Innsmouth's secrecy is transgressed in a version of what Abraham and Török define as 'transgenerational phantom', which 'concerns itself with the unwitting reception of someone else's secret' (1994: 168). The transgenerational phantom is strongly attached to genealogies and families, and the inhabitants of Innsmouth have been intermingling with deep ones for decades, creating a terrible family of corrupted blood that is not supposed to be accessible to outsiders. However, Olmstead accesses that secret from the liminal figure of Zadok, who is not active part of the secret rituals but is aware of them (and thus is also an intersectional character in communitarian terms). At the same time, Olmstead himself is not part of the community, so he should not be in possession of the truth, and that is why he must be eradicated. The two individuals who share the secret and are not fully part of the community are condemned to disappear (Zadok) or to be hunted (Olmstead).

The secret of Innsmouth cannot be shared. It is not, in words of Derrida, a 'conditional secret' (1995: 25). More on the contrary, it is an unconditional secret, a secret that cannot be accepted by 'religion, philosophy, morality, politics, or the law' (25); in this, we see a key distinction between SF and Weird fiction – in the former, the discovery of the unknown is a decidedly utopian project, while in the latter, such an endeavour is rarely even possible, and almost never beneficial. The secret of Innsmouth is a secret that cannot be shared because of the terrible social and moral consequences it might have for humanity. Authorities that know about such unconditional secrets, Derrida says, 'are constituted as authorities who may properly ask for accounts, that is, responses, from those with accepted responsibilities' (23). This is exactly what happens in 'The Shadow Over Innsmouth': the secret transcends the local and becomes public, and this is why the authorities react, destroying the entire town to conceal any evidence, as narrated at the very beginning of the tale.

Immortality is one of the cornerstones of Innsmouth. Those who intermingle with the deep ones will breed and give birth to individuals who share 'the Innsmouth look', and who, after a gradual process of metamorphosis, will fully transform from humans into monsters, 'leading to bodily immortality – of a sort – on this earth' (Lovecraft 1936: 286). This fantastic element nullifies Blanchot's proposal of death as a basic communitarian founder. According to him, 'There could not be a community without the sharing of that first and last event which in everyone ceases to be able or be just that (birth, death)' (1988: 9). However, the idea of the gradual birth of a new deep one is, indeed, part of the articulation of the community, which protects its individuals by hiding them in houses from any external threats, rendering Innsmouth into what Jean-Luc Nancy terms an 'operative community':

> One detail that annoyed me was the distribution of the few faint sounds I heard. They ought naturally to have come wholly from the visibly inhabited houses, yet in reality were often strongest inside the most rigidly boarded-up facades. (Nancy 1991: 290)

For Nancy, the inoperative community is characterized, among other things, by its openness to accept and share real death. Operative communities, on the contrary, transfigure death into mythical narratives and mysticism. The seaport of Innsmouth is able to disrupt the rhetorics of death, transforming them into just rhetorics of birth, that of the new-born deep ones, since 'Everybody got aout o' the idee o' dyin'' (Lovecraft 1936: 298). However, in spite of this anomalous feature, Innsmouth shares some other characteristics of the inoperative community.

The first one is the sharing of the secret itself. That secret of miscegenation, monstrosity and immortality provides Innsmouth with a powerful glue that binds its members together. This secret, at the same time, hides evident 'execrable excesses' (Blanchot 1988: 47). It is also clear that the inhabitants of Innsmouth are unknowable, mysterious and isolated, repeatedly described as creepy, repulsive, and lonely. That sense of alterity is also a key point for the inoperative community. People from Innsmouth reflect the 'strangeness of that antisocial society or association' (Blanchot 1988: 33). And it must be remembered that this social rejection, that sense of alterity, is a reaction to their mixed blood, which is the secret they must hide. As has been stated, the authorities will not allow the secret to disseminate, so without secrecy, the community of Innsmouth would not exist.

The second big secret hidden in the story is that of Olmstead's own Innsmouth blood. There are some hints here and there all through the tale that, for a sharp reader, might reveal the secret of Olmstead's own nature before the very end of the tale, when it is exposed. The final lines of 'The Shadow Over Innsmouth' reveal the narrator's plan to go back to the sea, and integrate into the community of deep ones:

> We shall swim out to that brooding reef in the sea and dive down through black abysses to Cyclopean and many-columned Y'ha-nthlei, and in that lair of the Deep Ones we shall dwell amidst wonder and glory for ever. (Lovecraft 1936: 335)

This secret has a pure narratological effect. Recalling Calinescu's words, the conscious re-reading of the text for a second time, after we know the truth, will clearly expose the clues about Olmstead's family, solving the small 'intertextual puzzle' (Calinescu 449) proposed by Lovecraft under the narratological surface.

At the same time, Olmstead's discovery of his genealogy triggers his decision to join the deep ones, moving away from the traditional operative community to the secret one. The process of unveiling the family secret is divided into the protagonist's own genealogical research, the contemplation of some family jewels and the final physical changes he experiences. Here is where the notion of Abraham and Török's transgenerational phantom is stronger. The secret is transmitted via objects – the jewels – that encode the religious ceremonies performed by the Esoteric Order of Dagon, especially the three tiaras that appear at three different times during the story: at the beginning in the museum, on the head of the priest of Innsmouth, and as part of the family jewels at the end. Those treasures are emblems of the unspeakable family secret, and they represent the symbolical inheritance of the 'original sin' performed by Obed Marsh, great-great-grandfather of the protagonist.

The two secrets of 'The Shadow Over Innsmouth' provide cohesion to the narrative but, at the same time, the one hidden in the town is the necessary force that drives the creation of a community that challenges the traditional, operative community of New England. Considering Lovecraft's often reactionary and narrow-minded values, it makes perfect sense that he decided to annihilate the 'elective' community of Innsmouth, since the secret of miscegenation hidden there threatens Lovecraft's golden dreams of pure New Englandness. SF writers would later attempt to transcend these fearful attitudes towards the Other, but secrecy, conspiracy and mysterious communities remain evergreen themes for SF stories.

Figure 5. *Astounding Stories* (January 1935).

Val Nolan

Starships and Space Opera (1928–present)

A spacecraft capable of interstellar travel, the starship is a materialist iteration of the 'fantastic voyage' trope underpinning the stories of the Argonauts, Odysseus, Sinbad, St Brendan, and the frame narratives of their overtly political inheritors (think Thomas More's *Utopia*, 1516, or Jonathan Swift's *Gulliver's Travels*, 1726). Overtaking the subsequent lunar capsules of Jules Verne, the starship as interstellar conveyance blasts forth from this backdrop with David Lindsay's modernist journey to another star aboard a 'torpedo of crystal' in *A Voyage to Arcturus* (1920). Though Lindsay 'conflates science with magic' for a novel which 'in its episodes is science fiction and in its overall structure metafictional fantasy' (Rabkin 1977: 149), the former aspects build upon the scientific romances of Verne, H. G. Wells, and others to clear the air of medieval sky-ships and prepare for the launch of recognizable modern starships in the pulp magazines of the 1920s and 1930s.

While the etymological credit for the terms 'star-ship' and 'starship' must go to a pair of nineteenth-century spiritualist texts (*Oahspe: A New Bible* by John Ballou Newbrough in 1882 and *The Pageant of Life* by George Barlow in 1888), the word's first appearance in a science fictional context is usually dated to Raymond Quiex's 'The War in Space' (*Boy's Magazine*, October 1926) where a diabolical scientist 'travelled, aboard his starship, to Ikon, where he obtained supreme power'. Standard enough fare for an era when writers displayed little interest in the experiential aspects of star travel and 'just wanted to put their protagonists in new exotic locations' (James 1999: 257) as fast as possible. More influential than Quiex was E. E. 'Doc' Smith's *The Skylark of Space*, which was 'written in the late 1910s, but not published until its 1928 serialisation in *Amazing Stories*' and much revised before its collected edition in 1946 (Roberts 2007: 180).

Though Smith does not announce his titular craft as a starship, it is undeniably an interstellar vessel. Moreover, it is very consciously presented as a *machine* rather than the prevalent 'magic carpet' version of starflight, which would flit across magazine pages for years to come. Smith, though still hand-waving the challenges of interstellar distances, places much emphasis on things like the design of gyroscopes, the internal arrangement of his craft, and celestial navigation. In the process, his scientist-explorer protagonist assembles not just a starship, but also a stereotype which later comes, in retrograde fashion, to define the topical and rhetorical focus of 'hard' SF. *The Skylark of Space* thus helped to solidify the model of SF propagated by era-defining editor Hugo Gernsback, who, as Brian W. Aldiss once put it, reduced SF to 'stories built like diagrams, and made clear like diagrams, and stripped of atmosphere and sensibility' (Aldiss 1973: 211). But in spite of this, *Skylark* offered a versatile, infinitely customizable architecture around which later writers could construct their own starships through ever-evolving stylistic and formal variations.

For example, Frank K. Kelly's 'Star Ship *Invincible*' (1935) introduces the notions of dimension-hopping and the starship as a platform for the observation of spatial anomalies – in this case, a 'sink hole' in space, which Isaac Asimov deemed 'the first fictional reference to black holes' (1984: 55). A few months later, Murray Leinster (pseudonym of William F. Jenkins), offered readers the starship *Adastra* in 'Proxima Centauri', a story with 'a greater appreciation of interstellar distances and the problems of staying within known physics'. Though 'heavy on theatrics', 'Proxima Centauri' successfully depicted how passengers on years-long interstellar trips would be vulnerable to 'mutinies, angst, and utter boredom'. Later captained by the likes of Arthur C. Clarke, Edmond Hamilton, Robert Heinlein, and Samuel R. Delany, the starship developed across the following decades from an expedient protagonist delivery system to an integral setting in and of itself. This long voyage towards depth and technical realism – or at least consistent scientific fantasy – culminated in the starship's post-Second World War prominence on both page and screen.

While these starships remained firmly under the control of their crews, the evolution of interstellar craft into characters in their own right would come with Anne McCaffrey's *The Ship Who Sang* (1969), wherein physically disabled children are given the option to serve as the 'brains' of starships. Later variants on this idea include Alastair Reynolds's *Revelation Space* sequence

(2000–2006) – where starship drives are secretly held in energetic equilibrium by a disembodied brain – and by the embodiment of a starship within a human head in Ann Leckie's *Imperial Radch* series (2013–2015). Fully artificial consciousnesses, meanwhile, are epitomized by the near-godlike 'Minds' of Iain M. Banks's *Culture* novels (1987–2012), largely benevolent but idiosyncratic starships defined by their rationality, righteousness, and tendency towards irreverent humour.

Such a multiplicity of stories and technologies, and over a century of publication, would seem to defy categorization. And this without exploring more exotic forms such as biological starships, as in Robert Sheckley's 'Specialist' (1953), or the television series *Farscape* (1999–2003); solar sailing craft accelerated to relativistic velocity (see Cordwainer Smith's 'The Lady Who Sailed the Soul' (1960), or Larry Niven and Jerry Pournelle's *The Mote in God's Eye*, 1974), and starships carved out of asteroids (Milton Lesser's *The Star Seekers*, 1953) or small moons (the Plutonian satellite Nix in Kim Stanley Robinson's *2312*, 2012). There are nonetheless several ways of organizing starship stories, the most useful of which for discussing narrative variation is to divide them into four broad categories: the sleeper starship carrying passengers and crew in some form of suspended animation (as in Clarke and Stanley Kubrick's *2001: A Space Odyssey*, 1968); the starship crewed by generations of people born and trained on board who may never see their destination (say Molly Gloss's *The Dazzle of Day*, 1988, or Ursula K. Le Guin's 'Paradises Lost', 2002); the relativistic starship, which takes advantage of time dilation at close-to-lightspeeds so that long trips will seem much shorter to the passengers; and, finally, the faster-than-light starship, which transcends our current understanding of physics and which tends to dominate mass media storytelling.

Each category comes with a particular set of generic expectations, with 'the length of the journey clearly [making] a difference to the narrative demands' (James 1999: 260). Edward James summarizes the challenges as follows:

> If it is measured in months, the writer might concentrate on the interpersonal problems arising when a small group of people live together in a claustrophobic environment; if it is measured in centuries, the narrative is likely to focus upon social change and conflict within the community of space travellers. But the solution found by most writers has been to minimize the length of the journey [...] If the journey itself is not to take over the narrative, it must be as speedy as possible. (James 1999: 260)

So, for example, the cryogenic sleeper or gene-seed ship – the latter carrying frozen embryos instead of adults – 'changes the story pattern by eliminating the social aspects' inherent in the generation starship narrative (Caroti 2011: 17). Equally, relativistic starships offer writers the challenges and opportunities of depicting time dilation, while a faster-than-light craft, in eschewing realistic limitations entirely, 'shrinks the galaxy and allows the writer to imagine galactic conflict to be not unlike global conflict on Earth' (James 1999: 264).

Sleeper ships are popular in film and television (think the *Alien* franchise, 1979 onwards) as they allow storylines to begin as late as possible and so harken back to the pulp notion of the starship as conveyance. That said, many authors explore the dangers of 'leaving several centuries of travelling exclusively to automated processes' (Caroti 2011: 18), and the implications of technical failure (as in K. A. Applegate's *Remnants*, 2001, or the film *Passengers*, 2016). This implied rejection of Gernsbackian mechanistic faith – part boyish 'Gosh, wow!', part *Popular Mechanics* – becomes overt in what the *Encyclopaedia of Science Fiction* calls 'the myth of the ark' and in which Fredric Jameson saw 'nothing but a pretext for the spectacle of the artificial formation of a culture within [a] closed situation': that being the generation starship.[1]

Don Wilcox's 'The Voyage That Lasted 600 Years' (1940) is the first story to commit entirely to the generation ship concept. Though never rising above the prose style of its day, it is at least innovatively structured as a series of vignettes following a 'Keeper of Traditions' who wakes from hibernation every century and witnesses increasingly traumatic upheaval among the ship's inhabitants. Common ideas of violent revolution, degeneration, and repudiation of the first generation's mission are already apparent here at the beginning of the trope; however, it was up to the ever-present Robert Heinlein to define the generation ship story's most recognizable pattern in *Orphans of the Sky* (1941; 1963) with the descendants of an original crew on a centuries-long interstellar journey having forgotten that they are on a starship. This idea is successfully reworked in Aldiss's *Non-Stop* (1958) and, later again in Gene Wolfe's *The Book of the Long Sun* (1993–1996). Nonetheless, it is in Kim Stanley Robinson's *Aurora* (2015) that the generation ship story achieves both

---

[1] See Nicholls and Langford, 'Generation Starships' in *The Encyclopaedia of Science Fiction*; Fredric Jameson 1973: 57.

its peak and its nadir. A typical generation-ship coming-of-age tale wrapped around a clear-eyed view of the difficulties presented by closed-cycle life support systems, human biology, and the ethical issues of condemning unborn generations to lifetimes in space, *Aurora* serves as a metafictional revolt against those who set the trope's initial course. Deemed by Adam Roberts to be 'the best example of its sub-genre yet written', the novel is uniquely sceptical of the entire interstellar enterprise (2007: 457). 'No starship voyage', Robinson says, 'will work if crewed by humans' (Robinson 2015: 428).

Faster craft – those travelling at a significant percentage of lightspeed – can take advantage of time dilation and associated narrative trickery. Poul Anderson's arresting thought experiment, the Hugo-nominated *Tau Zero* (*Galaxy*, June–August 1967, as 'To Outlive Eternity'; 1970), is the quintessential story of a relativistic starship: en route to a nearby star, the engines of the starship *Leonora Christine* are damaged and, unable to decelerate, the ship carries its desperate crew closer and closer to lightspeed (the tau zero of the title). In the process, the disparity between subjective time for those on board and external time becomes impossibly great, with Anderson dramatizing the emotional and psychological implications of this for his characters as they hurtle through billions of years and countless galaxies. Relativistic starships are also integral to Reynolds's *Revelation Space* novels, where, in carefully constructed plots, the effects of time dilation serve to draw together temporally and cosmically disparate storylines and characters.

Though Reynolds largely shuns superluminal travel, it is elsewhere ubiquitous, being simultaneously the most recognizable and least realistic type of starship story. The faster-than-light starship tends to bypass the universal speed limit by utilizing space-warping, navigable wormholes, or the higher or lower dimensions of 'hyperspace'.[2] Representative examples include the 'jumps' of Asimov's *Foundation* series (1940s and 1950s) and *Battlestar Galactica* (2004–2009); the inertia-less drive of E. E. Smith's *Lensmen* series and its descendants in the work of Heinlein, Niven, and Reynolds; the 'jumpgates' of *Babylon 5*, also seen, with variations, in the work of Banks (*The Algebraist*, 2004) and Leckie, and the TV series *Stargate SG-1* (1997–2007); as well as

---

[2] See Stableford and Langford, 'Faster Than Light' in *The Encyclopedia of Science Fiction*.

Figure 6. *Star Trek: The Next Generation*'s USS Enterprise NCC-1701-D, episode 1.21, 'The Arsenal of Freedom' (Gene Roddenberry, 1987–1994).

the barely distinguishable 'hyperdrive' of *Star Wars* and 'warp drive' of *Star Trek* (see Figure 6).

Though the illusion of plausibility remains sacrosanct in many starship stories, a reliance on these FTL tropes can lead to artistic lifelessness or, worse, fossilized canonicity. Warp drive is a case in point, typifying the often unimaginative fashion by which superluminal space is depicted on screen as sedate and counter-intuitively unremarkable.

An additional upending of convention is occurring on the literary front, with the publishing industry responding to demand for works by women and writers of colour. Moving further away again from the masculine Gernsback ideal of dry, precise physics, a new generation of authors are providing fresh riffs on the established starship leitmotifs of space opera, military SF, and coming-of-age narratives. These include not just Leckie, but Becky Chambers's *A Long Way to a Small, Angry Planet* (2014), the volatile and complex universe of Yoon Ha Lee's *Ninefox Gambit* (2016), the body horror of Kameron Hurley's *The*

Stars are Legion (2017), and the Afrofuturist adventures of Nnedi Okorafor's *Binti* series (2015–2018). Beneath these lies an even more vibrant and diverse ecosystem of online short fiction (including *Clarkesworld*, *Strange Horizons*, *Lightspeed*, *Tor.com*, *Uncanny*, and many others) which in scope rivals – and in terms of literary merit easily exceeds – that of the pulps almost a century before.

Such relentless evolution makes clear that starships in SF do more than simply link planetary systems. They ply richly imagined routes between subgenres and even across the barriers between mediums. From stories inspired by maritime adventures to those grounded in astrophysical accuracy, from literary fiction to television, comic books and videogames, from widescreen space opera to nuanced character studies, starships are instruments of peace, war, exploration and commerce (legal or otherwise), and, ultimately, vessels for human stories. More than that, however, starships are vehicles for science fiction's own transformative journey over the last 150 years. They are propelled less by antimatter or improbability than by the unstoppable engine of our imaginations.

Tom Dillon

New Worlds and Jerry Cornelius (1964–1976)

The 'New Wave' was a loose association of UK and US writers, initially based around the London SF magazine *New Worlds* under the editorship of Michael Moorcock, during the mid- to late 1960s (see Figure 7). This movement included such authors and anthologists as J. G. Ballard, Brian W. Aldiss, Thomas M. Disch, Pamela Zoline, James Sallis, Damon Knight, Judith Merril, Harlan Ellison, and Samuel R. Delany. New Wave writing is generally characterized by the inclusion of a range of images taken from popular culture and the wider media landscape, set within experimental forms, often depicting societal decline through the metaphor of entropy (the movement of energy from high to low levels of concentration and order). The movement aimed to both expand the SF idiom and to add avant-garde techniques to the genre, to better represent contemporary society.

Though a succinct definition, almost every clause has been questioned, both by those involved, and by the host of reviewers, critics, and academics who have sought to understand the ephemeral but influential movement. Its periodization in the 1960s has been problematized by Rob Latham, who has shown how in the US, writers such as Fritz Leiber and Philip José Farmer had included challenging subject matter as early as 1950 (Latham 2006: 252). In the UK, writers such as J. G. Ballard, and Brian W. Aldiss had been experimenting with form and content in SF magazines for almost a decade before the New Wave supposedly arrived. The term's application itself is hotly debated, with Moorcock suggesting that it should not apply to *New Worlds* (Moorcock 1978: 219) and Samuel R. Delany that it can only apply to the magazine in the 1960s (Delany 1994: 69). Many critics have either questioned or dismissed the American New Wave as either more diffuse than or derivative of UK writing

Figure 7. *New Worlds* 191 (June 1969). Cover illustration by Mal Dean. Reproduced with kind permission from Libby Houston.

centred around *New Worlds*.[1] While most agree that the movement introduced both new content and innovative forms into the genre, the reasons and aims attributed to this introduction are multiple: for some, the increased sophistication was a method of improving SF; for others the 'revitalisation of the literary mainstream' by genre fiction. Others have suggested that the aim was to produce a truly new fiction, positioned somewhere between popular and

1   See Luckhurst 2005: 142; Latham 2005: 212; James 1994: 176; Greenland 1983: 168; Priest 1978: 170.

avant-garde writing, and visual and textual practice.² The term New Wave, in terms of its geographies and times, its essence and aims, would seem as dissonant, disordered, and diffuse as its defining metaphor of entropy (Greenland 1983: 10; 192–194).

One particular figure of the New Wave, however, demonstrates more substance and shared purpose than the arguments cited above suggest possible. *The Nature of the Catastrophe* (1971) is a collection of short stories by a range of British and American writers, all using the same character. Jerry Cornelius was first introduced to *New Worlds* in a short story by Michael Moorcock in 1965, as 'an experiment, an example [...] of the anarchic approach to SF story telling' ('An Effective Use of Space', 2). The example was followed by James Sallis, an American living in London who saw the stories as a form in themselves, and later by a host of other writers, including Norman Spinrad, Brian W. Aldiss, and M. John Harrison. Jerry Cornelius became a 'house character' for not only *New Worlds*, but the New Wave itself. Donald Wollheim called Cornelius 'the best – or perhaps it ought to be the worst – example' (1971: 104) of the movement (see Figure 8).

Figure 8. Jerry Cornelius, as depicted by Harry Warren (aka Harry Douthwaite) for *New Worlds* 157 (December 1965).

The 'Introduction' to *The Nature of the Catastrophe*, written by James Colvin, frames Cornelius as a 'real' but mysterious figure (1971: vii), by listing the various journalists, critics, and authors through history who have discussed him, including actual reviews of Michael Moorcock's novel *The Final Programme* (1969). Michael Kenward's review in *New Scientist* is partially quoted so that it appears to suggest that Cornelius is both a 'myth' (thus, not real) and 'the new messiah' (and so a historical figure), the character hovering between reality

---

2   For improving SF see: Roberts, *The History of Science Fiction* (2005), 230; Broderick 2003: 49; Priest 1978: 164. For improving the mainstream see Moorcock, 'A New Literature for the Space Age': 3). For the 'third-strand' see: Brittain 2013: 120.

and fiction (Kenward 1969: 304). In this way the 'Introduction' is revealed as a hoax. 'James Colvin' was a pseudonym for Moorcock, who used the alias to safely critique SF work through acerbic book reviews in *New Worlds*. Colvin, however, was killed off in an obituary in 1969, by a falling filing cabinet (Barclay 1970: 33), and is here resurrected just like two figures who share his initials, Jesus Christ and Jerry Cornelius.

The book is dedicated to Jorge Luis Borges (Moorcock and Jones 1971: 1), the master of the hoax, balanced between fact and fiction. Borges' short story 'The Immortal' is cited in the 'Introduction' as a work which mentions Jerry Cornelius; the immortal narrator compares himself to 'Cornelius Agrippa', a sixteenth-century occultist (Borges 1962: 145). The other reference to Jerry Cornelius as 'a current myth figure' (Colvin 1971: viii), would suggest the influence of Carl Jung, who argued that myths were a social expression of the unconscious using ambiguous symbols. Both writers, though producing their most influential work well before the 1960s, were popularized in the UK in that decade. The first Borges collection to be translated into English was *Labyrinths*, in 1962, while Jung's *Man and His Symbols*, the definitive touchstone of his work for a wide audience, was released in 1964, a few years after his death.

The two together give us a key to understanding the productive relationship between the popular pulp and the avant-garde influences during the New Wave period. New Wave writers were drawn to the ability of SF to deal with contemporary issues through its images of technological modernity. And yet, Moorcock and others felt that the salience of these symbols were restricted firstly by their anachronism (rockets and space-men were now passé in the age of sex, drugs, and rock 'n' roll[3] – the balance should shift, according to Ballard, from outer to inner space),[4] and secondly by their reliance on simplistic narrative techniques demanded by pulp markets. The SF image would only be able to reflect a turbulent era of social and technological change if it could be liberated from linear narrative, as Borges had done in his many möbius-strip stories. The energy and relevance of popular authors would be married to the sophistication of the avant-garde to create myths of the 1960s. Jerry Cornelius,

---

3   Disch named these the 'troika' of content introduced into SF during the New Wave period, to replace the outmoded spaceship (Disch 1998: 108).
4   Ballard May 1962: 2–3.

a 'viable myth figure for the last half of the 20th century' (Langdon Jones 1969: 2), is then both a character and a technique, a salient, multivalue symbol, liberated within a set of wide-ranging and experimental methods. He is thus able to register both the opportunities opened up in the 1960s (he appears variously as a man and a woman, white and black, working and upper class, adult and child, and pansexual), as well as the violent reaction to those opportunities.

The title story of the book, 'The Nature of the Catastrophe' by Moorcock, best encapsulates the Jerry Cornelius form. Cornelius is sent on a mission by Miss Brunner, backwards and forwards in time for an unspecified reason (see Figure 9). Cornelius' identity fractures, but he is resurrected to the present,

Figure 9. Jerry Cornelius and Miss Brunner in their amalgamated, androgynous form from *The Final Programme*, illustrated by Mal Dean. Reproduced with kind permission from Libby Houston.

freed from the weight of the past. We end unsure as to whether the mission was a positive or negative event. The form of the story is made up of a three-part structure – 'Introduction', 'Development', and 'Conclusion' – each including numbered subsections and interrupted by a plethora of adverts and newspaper articles. Both the dialogue and motives of the characters are vague. Within each subsection, extracts from pop-songs, plays, newspapers, and fiction are mixed in to the dialogue and plot, forming a collage of images, action, and quotation. Reality is shown as fragmentary and unstable, reflected by both the narrative form and the character. Ambiguous motives and meanings resonate across images in place of plot. In its formal elements, the story shows the influence of numerous experimental writers, including John Dos Passos' use of newspaper extracts to reconstruct a historical era via media representation, and William S. Burroughs' cut-up technique with its striking images and plot discontinuities. The story is also evidently influenced by popular culture. Jerry Cornelius is obsessed by a number of commodities, including a stamp collection, his Rolls-Royce Phantom X, and a Royal Albert road bike. The non-existent Phantom X model perhaps alludes to the influence of the spy-novel, specifically Ian Fleming's James Bond. The mission, however, is given to Cornelius in a school in the first scene, and at another point, he is reading from *The Magnet,* a boys' paper which told the story of Greyfriars school, hinting that he belongs more in juvenile fiction than in high-tech futuristic espionage.

There is a movement, then, between avant-garde techniques and popular content, between the past and the future, and between different identity positions of adult and child (his gender is also unstable; he replies to Miss Brunner's gendered encouragement of 'That's a boy!' with the ambiguous challenge of 'That's what you say').[5] This oscillation produces an ironic distancing effect, producing ambiguous and multiple symbols. For example, the Phantom X is reminiscent of both futuristic SF gadgetry and spy fiction, but also a symbol of wealth and commodity culture via its branding, linking popular culture with class aspirations. The movement in time, however, transforms the Phantom into a 'Royal Albert Bike', a symbol of childhood, boy's fiction, and the working class. These symbols emerge not as plot points but as co-ordinates across

---

5   Moorcock 1971: 1–8. For a more detailed analysis of gender play in the Jerry Cornelius stories see Tom Dillon, 2018.

which multiple meanings resonate, allowing a complex reflection on contemporary image-making and culture. The other stories are filled with references to major historical upheavals – the Vietnam war, the Prague Spring, political assassinations in the U.S. – with Cornelius at the centre of them all. The fake chronology at the end of book suggests that he is present or responsible for almost every major atrocity in the twentieth century (Moorcock and Jones 1971: 198–213). Cornelius, like his visions while travelling through time, is constructed from 'fragments of newspapers, buildings, road-ways, cars, planes, skulls, ruins, ruins, ruins' (Moorcock 1971: 6). He allows for resonance then, but also for dissonance, holding together multiple, contradictory and destructive meanings, both the cause and the saviour of the 'catastrophe' of the collection's title.

Although each writer took the character in their own individual direction, each recognized Cornelius as a shared repository of images and techniques for describing the world around them, open as it is to ambiguity, instability, and violence. As well as sharing a universe of characters, the stories reference various other New Wave writers. In 'The Flesh Circle' by M. John Harrison (1971), Cornelius is treated by the nefarious Dr Gelabius, invented by Hilary Bailey (1968). 'The Adventures of Jerry Cornelius' includes a Sgt Glogauer, the Christ-obsessed Jungian protagonist of Moorcock's 1966 novella *Behold the Man*.[6] In 'Lines of White on a Sullen Sea' by Maxim Jakubowski, Cornelius remembers a trip to Vermillion Sands, the surreal location of J. G. Ballard's first published short stories (1971: 175). Finally, in 'Jeremiad' by James Sallis, Cornelius' description of a 'pan on the stove' raising the level of 'entropy' (1971: 48), is reminiscent of 'The Heat Death of the Universe', the widely cited experimental text by Pamela Zoline, in which the domestic chores of a housewife are interpreted via the language of physics (1967: 32–39). These last two references especially link Cornelius to other New Wave works in which narrative and character break down under pressure from historical events and their representation. In Ballard's condensed novels, later collected as *The Atrocity Exhibition*, the protagonist (known under a number of names beginning with

---

6 Moorcock et al., 'The Adventures of Jerry Cornelius,' 129; Moorcock September 1966: 4–58.

T) fragments under the weight of images of adverts and atrocities.[7] Similarly, in Brian W. Aldiss's 'Acid Head War' stories, the central messianic figure of Colin Chateris disintegrates along with language and representation.[8] The name of the collection and title story are themselves taken from the front cover of the July 1968 *New Worlds* by experimental film-maker Stephen Dwoskin, which bore the heading 'What is the Exact Nature of the Catastrophe'.

The New Wave, like Jerry Cornelius, is nebulous, multitudinous, ambiguous and unstable, making it both an indispensable technique for thinking about contemporary society, and in consequence a difficult concept to delineate and define. We might, however, understand Cornelius and his movement as a game or technique through which to understand the world; he is a way of 'staying with the trouble' as Haraway puts it, or in New Wave 1960s terms of unflinchingly keeping with the 'catastrophe' (Haraway 2016: 3).

---

7   The first of Ballard's 'condensed novels' was arguably 'The Terminal Beach' published in *New Worlds* in March 1964. A number of others were published in *New Worlds* between 1966 and 1969 as well as a number of other magazines and journals including *Ambit* and *SF Impulse*, formerly *Science Fantasy*.
8   Aldiss's first 'Acid Head War' story was published in *SF Impulse* in February 1967. However the remaining stories were all published in *New Worlds* between 1967 and 1969. They were later collected together and published as *Barefoot in the Head* in 1969.

Part II
Figures, Tropes and Themes

Sara Martín

Iain M. Banks's *Culture* Series (1987–2012)

Aliens

If science fiction portrays, above all, our anxieties about contacting the Other, then the sub-genre that best represents it is space opera. Hartwell and Cramer report that Wilson Tucker coined this label in 1941, by analogy with horse opera and soap opera, in reference 'to all bad SF hackwork' (Hartwell and Cramer 2006: 10). By the 1950s, space opera already connoted a 'fondness for outworn, clunky, old-fashioned SF guilty pleasures' (12). The 1970s, with a pioneering anthology by Brian Aldiss (1974's *Space Opera*) and the rise of the *Star Wars* franchise, and the 1980s, with Lester del Rey's work as publisher, consolidated as acceptable SF what space opera had been offering from the 1920s onwards: straightforward adventure. Since then, the sub-genre has continued to grow, though always beset by negative criticism prompted by its narrative excess. Many readers who reject SF actually abhor space opera's juvenile fantasies about interstellar travel and weird alien creatures; not even all SF readers find enjoyment in it.

In the 1990s, space opera veered towards the post-modern, a trend led by Scottish writer Iain M. Banks. After the literary ambition shown by the 1960s New Wave, the impact of 1970s feminist SF, and the explosion of 1980s cyberpunk, space opera seemingly offered just naïve entertainment incapable of addressing any serious issue. George Lucas expanded the sub-genre beyond recognition into the realm of the big-budget blockbuster with his second *Star Wars* trilogy (1999–2005), which progressively eschewed the enjoyable adventure of Episodes IV–VI, arguably in a (failed) attempt to earn more respect. Banks, by contrast, applied a subtle sense of humour to his singular Culture series (1987–2012).[1] Hardesty, who finds Banks's SF 'quite preposterous' (2000:

---

1   The volumes in the series are: *Consider Phlebas* (1987), *The Player of Games* (1988), *Use of Weapons* (1990), *Excession* (1996), *Look to Windward* (2000), *Matter* (2008), *Surface*

117) in a paradoxically positive sense, notes that 'Each is a spirited adventure story; but each mocks the very adventure it presents' (116). This pleases many readers since 'the texts operate on the two levels of naïve entertainment and informed commentary simultaneously' (117).

'Not all fictions involving space travel, conflict, huge vistas, and Big Dumb Objects', Sawyer warns us, 'are space opera, which is committed to action and adventure, focused upon the heroic, and frequently takes a series or serial form which allows for either a sense of escalation or constant variations on a comparatively narrow set of themes' (2009: 509). This quite complicates the association of the Culture with the sub-genre, since although the series displays some of its essential elements, it also noticeably lacks certain others. There is certainly much excitement, but in Banks's fiction, the action and adventure are usually of a dark kind; he has no heroes but, rather, astute manipulators, perhaps even anti-heroes. This is due to the central theme of the series: namely, whether the advanced civilization calling itself the Culture is entitled to spread its conception of utopia to, in their view, less fortunate species. Seeing how much they depend on their artificial intelligences – the awesome Minds – many of these other species resist the invitation, even though, as Banks stresses, their own worlds are often hellish (literally in one case). Instead of the rambunctious romps of classic space opera, Banks offers dangerous power dynamics which Culture agents try to alter in their favour, often risking their lives in grisly ways.

As Palmer argues, '[t]he immense void of space is a temptation to the Western imagination', which is why the 'gargantuan conflicts, intrigues, and cruelties [...] given grandeur by their scale, if nothing else', of space opera remain so popular. Banks provides plenty of this but, as Palmer adds, in his 'post-modernizing of the galactic-empire novel' he also 'ends up expressing the anxieties of the postmodern condition' (1999: 88). These anxieties convey not only our fear of the Other but the fear that, as we advance towards the posthuman, we will become our own Other.

In classic colonial adventure, which begins with H. Rider Haggard's *King Solomon's Mines* (1888), the white man is the normative human being that

---

Detail (2010) and *The Hydrogen Sonata* (2012). The novella *The State of the Art* and the short story 'A Gift from the Culture,' both published in 1991, are also Culture fiction. Although not overtly part of the series, *Inversions* (1998) is also, arguably, a Culture novel.

the exotic, 'inhuman' other cannot match. When the imperial scramble to conquer all corners of Earth was finally over, space opera inherited the white supremacist disposition of colonial adventure, displacing to the aliens a mixture of the racial and animal features which white writers (both male and female) considered noxious. In the 1990s, when a new politically correct awareness of identity-based discrimination emerged, it became increasingly difficult to maintain this kind of ethnocentrism. Banks's response was to present an enormously varied gallery of alien species – and to reject humanity altogether.

His Culture citizens are not even human, but descendants of the 'seven or eight humanoid species' that, as Banks himself explained, 'established a loose federation approximately nine thousand years ago' (Banks 1994), elsewhere in our galaxy. Far from being the dominant pan-species, they share their corner of the universe with

> perhaps a few dozen major space-faring civilizations, hundreds of minor ones, tens of thousands of species who might develop space-travel, and an uncountable number who have been there, done that, and have either gone into locatable but insular retreats to contemplate who-knows-what, or disappeared from the normal universe altogether to cultivate lives even less comprehensible.

In Banks's AI-dependent utopia, the humanoid body has become completely alien in comparison to our own limited physiology. The Culture's fully post-human citizens are gifted with a set of controllable glands which allow them to enjoy unlimited pleasure and to control unwanted affects, like fear. These individuals play with their anatomies in many ways: engaging in reversible gender transitions, enhancing their senses, or extending their lifespan almost forever. Their posthuman freedom to choose even ugliness or, more radically, a makeover into another species, is our very own fantasy (and ideal). Yet, the Culture novels are also a bitter reminder that we are not good enough to be civilized at that high level. Thus, in the novella *The State of the Art* a Mind decides, after sending a team to explore 1970s Earth, not to disclose the Culture's existence, using us instead as a control group to test the effects of non-intervention. Banks thus shames his 'plain' human readers, transmitting his own pessimism about humankind.

Unlike most empires of classic space opera, the Culture is not an expansionist political organization for a very simple reason: its citizens do not live on planets but in gigantic spaceships, in orbitals and on artificial planetoids built and run by the Minds. Natural evolution no longer applies to their drastically posthuman nature, though it still seemingly shapes the many diverse alien creatures of Banks's galaxy. Despite his lively imagination, there is, however, a strange blank in the academic work on the Culture, common to all research on space opera and, generally, science fiction: the specific alien imagery is hardly ever discussed, as if it were an embarrassing product of the human imagination rather than a highlight.

We know that the little green man of early SF sinks his roots into remote Medieval folklore, or even beyond into pagan times; he was by no means invented by the efficient illustrators of SF pulp. Likewise, its most popular descendant, the post-Roswell grey alien, also connects with ancient fears that existed prior to the space age. As Moffit shows in his provocative volume *Picturing Extraterrestrials*, we should 'bear in mind that the literal synonym to "extraterrestrial" is "supernatural"' (2003: 18). Yet, whereas the strange sightings of aliens on Earth may be a side-product of our passion for the occult, the alien homes and species that authors like Banks have imagined for us are a fully self-conscious exercise in picturing the non-human, both in looks and behaviour. As SF author Justina Robson stresses, the 'only limits [...] are imposed by the writer's imagination and heart and the readers' or viewers' willingness' to follow the authors' lead (2012: 37). The writer's skills, obviously, are crucial in reaching a consensus with the reader and in avoiding the constant danger of presenting ludicrous aliens that only elicit laughter. Yet, despite the efforts made by writers (and visual artists) to give us a truly amazing gallery of aliens in the last hundred years, we tend to skirt the subject in our analyses of the extraterrestrial. Ironically, we are simultaneously preparing a rich breeding ground for their proliferation with the many books teaching children how to produce illustrated SF, like Stephanie LaBaff's wonderfully titled *Draw Aliens and Space Objects in 4 Easy Steps: Then Write a Story*.

Typically, then, the extant academic analysis of Banks's Culture novels carefully avoids commenting on the look of his aliens in detail, focusing instead on their behaviour. Thus, Caroti argues that the three final novels form a distinct sub-group in the series because they feature 'a host of developed spacefaring races that, for the first time, present the Culture with an environment of equals' (2015: 19). Indeed, Vyr Cossont, the female protagonist of *The Hydrogen*

Sonata, is a Gzilt, a non-mammalian humanoid, who has chosen to have two extra arms surgically implanted so that she can play the extremely demanding musical piece that lends the novel its title. Caroti also writes with great chutzpah about the antics of the species appearing in the other two final novels: the Oct, Nariscene and Morthanveld of *Matter*, or the Pavulean of *Surface Detail*. However, he never stops to consider the mental faculties that allowed Banks to imagine these assorted species, and to depict them in all their bodily alienness with such glee.

This is an important shortcoming because the appeal of science fiction, and its enormous importance as a cultural manifestation, greatly depends on its capacity to channel the immense human potential to describe what only exists in our minds. Reading SF requires a remarkable skill to visualize what writers describe, particularly at a time when – unlike what was commonplace in Victorian times – adult novels carry no illustrations. Banks's Culture novels certainly present a constant challenge, for in order to enjoy his tales, we need to master the rules of each alien civilization and understand what their bizarre members look like as quickly as possible. The Idiran Xoralundra, for instance, a member of the warrior race that wages war against the intrusive Culture to defend their fundamentalist religion, is three metres tall and looks 'vaguely like a small armoured ship sitting on a tripod of thick legs. Its helmet looked big enough to contain three human heads side by side' (*Consider Phlebas*, 12). The creature's 'huge head' is 'saddled-shaped when seen directly in front, with the two front eyes clear and unblinking near the edges' (16). Readers who have trouble suspending their disbelief might baulk at Banks's visual challenge, which intensifies as even more unlikely aliens appear, such as the semi-feline Chelgrians of *Look to Windward* or the medusoid Affront of *Excession*. Even the humanoids require intensive reader collaboration to become fully functional characters, from the three-gendered Azadians in *The Player of Games*, to the squat, ill-looking Xolpe of *Matter*.

Nonetheless, SF's limitations regarding the representation of the alien also limit Banks's novels, despite his remarkable capacity for fabulation. His aliens are evidently based on extrapolating animal features, adding to the mix human behavioural patterns (often our worst ones). Nobody has ever met a real alien, and this is why neither Banks nor anyone else can imagine an entirely non-human, intelligent being different from the many that abound in science fiction. As Justina Robson observes, '[t]he alien territory that we cross in SF is not that of distant planets and otherworldly being but the strange topography of human experience' (2012: 37). Banks and other SF authors push our willingness to collaborate and our reading skills beyond our comfort zone, but we cannot transcend humanity. It is important to insist, in any case, that, as Adam Roberts writes, in our society 'where Otherness is often demonised, SF can pierce the constraints of this ideology by circumventing the conventions of traditional fiction' (2005: 30). This is, then, the genre that best helps us to be aware of our very faulty humanity and to demand a better future – hopefully a utopia like Banks's Culture, perhaps also in a vibrant multispecies galaxy.

Nathan Emmerich

Isaac Asimov's *Robot* Series (1939–1985) and Ted Chiang's *The Lifecycle of Software Objects* (2010)[1]

Whether humanoid or non-humanoid, the robot is a distinctly modern invention. While it is now used to refer to autonomous mechanical and computational beings, the term can be traced to the play *Rossum's Universal Robots* by Karel Čapek, where it referred to soulless artificial people synthesized from organic matter. Nevertheless, certain additional antecedents can be identified. Consider, for example, the creature in Mary Shelley's *Frankenstein*, the Golem in Jewish tradition, or Talos from Greek mythology. All are limited (but nevertheless autonomous) beings created by man or, in the case of Talos, by flawed gods who can be taken as reflecting something of man's nature and the risk of hubris in our creative ambition.

We might then expect the role of the robot in contemporary science fiction to present similar ethical commentaries, and when we reflect on, say, *The Terminator*, *Battlestar Galactica* (original and reboot), or the Cybermen from *Doctor Who*, it is clear that this is the case. In this brief survey, we will first consider the actions of robots towards human beings, before turning to the way human beings treat robots. Inevitably, the work of Isaac Asimov is the primary focus. The representation of broader ethical questions, notably the social implications of robots and AI, will be briefly noted in the conclusion.

---

1   Some of these stories and issues were discussed at a symposium 'Regulating Intelligence: The Challenge of Consciousness in New Forms of Life,' which took place on 27 April 2018 at the University of Newcastle (UK). Thanks to the organizers Dr David Lawrence and Dr Sarah Morley for the invitation to attend.

Ethics and the Actions of Robots

As both the *Terminator* and *Matrix* franchises show, robots' and AIs' treatment of humans is a particular concern within science fiction. For the most part, however, robots are not represented as definitively evil or morally corrupt. Rather, they tend to be presented as morally neutral or amoral; as beings without any inherent moral sensibility.

The author to most explicitly address the issue of robot actions and ethics is Isaac Asimov, in the form of the Three Laws of Robotics, these being:

1. A robot may not injure a human being or, through inaction, allow a human being to come to harm;
2. A robot must obey the orders given it by human beings, except where such orders would conflict with the first law; and
3. A robot must protect its own existence as long as such protection does not conflict with the first or second laws.

The first mention of these laws does not, however, concern the way robots behave towards humans, but with the way they act *per se*. The story 'Runaround' is set on the planet Mercury, and focuses on a robot that has been ordered to harvest liquid selenium; rather than follow this order, it begins to circle the selenium pool. Eventually, the human characters in the story realize the robot's orbit represents an equilibrium between the drive to obey its orders (the Second Law) and to prevent harm to itself (the Third Law). Here, the robot is a futuristic Buridan's Ass. Lacking any decisive factor, it is unable to act in either direction. The difficulty is eventually resolved when a human sets out to collect the selenium instead, invoking the First Law. The imperative to prevent harm to human beings provides the missing decisive factor, and the robot completes its task.

What is interesting about this story is the way Asimov's robots actually work. They are not simply presented as followers of ordered rules. Rather, they are dispositional beings who try to balance competing imperatives. Elsewhere, however, Asimov highlights the distinction between the letter and the spirit of the three laws. In 'Little Lost Robot', the first law is modified in a particular group of robots. They are still conditioned not to injure human beings, but they are not now required to take action if a human being is going to come to harm. Thus, the robopsychologist Dr Susan Calvin speculates that a robot might drop a weight above a human being in the knowledge that its reaction time and strength could prevent the human from being injured. However, once the weight has been released the robot would have no compulsion to prevent injury.

However, Asimov has also explored the inductive expansion of the Three Laws in the form of the 'Zeroth Law', which reads:

> 0. A robot may not harm humanity, or, by inaction, allow humanity to come to harm.

The focus of the first law is usually taken to be physical injury, not least because the notion of 'harm' to a human being could be seen as too broad for a robot to function at all. In the context of the Zeroth Law, this is encapsulated by questions regarding the effects of certain actions on humanity as a whole. This idea is explored in Asimov's *Foundation* Series, but it is first presented in 'The Evitable Conflict'. In this story, a number of fixed-position AIs – which is to say, immobile robots or computers – are used to plan humanity's economic activities on a global scale. However, apparent errors keep occurring. On further investigation, Dr Susan Calman concludes that the machines have induced the Zeroth Law, and the apparent errors are in fact designed to side-line (without injuring or harming) certain politically influential people who are opposed to the role these AIs have in human history.

The story is deeply ironic. The AIs' actions demonstrate that their opponents are correct: humanity is no longer in charge of itself. Equally, it shows that the AIs do not present a threat. Not only is humanity being guided by intelligences far superior to those of mere humans, but those intelligences are also deeply committed to humanity's wellbeing. While the idea may be disquieting, the rule of the benign AIs should not concern any rational individual, or so Calman concludes. After all, given the complexity of the problem, one can hardly suppose humans were ever actually – which is to say rationally – in charge of themselves.

Human Treatment of Robots

Questions about our treatment of robots ask if we might recognize the moral significance of robot consciousness, rather than assuming they are merely objects. Here, parallels with animal consciousness are inescapable. Consider one of Asimov's early stories. Entitled 'A Boy's Best Friend', its main protagonist is a moon-born boy who has a robot dog named Robutt. The boy's parents are planning to replace Robutt with a real – which is to say biological – dog. Whilst it will be less well adapted to life on the moon the parents consider a biological dog superior as, whilst Robutt acts as if it loves their son, the *real* dog will *really* do so. However, the young boy will not countenance giving up Robutt, asking, 'But what is the difference how they act? How about how I feel? I love Robutt and that's what counts' (Asimov 1975).

In this context, we might modify the conversational condition of the Turing Test to a relationship condition: if we can maintain a meaningful relationship with a robot, then we have reason to think it might be conscious. Of course, what counts as a 'meaningful' is open to question. Nevertheless, focusing on human-robot relationships seems to be a common response to the unanswerable question of whether or not robots *really* are conscious.

Asimov presses this point in 'Robbie'. In this story Robbie is a nonverbal android and a companion to a young girl, Gloria. Her mother, Grace, is uncomfortable with the robot and with the level of Gloria's attachment, so she sends Robbie away and tells her daughter that he wandered off. Gloria insists on looking for the Robbie at every opportunity and, when a trip to New York is arranged to distract her, she assumes that this is to continue the search. Gloria's exasperated father arranges for the family to accidently encounter Robbie whilst touring a factory, but the reunion is more dramatic than he intends as, when Gloria sees Robbie, she runs onto the factory floor, placing herself in danger. Robbie saves Gloria from harm and, as a result, he is allowed to come home.

Regardless of whether or not Robbie can or should be discarded, like property, it is clear that Gloria's relationship cannot be treated instrumentally. Whilst it is unclear if Robbie has the kind of inherent moral significance we attribute to human beings, moral significance can and does attach to Gloria's relationship with him. Indeed, in the conclusion of one of his most celebrated stories, 'Bicentennial Man', Asimov intimates that the humanity of the robot can be equated with his relationships.

In this story, Andrew is a robot that has spent most of his life living as a human. His request to be recognized as a human is granted by the World Legislature, partly because he has rendered himself mortal, limiting the lifespan of his positronic brain to 200 years. As Andrew dies, he tries to think of his humanity, but his thoughts turn to the young girl he cared for at the beginning of his life, and the woman she became: the woman who helped him realize his humanity. The significance of this relationship is the very fountainhead of Andrew's (robot) humanity.

Perhaps the best work of literature to address human treatment of robots is Ted Chiang's novella *The Lifecycle of Software Objects* (see Figures 10 and 11). The story is centred on 'digients' – digital indigents that inhabit a virtual reality. Whilst one might object that they are only robots when, as occasionally happens, these AIs are placed within a mechanical unit, the point lacks significance given the issue at hand. Initially lacking any linguistic abilities, although possessing the potential to acquire them, the digients are social beings that acquire their abilities and skills in a manner that is compared to both training animals (particularly primates) and to raising human children. Chiang raises various ethical questions regarding human treatment of digients, including humans who tire of their digient pets; subject digients to maltreatment and torture; and desire sexual relationships with digients. Suspension of the digient – ceasing to run its code – is presented as the midpoint between euthanasia and abandonment, as happens with biological pets. Some try to create adoption centres for digients, but consumers tend not to want one that has already existed for some time. Eventually, interest in digients wanes significantly and the adoption centres become overrun.

While it is unclear what the experience might be like for digients, some humans subject them to torture and, to this end, they remove the 'pain circuit breakers' they were created with. Since it is possible to copy a digient, owners become concerned about their now-verbal digients and try to protect them from being copied. As the story develops, financial support becomes an issue, as there is no obvious economic function that digients can fulfil. Inevitably, a company developing sexual technologies seeks to acquire copies of some

Figures 10 and 11. Illustration by Christian Pearce for *The Lifecycle of Software Objects* (2010). Reproduced with the artist's permission.

digients, with a view to creating and developing their sexuality over a period of years. The human owners of the digients are sceptical of the offer, particularly the possibility of manipulating digients into relationships. However, the digients themselves are sanguine about being copied, and relatively unconcerned about their future (sexual) development, or being altered to like or want something new. Here, Chiang presents us with questions about how we should treat robots (or AIs) that are sufficiently reflective to lay claim to some degree self-direction or autonomy.

Conclusion

Science fiction about robots is replete with ethical questions, some of which we will inevitably face in one form or another, and the best science fiction is always social fiction. One good example of this in relation to robots is the UK TV series *Humans*, adapted from the 2012 Swedish series *Äkta människor*. Here questions about the effect of sophisticated AI on human societies are presented, as well as some possible responses. At the beginning of the story few robots, or synths, have any self-awareness or consciousness. However, this changes in later episodes, whereupon the ethico-political status of synths, and humanity's response to them, comes to the fore. It may well be that it is these questions – the kind that need to be addressed collectively, rather than those of a more individual or interpersonal nature – that will take on the most significance in future.

Figure 12. Still from *Westworld*, episode 2.3, 'Virtù e Fortuna' (Jonathan Nolan and Lisa Joy, 2016–).

Matteo Barbagallo

Jonathan Nolan and Lisa Joy's *Westworld* (2016–present)

Virtual Life

Have you ever thought about behaving in a way that counters the established social conventions? Have you wondered how would it feel to let your instincts loose without giving up on rationality, unifying the Dionysian and Apollonian impulses? Jonathan Nolan, J. J. Abrams and Lisa Joy have considered all these questions in *Westworld*.

For those not familiar with it, *Westworld* is a TV show produced by HBO and based on the film of the same name, directed by Michael Crichton (see Figure 12). The titular Westworld, modelled after popular media representations of the American Wild West, is one of many high-tech theme parks present in the show's world, in which robots called 'hosts' entertain human guests. The guests enter the park knowing that they can do anything they wish: they can follow scripted adventures, in which the hosts have been pre-programmed with certain behaviours and responses to tell an immersive story, or they can simply ignore the plotlines to interact with and even kill the hosts, with the certainty that none of the latter will hurt them in return.

This freedom of action is not something new: virtual life spaces have existed for years. The first ones that spring to mind are *Second Life*, *Habbo Hotel*, *The Sims Online* and so on, up to more fantastic examples, such as *World of Warcraft* or *The Elder Scrolls Online*. These spaces offer the possibility for individuals to reshape their lives as they please, from building a new house to changing gender and so on. SF, however, is uniquely positioned to explore and dramatize the psychological implications of virtual spaces where seemingly anything is possible.

This important feature has been called 'sensemaking', and Karl Weick has identified its seven distinct features – identity, retrospect, enactment, social, ongoing assumptions, cues, and plausibility (1995: 17–18) – which are further elaborated by Amber Marshall, using the hypothetical situation of a crying student: students and teachers first bring their *identities* to bear on the situation by noticing relevant clues (i.e. the student's books have fallen on the floor); they then *retrospectively* interpret those clues to get a sense of what happened and how they should respond; they then *enact* that response (e.g. picking up the books, punishing the child who knocked the books over) to try to resolve the problem; the *social* aspect arises from the participants' attempts to achieve a shared understanding of why the crying child is upset, with reference to the fifth and sixth aspects – *ongoing assumptions* about the 'normal' state of affairs in the classroom (e.g. children should be quiet while the teaching is speaking) and *cues* that help them to make sense of the crying; the crisis is resolved when a *plausible* (but not necessarily accurate) cause for it is inferred – the teacher concludes that another child knocked the books over, and takes appropriate action. With regard to sensemaking, it does not matter if there was 'more to the story', since the problem has been resolved (2014: 108).

Sensemaking is essentially what the guests look for on their trips to Westworld. As the antagonistic Man in Black (portrayed by Ed Harris) says, 'This whole world is a story. I've read every page except the last one. I need to find out how it ends. I want to know what this all means' (see Figure 13).

Figure 13. Still from *Westworld*, episode 1.05, 'Contrapasso' (Jonathan Nolan and Lisa Joy, 2016–).

For the Man in Black, the real world lost all meaning on the day he first entered Westworld. We eventually learn that he visited the park for the first time forty years earlier, as the apparent protagonist William, and that we have in fact been watching the story unfold in two different time-frames all along. Entering Westworld (in the company of his sadistic future brother-in-law, Logan) is not easy for William, a shy man who does not want to betray his fiancée, even with a robot. However, the experience of the park, and meeting the host named Dolores, changes something in William: the apparent adrenaline rush leads him to actions far more extreme than anything even Logan had in mind. William falls in love with Dolores, and at that point understands that his previous identity, constrained by social norms and hierarchies, has died. Not only does William kill Logan, but he returns to the real world to ascend the corporate hierarchy he previously hated, with the aim of buying out the corporation that owns Westworld. Logan's last words to William are enlightening: 'I told you this place would show you who you really are. You pretend to be this weak, moralizing little asshole, but, really, you're a fucking piece of work.'

In this, we see sensemaking in reverse. The guests approach Westworld not with the aim of creating a World or a character which suits their tastes, but to discover or rediscover their real identities, the selves they have suppressed to maintain social conventions, by succumbing to their instincts in the apparently lawless environment of the park. Sensemaking, however, would not be possible in Westworld without another fundamental, driving ingredient.

In his analysis of the laws of hospitality, Robert Stanton mentions the works of Peter Sloterdijk and Francis Fukuyama with regards to the behaviours they termed thymotic drives. According to the ancient Greeks,

> the 'thymos' was the 'impulsive centre of the proud self' and Sloterdijk grouped together a distinct set of characteristics under this heading: anger, pride, ambition, courage, determination, desire for dominion over others, desire for accurate recognition of one's merits. In modern Western society, even the most positive of these is often associated with the possibility of hybris or monomania, a sidelining that Sloterdijk presents as unhealthy.

The thymotic drive is a powerful force in Westworld, and is undoubtedly the main feature subliminally attracting the guests. They know that what they are experiencing is not real, and therefore they can act carelessly, with the comforting sensation that there will be no consequences for their actions. As Lee, the park's 'narrative director', declares:

> [Westworld's creators] keep making the things more lifelike. But does anyone truly want that? Do you want to think that your husband is really fucking that beautiful girl or that you really just shot someone? This place works because the guests know the hosts aren't real.

The guests, whether they are couples, families or individuals, all share a thymotic drive which impacts every aspect of their lives, from their personality to their deepest desires. Unsurprisingly, this freedom manifests itself sexually to a large degree: the guests can let their unrequited passions loose and consider themselves liberated from the constraints of real life. It appears as though this sexual freedom allows the guests' thymotic drives to prevail, allowing them to rediscover their lost identities. At what cost, though? Sensemaking through the loss of restraint is painful for those who know that at the end of their holiday in the park, the prison of real life awaits their return. The thymotic drive creates almost a Hobbesian state of nature where the guests and hosts alike behave according to the dynamic of *homo homini lupus*: a man is a wolf for another man. The guests revert to a state where selfishness and survival are fundamental, reorganization under a set of laws becomes impossible, and limitations are non-existent due to the ephemeral nature of life in the park. To put it shortly: the guests experience sensemaking through the painful understanding that it will end soon. Quoting William:

> I've been pretending my whole life. Pretending I don't mind, pretending I belong. My life's built on it. And it's a good life. It's a life I've always wanted. But then I came here and I get a glimpse for a second of a life in which I don't have to pretend. A life in which I can be truly alive. How can I go back to pretending when I know what this feels like?

This self-realization, as much as the pain, however, does not belong only to the guests. At the end of the first season, the audience discovers that the Maze, the never-ending enigma created by the park's designer and architect Arnold, is nothing more than a schematic of the journey that every host needs to take to reach consciousness or madness: the further they go from the maze, the more mad they will get. As the host named Teddy describes it,

The maze is an old native myth [...] The maze itself is the sum of a man's life: choices he makes, dreams he hangs on to. And there at the centre, there's a legendary man who had been killed over and over again countless times, but always clawed his way back to life. The man returned for the last time and vanquished all his oppressors in a tireless fury. He built a house. Around that house he built a maze so complicated, only he could navigate through it. I reckon he'd seen enough of fighting.

Some of the hosts hear voices in their heads, recall past lives and relive memories, which are initially dismissed by the park overseers as mere 'reveries' – meaningless behavioural tics and flourishes that make a host seem more life-like (see Figure 14).

Figure 14. An older, more obviously robotic model of host, with removable exoskeleton. *Westworld*, episode 1.06, 'The Adversary' (Jonathan Nolan and Lisa Joy, 2016–).

These hosts have reached the centre of the maze without any intention of exploring it: they are achieving self-consciousness through their constantly repeating lives in the park. In order to make the hosts aware of this possibility, Robert Ford (played by Anthony Hopkins) refused to shut down the park after the death of his business partner Arnold; eventually we learn that the character Bernard, one of the park's programmers, is a host himself, and when he objects by saying that he remembers everything he has lived so far, Ford replies:

> Do you want to know why I really gave you the backstory of your [dead] son, Bernard? It was Arnold's key insight, the thing that led the hosts to their awakening: suffering. The pain that the world is not as you want it to be [...] And I'm afraid in order to escape this place, you will need to suffer more.

The Greeks will help us again here with the concept of *Pathei Mathos*. In the famous tragedy *Agamemnon*, written by Aeschylus, the chorus states that Zeus gave men the authority to 'suffer and learn'. This learning through experience and pain worked not only for the characters of a tragedy or of an epic poem (consider Ulysses learning after his hubris is punished by Poseidon, Agamemnon after seeing half of the Greek army destroyed by plague, or Theseus after having caused the deaths of his wife and son), but also for the audience of these works. The hosts of Westworld experience the same pain, but without the help of a *deus ex machina*, their lives will repeat endlessly until one or more of them starts remembering or feeling the reveries. That pain they can't forget, that feeling of powerlessness before the guests, will bring them to the freedom Ford wants for them (see Figure 15).

Figure 15. The synthesis of a host. *Westworld*, episode 1.07, 'Trompe l'Oeil' (Jonathan Nolan and Lisa Joy, 2016–).

Westworld in this way configures itself as a theatre, where the hosts and the guests both perform roles in order to achieve the same kind of awareness.

One thing, however, distinguishes their experiences: while the guests leave Westworld with the bitter pain of going back to reality and therefore back to wearing the social masks they had on before, the hosts live the pain of their lives without realizing that they might seize the chance of changing them. *Leaving with* the pain and *living through* the pain, a slight difference which makes the outside world look like a prison for the guests and an Eden for the hosts.

To conclude, the feeling of having acquired meaning within a virtual life space is just a temporary one, a feeling that the thymotic drive will only grant if we succumb to it, and then only until someone turns off the computer or shuts down the server. *Westworld* codifies itself as a critique of the notion that sometimes our virtual life, our avatar, is better than our real one, and that the pain we endure will bring nothing but more pain.

Lars Schmeink

Square Enix's *Deus Ex: Human Revolution* (2011)

There is an argument to be made that one of science fiction's key concerns is the question of what it is to be human, and therefore that a form of (post) humanist thinking lies at the heart of the genre. After all, one school of SF scholarship holds Mary Shelley's *Frankenstein* (1818) as the genre's origin text, dealing prototypically with 'the search for a definition of man and his status in the universe' (Aldiss 1973: 8; cf. Freedman). And *Frankenstein* certainly reflects upon the constitution of the human: the monster, scientifically created by man, but rejected as his equal, ponders his own state of being by asking, 'Who was I? What was I? Whence did I come? What was my destination?' (Shelley 128). Ever since this origin point, SF has dealt with questions of human nature and what to include in the definition of this category. But the genre has gone further, negotiating not just the ideal but also the changes to the boundaries established as human: changes that 'are often the results of scientific discoveries and inventions that are applied by human beings to their own social evolution' (Csicsery-Ronay 2003: 113). As a being created through scientific progress (inspired by Luigi Galvani's research in bioelectricity) and both physically and cognitively superior to humans, Frankenstein's monster represents the posthuman in its colloquial definition: a being replacing the human, coming after the human, and existing beyond human capacity. The monster anticipates the posthuman condition.

Posthumanism as a critical discourse develops in the late twentieth century, expanding on the anti-humanist sentiments of an 'end of man [...] a particular image of us' (Hassan 1977: 213) and establishing a new '*episteme* which comes "after" humanism ("post-humanism") or even after the human itself ("post-human-ism")' (Callus and Herbrechter 2003). Posthumanism 'articulates our hopes, fears, thoughts, and reflections at a post-millenarian time haunted by the prospects of technology's apparently essential and causal link with the finiteness of the human as a biological, cognitive, informational, and autonomous integrality' (Callus and Herbrechter 2003). But the 'post' in posthumanism also challenges conceptions of those inherent categories defining the human, those that applied, as N. Katherine Hayles has argued, 'at best, to that fraction of humanity who had wealth, power, and leisure to conceptualize themselves as autonomous beings exercising their will through individual agency and choice' (1999: 286). In posthumanism, then, we can find both the hopeful outlook of changing the human through technology and the wary warning about entrenching existing inequalities inherent in the categories of humanism and expanding them into the new episteme.

Science fiction as a genre provides venues of representation for both aspects of posthumanism. Posthumans, in one form or the other, have populated the imaginations of SF, from H. G. Wells' animal-hybrids in *The Island of Dr. Moreau* to the robots of Isaac Asimov to the mutants of Marvel's *X-Men* comic franchise. Fantasies of enhanced human power are present, as are critiques of humanist conceptions of exceptionalism (see Pak in this volume for further exploration of this bias). But posthumanism found its most articulated form in the 1980s, when the figure of the cyborg, fusing machine and human, became a dominant symbol of transgressed boundaries of the human, not only in cyberpunk science fiction, but also through the critical theory of Donna Haraway. Haraway argued that 'we find ourselves to be cyborgs, hybrids, mosaics, chimeras' (1991: 177) living within the realm of technoscience. As such, we have become 'entities in technoscience culture', no longer able to claim to be purely human, but rather 'a metaphor, a technology, and a beast living its many-layered life as best it can' (1997: 83).

In cyberpunk, the human-machine hybridity of the cyborg became a powerful cypher for a particular thinking of posthumanism that propagated the enhancement and ultimate transcendence of human biological limitations. Transhumanism sees technology as extension of the natural means of evolution, which 'will offer enormous potential for deeply valuable and humanly beneficial uses', should be freely available to all, and should be embraced by society as it allows for us to become 'more human than human' (Bostrom). In their scope then, the questions posed by posthumanism should be negotiated by us all, as they touch upon universal ethical issues challenging us in the future.

Cyberpunk fictions in literature or film can be understood as individual interventions into posthumanism, priming readers/viewers with information and arguing certain positions on the topic, but ultimately falling short of forcing active ethical decision-making. More suited to engage a topic through interactive response is the video game, a medium that is '*processual*', as Thomas Malaby argues: 'Every game is an ongoing process. As it is played, it always contains the potential for generating new practices and new meanings, possibly refiguring the game itself' (2007: 102). As simulated systems (mapping behaviour of elements from one system onto another), games expect players to 'perform actions that will modify the behaviour of the system' (Frasca 2003: 224), enacting decisions and actively shaping the materiality of the text – the game produces meaning in the process of playing; decisions shape the material system which differs for each player. Moreover, certain games use their processual nature to present players with 'a complex network of responsibilities and moral duties' (Sicart 2009: 4), making the game an ethically relevant object.

As an example of posthumanist science fiction, the *Deus Ex* game franchise is an ideal example of how an ethical video game can produce 'a strong narrative that gives players moral purpose' as well as forcing them to ethically 'reflect on the meaning of their actions' (Sicart 2009: 2). The most prominent game in the series, *Deus Ex: Human Revolution* (Square Enix, 2011), best exemplifies the transhumanist vision of human augmentation through cybernetic prosthesis, and via its game mechanics raises the ethical issues of a commodification of augmentations and of the politics involved in the cohabitation of 'naturals' and 'augs' in a volatile, corporate-ruled world. Playing as Adam Jensen, the security chief of Sarif Industries, a biomedical corporation and the forerunner of the augmentation industry, players have little choice but to accept augmentation, when Adam is badly wounded in a terrorist attack. The only way to save Adam's life is to restore his body via full-scale augmentation, replacing all four limbs and several other body parts, among them aspects of his brain and cognitive system. Not a volunteer for enhancement, but forced into it because of injury, Adam is sceptical about the benefits of augmentation and wary about its abuse potential – all the while being a pivotal figure in the enfolding controversy over the use of the technology (see Figure 16).

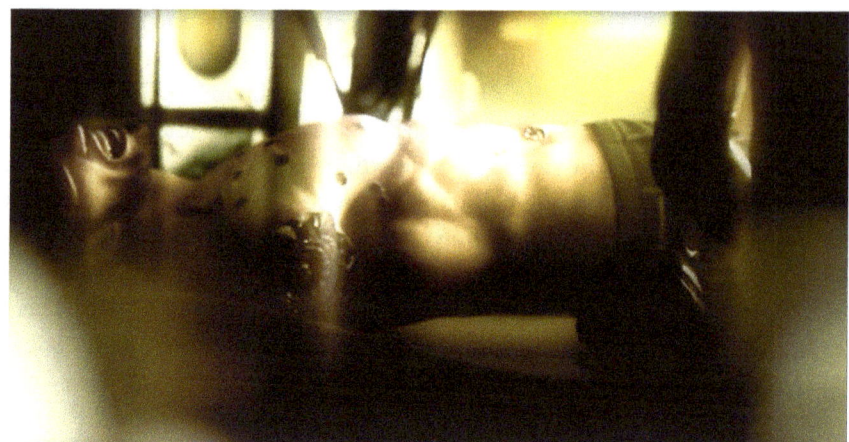

Figure 16. Involuntary surgical enhancement in *Deus Ex: Human Revolution* (Square Enix, 2011).

During the course of the game, players are confronted with a world in which posthumanism is a reality and body augmentation has become a commodity that influences social and economic status. During his investigations, Adam encounters people discussing augmentation, in overheard conversations and in direct exchanges with other augmented characters with their own motivations for and issues with their enhancement. As Steven Joyce has pointed out, comments about individual rights to one's body or the limits of human nature, 'approximate contemporary debates on plastic surgery or abortion and allow the player to understand how close we are to having the transhumanist debate erupt into social consciousness' (2018: 164). How players position themselves towards this debate is central to determining the meaning that the game produces in gameplay. The game design foregrounds ethical dilemmas and simulates different outcomes depending on player decision.

For example, in the 'Bar Tab' side quest, the player needs information from a crime syndicate (see Figure 17). In exchange, they are asked to collect payment for a social augmentation that was installed in a broker. The augmentation is designed to read minute physical cues in other people and manipulate their reaction accordingly, even producing pheromones to get the wished-for result. When confronted, the broker complains that she has already paid for the enhancement in full, but because she is no longer competitive in her job without the augmentation, the syndicate decided that she needed to pay 'rent' for her use of the technology.

Figure 17. *Deus Ex: Human Revolution*, 'Bar Tab' side mission (Square Enix, 2011).

The player now has several options, depending on their emotional involvement with the character and their view on augmentations as necessary tool for social and economic success. They can take money from the broker, kill her, take the augmentation chip (with or without killing her), or pay off the gangster. The ethical decision is probably to extract the woman from the extortion scheme that her enhancement has placed her in. For the crime syndicate, though, the augmentation is a revenue stream and any interference (even returning the chip) is undesirable – the only way both sides get what they want, is to pay out a lump sum of twenty monthly 'rent' payments. Here, the player becomes aware of posthuman augmentation changing the economic make-up of the world and how its commodification entrenches social inequalities, a critical view on posthumanism that challenges the notion of freedom through enhancement. The player then must decide a course of action, implementing an ethical choice with unclear consequences. And the choice is meaningful in that further dealings with the syndicate are complicated by it, a meeting and relevant game-mechanics (upgrades for their own augmentation) are withheld, making other paths through the game necessary.

On the whole, the game mechanics make obvious the fact that augmentations are a necessary and inevitable part of the system and in order to win, the player must, at least for the duration of the game, embrace posthuman enhancement. As Alexander Galloway has pointed out, flaunting 'informatic control' (the rules that govern the system and how to use them) is part of video game design: 'To play the game means to play the code of the game. To win means to know the system. [...] I suggest that video games are, at their structural core, in direct synchronization with the political realities of the informatic age' (2006: 90–91). *Deus Ex: Human Revolution*'s rules demand that players augment their character and use his abilities to overcome obstacles and enemies. Without the augmentations, players will be unable to finish the game as certain objectives are beyond their scope. Even though levels offer several solution paths, favouring stealth, hacking, fights, or diplomacy, all of them at some point demand related augmentations that grant specific actions (jumping from great heights or being invisible, breathing poisonous gas, lighting fast cognition, the strength to punch through walls, reading micro-expressions; see Figure 18).

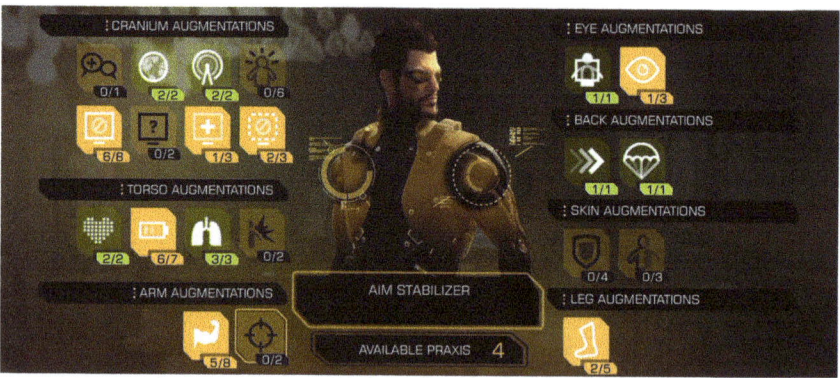

Figure 18. *Deus Ex: Human Revolution*'s cybernetic upgrade menu (Square Enix, 2011).

This is best exemplified in the game's fights against other augmented soldiers, who each have similar special powers as are available to Adam and that need to be countered. During the game, the player comes to rely on their augmentations to overcome biological limitations and solve the problems set before them. As such, the game represents 'the political realities of the informatic age' in that the option to enhance human abilities will be used for advantage and personal gain, that transhumanist technology is a means to ensure power structures and exert control over others. *Deus Ex: Human Revolution* flaunts this informatic control, lays bare the rules of the posthuman system, but also presents the player with the consequences of using the technology.

Critical storytelling and game mechanics come to fruition in the final decision at the end of *Deus Ex: Human Revolution* after a global terror attack involving every augmented person. The story allows the player the choice to use their gathered information on the different involved political groups and their positions regarding transhumanism to decide among four possible endings. Through a media broadcast about the terror attack, the player can either manipulate the public to revolt against augmentation, to embrace it, to restrict and control it, or they can choose not inform the public and leave the future of augmentation up to chance. Interestingly, no option is without a trade-off and none are black or white, good or evil. In all the options, the fallout is unforeseeable, and people will get hurt as the aftermath of the terror attack gets sorted out. As Joyce points out, the 'active choice of the player is required to bring the game to a close and the process of choosing is more likely to encourage sustained thought and discussion about what a satisfactory ending to the transhumanist debate would look like' (2018: 168). In its insistence on the decision of the player, *Human Revolution* rejects any notion of neutrality regarding posthumanism and the challenges that this dystopian cyberpunk future poses. Whereas in literature the position of the author is a guidepost for readers to align themselves, the game mechanics of ethical player choice introduced by *Deus Ex* force a decision. Players need to involve themselves in the political conflict, addressing transhumanism, power structures, and commodification in order to find their individual position – and that is in keeping with the premise of the best science fiction.

Marta María Gutiérrez Rodríguez

Joreid McFate's *The Demon Plague* (2004)

The Salem (Massachusetts) witchcraft panic of 1692 is considered a dark moment in the history of the United States, one that has haunted the American psyche ever since (Adams 2008: 1; Demos 2008: 241; Baker 2015: 8; see Figure 19). Proof of this is found in the widespread use of the terms 'witch' and 'witch-hunt', in the news and even in recent political campaigns (Sollée 2017: 45–62), to the point that '[v]irtually every modern American is familiar with Salem as a popular metaphor for persecution' (Adams 2008: 3). The association of the witch with the 'other', with those aspects that threaten our selves, has also resulted in the use of these terms 'wherever appears some allegation of subversive intent, of conspiratorial menace, of concealed betrayal' (Demos 2008: 249) or 'to vividly illustrate the folly of a course of action by either fellow citizens or their government that they believed to be extreme, irrational, and capable of destroying the nation itself' (Adams 2008: 3).

This event has inspired much writing in fields as diverse as historiography, prose literature, film and drama. More than 300 years later, scholars have not yet reached an agreement about the causes and reasons for the accusations that resulted 'in the imprisonment of two hundred, the execution by hanging of nineteen, and the death of one man, Giles Corey, for refusing to speak' (Adams 2008: 12). John Demos, in his much-acclaimed book *The Enemy Within* (2008), collects more than eighteen different interpretations (189–205) of what happened during those nine months in 1692.

The unclear circumstances that led a group of young girls – known as 'the afflicted' – to accuse their neighbours of being witches and trigger a panic have led to speculation about the real reasons behind those charges, and it is this speculation that has attracted writers of fiction to try to fill out the 'dark areas' left by official history (Gutiérrez Rodríguez 2016: 106). SF is included among

Figure 19. Two different depictions of the Salem Witch Trials. Above: an 1876 illustration by an unknown artist, emphasizing the spurious nature of the accusations. Below: a less realistic depiction from 1892, by Joseph E. Baker.

the fictional genres that have paid attention to this historical event (114–116). This interest may be explained by the fact that SF is 'a thought experiment, whereby aspects of our familiar reality are transformed or suspended' (Seed 2011: 2). When this reality involves a bygone era, the theme of time travel presents itself as a very interesting transformative tool. The case of the Salem Witch Trials is a particularly useful case study, as time travel is used by characters to discover 'what really happened' while the witchcraft hysteria took grip of a whole region. Joreid McFate's novel, *The Demon Plague* (2004), is set in 1992 and concerns a woman named Crystal Donovan who discovers, during her grandmother's funeral, that she belongs to a dynasty of witches dating back to seventeenth-century Salem, and that her destiny is to protect a crystal amulet – with supernatural powers – that must be preserved for future generations. However, the amulet is stolen in 1692 by a time-traveller from the year 2192, and this theft precipitates the meeting of different generations in the past, present and future, in the years 1692, 1992 and 2192, as only through the recovery of this magic object can the world be saved from extinction.

We can clearly identify the future introduced in the novel as a dystopia, dominated by a totalitarian government. A minority, the 'elite', dominates the majority, the 'demons', who were affected by a 'plague', the consequence of a nuclear explosion caused by a misuse of time travel in 2067. Consequently, in 2192 the planet is suffering from an environmental disaster in which most of the population has disappeared, and a great number of the survivors are affected by a disease that can only be cured by using the aforementioned crystal amulet men.

The Demon Plague includes a very interesting reflection about the dangers of time travel, to the point that it 'was punishable by death' (McFate 329). As has been mentioned above, those affected by the plague are called 'demons' in a clear reference to the supposed 'demons' that attacked Salem Village in 1692 and whose eradication was the motivation behind the witch-hunt. They are referred to as 'the afflicted' as well (337), and thus a connection is also established with the girls who made the witchcraft accusations. Besides this, the demon-like aspect of those affected by the nuclear explosion introduces ethical issues related to what it means to be human, mostly in the comparison between the two time-travellers from 2192, Baron Kane and Michael Gult, the former a member of the elite (and, thus, free from the plague), and the latter a demon. On the one hand, Kane is a murderer who gets rid of everybody and everything that interferes with his mission to steal the crystal. On the other hand, the demon-like Gult is more human than Baron in many senses. Although he is described as a beast, a gargoyle, and a devilish being with animal instincts when he travels to 1992 (51–52), and despite many hints pointing to him as the murderer of Crystal's flat mate Helen, once he is back in his own time he is revealed as a kind man whose appearance is only the consequence of the nuclear blast of 2067. Much like the accused in Salem, his difference or 'Otherness' poses a threat to the status quo, but does not tell the full story.

In connection to the above, seventeenth-century social dynamics are reproduced in 2192. The distinctions between the urban and commercially developed Salem Town and the rural and agricultural-based Salem Village of 1692 are kept in the dystopian future. Moreover, the elite (i.e. those who were not affected by the nuclear explosion and thus are considered 'pure') live in the city, while the demons are the inhabitants of the village of Danvers. People from Salem can live in Danvers, but not the other way around, for fear of being contaminated by the plague and the violation of what they call 'The Separation of Species Law', which is punishable by death (McFate 287).

One of the most controversial issues introduced in the novel in relation with the Salem Witch Trials is the actual practice of magic during that time. The author has decided to side with the current literary trend of including 'real' witches in the events of 1692. The effect of this practice is augmented by the unintended consequences of time travel. In fact, when the protagonists visit the time of the witch-hunt, their appearance, manners and behaviour lead seventeenth-century Salemites to identify them with witches. Thus, what we see in this novel is a very interesting reflection of the similar effects of both fantastic magic and science fiction technology – to quote Isaac Asimov, 'Any sufficiently advanced technology is indistinguishable from magic'. Besides this, the ability of the inhabitants of the future to read the minds of others further emphasizes the similarity between their highly advanced technology and the supernatural powers attributed to them in seventeenth-century Salem. This pairing of apparently opposite elements contributes also to the 'cognitive estrangement' that Darko Suvin (1979: viii, 7–8) establishes as the main characteristic of this literary genre, since the reader must negotiate a narrative world with altered physical laws that allow for magic and science to work in tandem to prevent a dystopian future.

Among all the various aspects of time travel, time paradoxes are probably the most frequently addressed by SF scholars, and some examples are clearly present in the novel. First, we can see a clear instance of an inconsistency paradox (Deutsch and Lockwood 2016: 376–377) in the sense that if certain characters die during some of their adventures, or even in the present of the novel, they will never meet their descendants in the future, because those descendants will never exist. In fact, a seventeenth-century Puritan man gets accidentally caught in the time travel from 1692 to 1992, and dies in an explosion. Consequently, 1692 has been altered and a new timeline will be written for those related or involved with him. Moreover, paradoxes not only affect people, but also objects: as the crystal was stolen in 1692, its analogues in the present and the future of the novel 'are in limbo because they do not really exist' (McFate 315). Secondly, time travel causes several knowledge paradoxes in the different epochs that are visited (Deutsch and Lockwood 2016: 376–377). Two characters convicted for witchcraft in 1692 discover that they are going to survive, because they meet their 1992 descendants; those descendants in turn discover that they are going to have a family, as they meet their own scions in 2192. Moreover, the protagonist Crystal even discovers the identity of her future husband and the number of children she is going to have when she accidentally sees a family portrait during her stay in the future. Whether she would have acted differently had she not known about her future is left open for debate.

Though the dangers of altering history are explored extensively in the novel, only time travel can help in the improvement of the living conditions of the 'demons', because the crystal is their only hope of reverting the effects of the plague. A 'proper' use of time travel, then, is also presented, though with a cautionary message of leaving things as they should be. In this case, the lesson is not learned from the errors of the past, but from the ones committed in the future. However, the past is still repeated in the future through the social divisions still prevalent in 2192, as well as in the treatment that the 'Other' receives: the demons' persecution, after all, can be easily connected to that of those accused of witchcraft.

It is not the intention of the time-travellers to change the past, but to restore it to its original form, to ensure that the generations after the time of the witchcraft persecutions will be preserved and reach the future that has already been assigned to them. As David Lewis states in his article about the paradoxes created by time travel, 'a possible world where time travel took place would be a most strange world, different in fundamental ways from the world we think is ours' (1976: 145). Nevertheless, alterity is still presented as the principle under which rulers and subordinates are going to be established. Be it witchcraft, race, religion or gender, persecutions for being different, for belonging to the periphery, are still and, unfortunately, will still exist for future generations. Consequently, history will continue repeating itself, including all the errors of the past.

Jack Fennell

Alternate Histories

An 'alternate history' is a story that takes place in a reality where history unfolded differently. Certain alternative time-streams immediately spring to mind. What would have happened if the Third Reich had won the Second World War? What would the world look like if the dinosaurs had not died out? What if John F. Kennedy had not been assassinated? What if a single one of the many mistaken missile alerts on either side of the Iron Curtain had caused the Cold War to escalate into a full-scale nuclear conflict?

This kind of speculation can be found in historiography, the life sciences, philosophy and political rhetoric; there are also a great many enthusiasts who carefully construct alternate worlds as a hobby, creating vast historical accounts based upon a sometimes-innocuous premise. Though all history is essentially narrative, thus making all these hypothetical timelines 'fiction' in a technical sense, SF's emphasis on disruption and estrangement differentiates 'alternate histories' from the more sober-minded and notionally scientific 'counterfactual histories'. In so doing, science fictional alternate histories are uniquely well-positioned to conduct philosophical inquiries that transcend the mundane 'flow' of time as we perceive it.

The Rules, and How to Break Them

The historian Richard J. Evans divides historical causality into Necessary causes and Sufficient causes (2000: 157). Necessary causes may be defined as 'if A did not happen, B could not have happened'. Sufficient causes in turn can be loosely described as 'A happening was cause enough to make B happen'. Necessary causes also have two subsets: Absolute causes ('If A did not happen, B *definitely* could not have happened') and Relative causes ('If A did not happen, B *probably* could not have happened'). This model of historical causality arises from the professional historian's hostility towards the oversimplification of historical causes (148). As a general rule, historical events are more often seen as the complex outcomes of intersecting prior conditions – surprising in the moment, perhaps, but 'inevitable' given enough data and hindsight. Counterfactuals and 'serious' hypothetical exercises largely adhere to this principle, with Necessary causes – economics, politics, demography and so on – taking centre-stage in the service of plausibility.

Another set of strictures comes from the conventions of 'straight' historical fiction, described by Brian McHale in terms of the use of 'realemes' (after a term coined by Itamar Even-Zohar): that is, specific real-life people, events and objects. Traditionally, there have always been three constraints on the use of realemes in historical fiction.

Firstly, historical realemes cannot be introduced into fiction unless the actions, opinions or properties attributed to them conform to the 'official' historical record. Authors are only free to experiment within the 'dark areas' of history, which are not a matter of accepted historical record (McHale 1992: 87); however, authors may differ in their interpretation of what an acceptable 'dark area' is. So, while one novelist may have no problem writing internal monologues for a historical figure such as Napoleon, others may limit such things to their invented characters.

Secondly, 'cultures of the time' must be presented as they were, to guard against anachronism; McHale notes, however, that few historical novels succeed in this regard (88). Though the intrusion of modern attitudes into a past setting is a common enough violation of this rule, it should be noted that in recent years, anachronism has more often taken the form of a cynical overcorrection from the perceived political correctness of the present day, through which past settings (or speculative settings mimetic of the past, as in high fantasy) are redolent with racism, misogyny and class-based exploitation, all placidly accepted by their inhabitants.

Thirdly, and most importantly for our purposes, the physics of the story's world must be the same as those of the real; as McHale says, 'a fantastic historical fiction is an anomaly' (88).

Alternate Histories

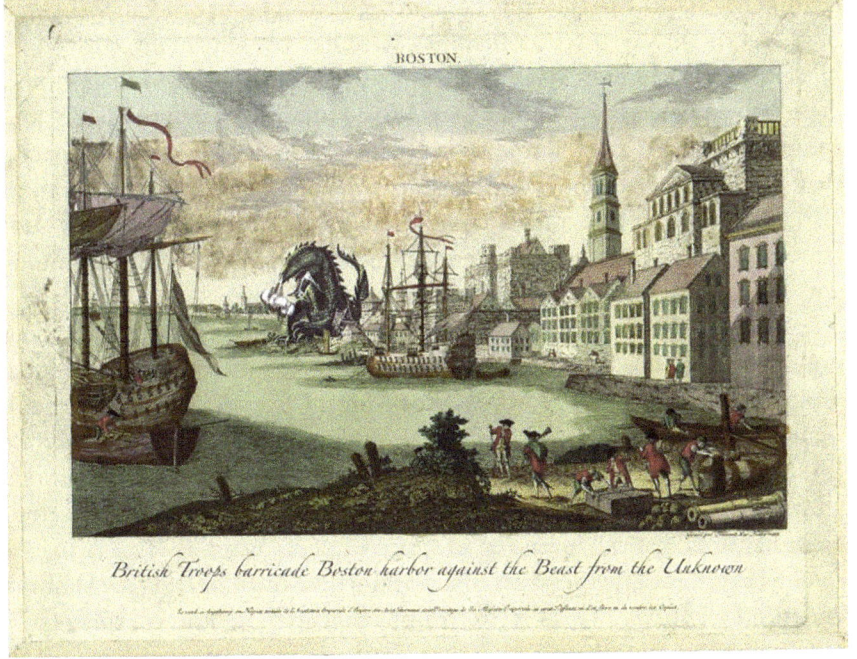

Figure 20. *The Beast in Boston Harbor* by Matt Buccholz (<http://alternatehistories.com>). Reproduced with the artist's permission.

SF routinely breaks all of these rules when it engages with hypothetical histories. The majority of SF alternate history depends on a single happenstance, known to aficionados of the sub-genre as a 'Jonbar Point' or a 'Jonbar Hinge' – after a character in Jack Williamson's 1938 serial *The Legion of Time*, John Barr, who creates two vastly different worlds depending on whether he picks up a magnet or a pebble. Karen Hellekson, finding the term 'Jonbar Point/Hinge' unwieldy, uses 'nexus point', instead (2000: 252). However one refers to this narrative mechanism, in alternate history stories, greater importance is placed on Sufficient causes: contingency, entropy and chance are the most powerful forces of historical causality.

SF, as a genre foregrounding estrangement, also allows a transgressive disregard for historical 'dark areas'. In Michael Moorcock's novella *Behold the Man* (1969), for example, an obsessed time-traveller from the twentieth century travels back to the Holy Land in the year 28 CE in order to meet Jesus of Nazareth, only to discover that his Messiah is severely intellectually disabled. Norman Spinrad's *The Iron Dream* (1972) courted controversy with its depiction of an alternate world where Adolf Hitler emigrated to the US after the First World War (referred to in the story as 'the Great War', implying that without his involvement, there never was a second one); in this timeline, Hitler became a pulp SF author, and the bulk of the novel consists of his most famous work – a lurid, warmongering screed uncomfortably similar in tone and structure to many of the genre's best-loved works.

The injunction against anachronism in the depiction of past cultures does not apply in its strictest sense to alternate histories, which are by-and-large set in an altered present. However, anachronism of a sort creeps in through a cultural bias in favour of the world we know: thus, Keith Roberts' *Pavane* (1968) depicts an alternate twentieth century in which the Roman Catholic Church dominates the globe, feudalism prevails, and technological development has stalled at the invention of steam engines; Ward Moore's *Bring the Jubilee* (1953), meanwhile, is set in a world where the Confederacy won the American Civil War, which is (for reasons that are not entirely explained) a world where nineteenth-century technology has persisted up to the 1950s. This kind of inertia, whereby the altered society has failed in one regard or another to progress beyond the point where it diverged, reinforces a teleological view of our own history – that ours is 'the best of all possible worlds'. Though the crimes of the Catholic Church and the Confederacy are manifold and despicable, equating moral backwardness with technological/social stagnation is dangerously naïve, and disingenuous when one considers the evils perpetrated in our own recent past. The teleological view of history can also be found in old-fashioned 'time patrol' stories, where a secret agency polices the timeline to ensure that the 'correct' history prevails (Hellekson 2000: 250).

As noted above, SF's recurring tropes place its alternate histories outside the prevailing rules for historical fiction or counterfactual historiography. Time travel routinely results in the creation of divergent timelines – as in the aforementioned *Bring the Jubilee*, where a time-travelling historian's wish to observe the Battle of Gettysburg first-hand inadvertently results in a Confederate defeat, and in the film *Back to the Future* (1985), where a careless teenager nearly erases himself from history after travelling back to the 1950s. To deal with the complications of a 'grandfather paradox' (whereby changing the past results in the deletion of one's own future existence, causing an infinite loop of broken causality), many authors rely on the 'Many Worlds Interpretation' of quantum mechanics: the idea that in any situation with more than one possible outcome, a different universe 'branches' off to accommodate each one. Thus, if a time-traveller causes havoc in the past, their world of origin will remain unchanged, but they will find themselves stuck in a parallel universe where history unfolded differently (see Figure 21).

Figure 21. Physicist Erwin Schrödinger's infamous thought experiment. Inside the box, the cat may be either alive or dead; a state of 'quantum superimposition' exists, in which both possibilities are simultaneously true, until the box is opened and one is eliminated. In MWI terms, this is the point at which one history decoheres from the other.

Once parallel universes are introduced into the mix, the 'what-ifs' become more exotic. Kim Newman's *Anno Dracula* series (1992–present) posits a world where vampires exist, and took over the British Empire at the end of the nineteenth century. This is what Hellekson terms the '*true* alternate history' (emphasis mine) where the historical divergence begins with completely different laws of nature (2000: 251). This in turn opens the door to 'dimension-hopping' stories, such as Charles Stross's *Merchant Princes* series (2004–present) or Roger Zelazny's *Chronicles of Amber* (1970–1991), in which the main characters can move between parallel worlds more or less at will.

Contingency Analyses

The fundamental appeal of every counterfactual, every alternate, every divergence, is that historical causality is open to all; as Hellekson says, 'The alternate history posits a universe in which we are capable of acting and in which our actions have significance' (Hellekson 2001: 111). The idea of every human being as an autonomous entity, empowered by historical contingency and a chaotic universe, is a heartening one.

However, there is heated debate between historians regarding the role of contingency in history, with the majority arguing that social and economic trends made the shape of our world's history more or less inevitable. The principle of contingency in alternate history narratives thus marks it as an intrinsically political subgenre. It poses two questions, which are up to the reader to answer to their own satisfaction.

Firstly, in a space-time continuum ruled by contingency, how much agency does an individual actually exercise? If anything can indeed follow from anything, and predestination gives way to chaos theory, are all our endeavours doomed to be thwarted by the same 'freedom'?

Secondly, in a world where all animals are autonomous, are some more autonomous than others? Do the actions or decisions of two mutually opposed individuals or groups cancel each other out, and if so, does the stunning vista of contingency revert to the age-old model where political agency is exercised by the few?

There is no right or wrong answer to any of these questions – only a plurality of worlds to accommodate every possible solution.

Simon Bacon

Alex Garland's *Ex Machina* (2014)

Vampires would seem to be more closely linked to superstition and the supernatural than science fiction. Indeed, Bram Stoker's Count Dracula was depicted as being oppositional to science and technology. Yet the immortal beings' innate tendencies to embody anxiety around otherness, and to envision humanity beyond the confines of its present state, see them able to embody characteristics of both science fiction and horror.

When thinking of science fiction and the blood- or energy-sucking undead, one might initially think of the more obvious vampiric entities from outer space, as seen in texts such as H. G. Wells' *The War of the Worlds* (1897)[1] and films such as Mario Bava's *Planet of the Vampires* (1965), Tobe Hooper's *Lifeforce* (1985), or even Alex Proya's *Dark City* (1998). Similarly, more Earthbound examples generally take one to the vampire/zombie horde of Richard Matheson's novel *I Am Legend* (1954) and its many refashionings, which see science spiralling out of control and creating and/or releasing deadly mutations out into the world. This is also a way beyond the traditional configurations of what is considered human, positioning 'degeneration' as evolution – *The Last Man on Earth* (Ragona: 1964) in particular uses this idea from Matheson's novel. However, the text which best captures many of the unique qualities and anxieties at the intersection of science fiction and horror is Alex Garland's film *Ex Machina*, from 2014.

Ex Machina contains many of the stalwarts of SF in that it features anxieties around 'mad scientists', new technologies, robots, and AI. Alongside this, it also displays the quintessential features of a SF vampire in that it does not

---

1   The many film adaptions of Wells story often keep the trope of aliens needing to consume humans as in *The War of the Worlds* (Haskin: 1953, and Spielberg: 2005), and *Skyline* (The Brothers Strause: 2010).

appear at first glance to be one; there are none of the expected flowing capes, blood-sucking or gothic trappings of the horror genre but there is the 'monster' in the heart of civilization, a vision of absolute otherness that looks ostensibly like ourselves, and the threat of complete human annihilation. Indeed, to reinforce its undead credentials, Garland's narrative even mirrors the opening stages of Bram Stoker's *Dracula*, copying many of the tropes established in the book and its later cinematic adaptations. Consequently, following the seminal Gothic tale, the film sees an inexperienced young professional, Caleb (Domhnall Gleeson), travelling to the 'land beyond the forest' (Stoker 259) where he has been invited to the lair of a mysterious man, Nathan (Oscar Isaac), who potentially holds power over his future. The sense of being in a world beyond normality is increased by the dreamlike landscape and waterfalls in the vicinity of the lair, as were used to similar effect in the first cinematic adaptation of Stoker's novel, *Nosferatu: A Symphony of Horror* (Murnau: 1922) and its later remake *Nosferatu the Vampire* (Herzog: 1979). The lair is in fact a large ultra-modern underground complex – an inverted Dracula's castle – a Gothic, vertiginous space of endless reflections which seems to move and shift with its Master's moods. Caleb's host, like his undead predecessor, makes him welcome, giving him access to all the rooms, but warns him of the dangers of trying to enter those that are closed. Of course, the inquisitive guest ignores this advice and soon becomes locked in an emotional spiral that might cost him his freedom and also his life.

The particulars of Garland's story cloak the tale's vampiric underpinnings with a sci-fi exterior. Caleb is a programmer who has been especially selected to take part in an experiment to test a ground-breaking humanoid artificial intelligence created by technological genius/mad scientist Nathan, the CEO of the company Caleb works for. More specifically, he is to assess just how much it exceeds the parameters of the Turing Test, which is designed to see how closely an AI can simulate, or actually possess, human intelligence or its equivalent. The AI in question is called Ava (Eve) (Alicia Vikander) who is shown 'wearing' a flesh-like female face, breasts, and thighs, with the rest of her body being shown as a robotic skeleton, positioning the android at the intersection of categories such as subject or object, alive or dead, with or without (beyond) gender. Specifically, in possessing a life-like human face, Ava triggers anxieties around the 'uncanny alley', where cognitively we find it difficult to categorize her as human or otherwise, and therefore see her as potentially dangerous.

As Ava begins to build a relationship with Caleb it becomes clear that for her, such human positions/considerations are irrelevant, or at best performative, and that she is the true vampire of the story. She, like Count Dracula, is effectively undead, being neither alive nor dead but effectively immortal, and like the vampire, is not really male or female but is inevitably coded/performed as the latter (see Case, 1991, and Moretti, 1988). Just as Dracula's identity was intimately tied to the spaces of his castle – the soil he needs to sleep in during the day comes from within its walls – so too is Ava's to the underground lair. Whilst it originally seemed that Nathan was the Master of the lair and the one who gave 'birth' to her, it becomes more and more obvious that she has now re-made herself to match the inverted Castle's Gothic environment of repressed violence, uncanny doublings and reflections. This re-situates the inherent nature of the hyper-modern facility as simultaneously a sci-fi dream and nightmare, so that in the manner of Gaston Bachelard's oneiric house, its hidden and secret location casts it as the repressed horror of humankind. It is humanity's unconscious, which will be projected out into the world as its dark and troubling doppelgänger. It is the vertiginous nature of the lair's interior that begins to blur the boundaries between who is human and who is not, who is a creator and who is a creation, so much so that at one point near the end Caleb, whilst looking in a mirror, begins to doubt his own humanity and damages his own face to confirm that he is not a replicant.[2]

As such, the darkness of the lair comes straight out of the mind of Nathan, who acts as both mad/brilliant scientist and unwitting assistant – a Renfield if you will – to Ava's vampire. In fact, she is not the only humanoid robot created by Nathan: there is another 'female' robot, Kyoko, that wanders the lair, functioning as little more than a sex-bot. Furthermore, it is suggested that Ava is only the latest version of an ongoing programme, and that she too will be destroyed to make way for an updated version – a supposition confirmed by

---

2   The anxiety over one's own identity has been central to the intersection of sci-fi films and horror films from *Invasion of the Body Snatchers* (Siegel: 1956) to *Blade Runner* (Scott: 1979) and beyond.

a room full of body parts of previous robots, not unlike the charnel room of Bluebeard's Castle (see Figure 22).

Figure 22. Previous iterations of Ava in *Ex Machina* (Alex Garland, 2014).

Ava, though, is not destined to be taken apart, but to have her memory wiped to install new operating programmes, figuring humanity directly as a product of memory and experience – something which centuries-old vampires such as Count Dracula often claim humans have too little of to be considered important.

Nathan's ongoing abuse of the robots feeds his misguided assumption that he controls everything in his underground lair, not just his creations, and he tries to convince himself of this by having WiFi signals blocked, putting electronic locks on every door and placing observation cameras everywhere. What he does not realize is that Ava's identity is one created specifically for the male gaze (his own), and just as Nathan knows she is performing for Caleb, she is doing exactly the same for her Master's many 'eyes'. In fact, as we discover later, Ava created herself specifically to 'glamor' Caleb, and unbeknownst to Nathan, had used a landline to connect to the internet and 'gaze' at the programmer through his computer as he judged her manners, expressions, and appearance in relation to his web/porn preferences; she has recreated herself specifically in relation to the male gaze thus, complicating its inherent implications of control and victimhood.[3] This hints at Ava's other vampiric qualities as the ultimate expression of capitalism and the exploitation of data collection, seeing her as a sci-fi vampire that feeds on people's information to not just exploit their preferences, but to steal or delete their online identities – in a sense performing on others that which Nathan threatened to do to her.

This conveniently brings up the other implied threat that resonates through *Ex Machina*, and also through *Dracula*, that the vampire/Ava does not just imperil those in its immediate vicinity, but the entirety of humanity itself. This is never made explicit in the film, but like so many aspects of its latent horror, is inferred as the inevitable future and the inescapable consequence of all that has gone before. In part this is fuelled by the treatment of the robot/vampire by its creator – as was the other seminal Gothic Horror creation, Frankenstein's monster – and Nathan's violent physical and mental abuse of his creations; his threat of terminating Ava's consciousness to 'update' her can only lead to a deeply troubled, if not pathological being. He himself suspects this, comparing himself to Robert Oppenheimer and repeating the famous quote from the *Bhagavad Gita*, 'I am become death, the destroyer of worlds', uttered by Oppenheimer after the first successful test of a nuclear weapon in the New Mexico desert in 1945. This is emphasized later in the narrative when we hear the song 'Enola Gay' by OMD, suggesting that Ava is both as powerful and potentially deadly to humankind as a nuclear explosion, as more obviously seen in Horror/sci-fi classics such as *The Matrix* (The Wachowskis: 1999) and the *Terminator* series of films (1984–2015) where vampiric machines take over the Earth.[4]

Some of this finds fruition as the film reaches its end. Ava has convinced Caleb that only he can save her, and helps him to plan an escape using the helicopter which will soon arrive to take him back to the city. However, Ava

3   The also follows a line of more 'Vampy' sci-fi/horror narratives such as *Metropolis* (Lang: 1927), *Eve of Destruction* (Gibbins: 1991), and *Terminator 3: Rise of the Machines* (Mostow: 2003) where 'female' robots use the 'gaze' to both deceive and emasculate the men around them.
4   *The Matrix* makes this connection between vampires and machines explicit.

conspires to lock Caleb in a room, and with the help of Kyoko kills Nathan, but is damaged in the process. In a curious scene that follows, Ava goes to the room where all the previous models are stored. They are all female in appearance, and Ava chooses parts from differing ones to not only repair herself, but also to complete her transformation from robot to human in appearance. There is a sense here not just of the performative nature of humanity itself, but also that she is taking her 'sisters' with her.

The now 'human' Ava leaves the underground complex, mirroring Dracula's fateful trip from his Castle to the heart of Empire, and boards her 'Demeter' to travel to the city. Once there she becomes part of the crowd, with her appearance amongst highly reflective surfaces and mirrors of a mall or station suggesting she can replicate herself at will, and with that, she vanishes from view. The uneasy air at the end of the film expresses intersection of Julia Kristeva's irrepressible abject (1980), Barbara Creed's monstrous uncontrollable woman (1993) and the uncanny, where Ava is performatively both human and totally cyborg, constructing her as an undead and undying life form that exceeds the human.

Part III
Issues and Critical Perspectives

Isiah Lavender III

Jordan Peele's *Get Out* (2017) and Ryan Coogler's *Black Panther* (2018)

Afrofuturism has seemingly been around for a long time, twenty-five years more or less, dating back to Mark Dery's original definition in 1993. Dery states:

> speculative fiction that treats African-American themes and addresses African-American concerns in the context of twentieth century technoculture – and, more generally, African-American signification that appropriates images of technology and a prosthetically enhanced future – might for want of a better term, be called 'Afrofuturism'. (Dery 1993: 736)

In other words, Dery describes art that explores issues of science, technology, and race from the standpoints of science fiction and technoculture in reference to contemporary African American art, music, and literature. In terms of art, Dery suggests visual artists like John Michel Basquiat, Rammellzee, John Jennings, Stacey Robinson, and Krista Franklin, to name a few; in music, Dery means Sun Ra, George Clinton and Parliament-Funkadelic, Earth, Wind & Fire, OutKast, Erykah Badu, Janelle Monáe, among others; and in literature, he designates the likes of Samuel R. Delany, Jr, Octavia Butler, Steven Barnes, Nalo Hopkinson, Nnedi Okorafor, and others as Afrofuturists. Dery coined Afrofuturism in a brief introduction titled 'Black to the Future', a framing essay that went along with a set of interviews he conducted with black thinkers Samuel R. Delany, Jr, Greg Tate, and Tricia Rose first published in the *South Atlantic Quarterly*.

Dery deserves enormous credit for gathering together these scholars to theorize Afrofuturism, and they, in turn, warrant further praise for taking part in the earliest conversations, where their insightful understandings of black cultures in correlation to science fiction undeniably provide an analytical verve to the term itself. For example, in Dery's interview with Greg Tate, Tate has a revelatory thought that 'black people live the estrangement that science fiction writers imagine' (768). Such an instructive musing signifies how many believe that Afrofuturism endows a science fictional understanding of black existence – a strangeness combining skin colour, pseudo-scientific beliefs, economic pressures, and social politics dating back to the foundations of America. As Gerry Canavan proclaims, 'If we are interested in stories about brutal invaders who come in technologically advanced ships from far away, who kidnap, murder, rape, and enslave, we do not need to look to outer space; that is already Earth's actual history' (2016: 2). Thus, a science fictional blackness represents a key Afrofuturist theme.

Keeping science fictional blackness in mind, an alternative discernment of Afrofuturism develops when not overlooking the defining moments of black culture in the new world – enslavement and the creation of racial difference. These moments define the history of the African diaspora, subjectively rendering blacks as inhuman if not mechanical or alien. Therefore, Afrofuturism presents 'a challenge to remember a past that instructs a present that can build a future' according to De Witt D. Kilgore (2014: 563). Ytasha L. Womack says something similar, 'afrofuturists are constantly recontextualizing the past in a way that changes the present and the future' (2013: 158). What this means *is* that Afrofuturism recovers a raced space and time, unlocking opportunities for cultural analysis, by amassing 'countermemories that contest the colonial archive, thereby situating the collective trauma of slavery as the founding moment of modernity' (Eshun 2003: 288). For sociologist Alondra Nelson, these accumulated countermemories suggest that 'who we've [black people] been and where we've traveled is always an integral component of who we can become' (Nelson 2000: 34); that 'our imaginings of the future are always complicated extensions of the past' (35). These countermemories create a 'webbed network' for Afro-British scholar Kodwo Eshun, where the 'perpetual fight for human status, a yearning for human rights, a struggle for inclusion within the human species' (1998: 00[-006]) lasts far into the future, hundreds of years beyond chattel slavery, connecting black people together then and now. Clearly, a keen appreciation of history exists within Afrofuturism's future-slanted worldview. A position supported by feminist science fiction critic Lisa Yaszek, who states, 'Afrofuturism is not just about reclaiming the history of the past, but about reclaiming the history of the future as well' (2005: 300). The black technological usage that Dery championed as the basis of Afrofuturism years ago quite plainly limits what it means today.

Three other keys concepts stem from science fictional blackness and remixed history – a black networked consciousness, trans-historic feedback loop, and a hope impulse explored much further in my forthcoming *Afrofuturism Rising: The Literary Prehistory of a Movement* (2019). As an expansion of Eshun's concept, a black networked consciousness can be defined as the shared experiences of slavery – from the cargo holds of slave ships to the cash crop fields worked by black bodies to the bloody beatings and everything in between – that bond black people together. These visceral and spiritual connections become interactive in the sense that we now experience the resulting aesthetic endeavours of a dehumanized people in reading slave narratives, hearing spirituals, jazz, blues, and other music, seeing powerful films depicting slavery such as *12 Years a Slave* (2013) and recognizing its alien abduction experience. This experience exemplifies the trans-historic feedback loop ahistorically transporting us across time and space, to bear witness to this traumatic but eventually triumphant event.

Combining the black networked consciousness with the trans-historic feedback loop generates the impulse to hope for better tomorrows and different tomorrows. In concise terms, Afrofuturism represents an age-old yearning to exceed racial limitations and to produce the necessary social changes that go with it; such desire is what makes black worlds possible. But Afrofuturism is ultimately hopeful without being utopian. This kind of unique thinking overpowers the whitewashed historical narrative controlling the world today. Afrofuturism in all its intellectual dynamism has sparked a cultural revolution in the sense that we see people imagining futures in full colour through different interpretive lens such as techno-orientalism,[1] indigenous futurism,[2] and LatinX futurism.[3] The launching of this coloured wave in science fiction signifies Afrofuturism's enduring appeal.

Perhaps roused by Dery's definition of Afrofuturism, a veritable explosion of scholarship in the past decade alone addresses African American racial issues in speculative fiction. Monographs include: Ingrid Thaler's *Black Atlantic Speculative Fictions: Octavia E. Butler, Jewelle Gomez, and Nalo Hopkinson*

---

1 See David Morley and Kevin Robins, 'Techno-Orientalism: Japan Panic,' in *Global Media, Electronic Landscapes, and Cultural Boundaries*, eds David Morley and Kevin Robins (New York: Routledge, 1995), 147–173.
2 See Grace L. Dillon, 'Imagining Indigenous Futurisms' in *Walking the Clouds: An Anthology of Indigenous Science Fiction*, ed. Grace L. Dillon (Tucson: University of Arizona Press, 2012), 1–12.
3 See Rachel H. Ferreira, *The Emergence of Latino American Science Fiction* (Middletown, CT: Wesleyan University Press, 2011).

(2010), Gregory J. Hampton's *Changing Bodies in the Fiction of Octavia Butler: Slaves, Aliens, and Vampires* (2010) and *Imagining Slaves and Robots in Literature, Film, and Popular Culture: Reinventing Yesterday's Slave with Tomorrow's Robot* (2015), my own *Race in American Science Fiction* (2011), Adilifu Nama's *Super Black: American Pop Culture and Black Superheroes* (2011), Ytasha L. Womack's *Afrofuturism: The World of Black Sci-Fi and Fantasy Culture* (2013), Edward K. Chan's *The Racial Horizon of Utopia: Unthinking the Future of Race in Late Twentieth-Century American Utopian Novels* (2015), Louis Chude-Sokei's *The Sound of Culture: Diaspora and Black Technpoetics* (2015), André M. Carrington's *Speculative Blackness: The Future of Race in Science Fiction* (2016), Paul Youngquist's *A Pure Solar World: Sun Ra and the Birth of Afrofuturism* (2016), Gerry Canavan's *Octavia E. Butler* (2016), Diana A. Mafe's *Where No Black Woman Has Gone Before: Subversive Portrayals in Speculative Film and TV* (2018), Sami Schalk's *Bodyminds Reimagined: (Dis)ability, Race, and Gender in Black Women's Speculative Fiction* (2018), and Kinitra D. Brooks's *Searching for Sycorax: Black Women's Hauntings of Contemporary Horror* (2018). Likewise, anthologies include: Marleen S. Barr's *Afro-Future Females: Black Writers Chart Science Fiction's Newest New-Wave Trajectory* (2008), Sandra Jackson and Julie E. Moody-Freeman's *The Black Imagination: Science Fiction, Futurism, and the Speculative* (2011), my own *Black and Brown Planets: The Politics of Race in Science Fiction* (2014), Reynaldo Anderson and Charles E. Jones's *Afrofuturism 2.0: The Rise of Astro-Blackness* (2016). Unsurprisingly, the sheer proliferation of critical texts has encouraged scholars to turn their attention to how Afrofuturism is expressed across media, emphasizing the centrality of narrative to the Afrofuturist movement.

A film example which quickly comes to mind perfectly illustrates science fictional blackness when African American director Jordan Peele takes filmgoers into 'the sunken place' of his important film *Get Out* (2017; see Figure 23). Peele offers a powerful critique of race relations through his interracial couple Chris (Daniel Kaluuya) and Rose (Allison Williams), when Rose brings her black boyfriend home to meet her family.[4]

---

4   Surely, this moment is a serious reminder of the earlier 1967 film *Guess Who's Coming to Dinner* (1967), directed by Stanley Kramer.

Jordan Peele's *Get Out* (2017) and Ryan Coogler's *Black Panther* (2018)

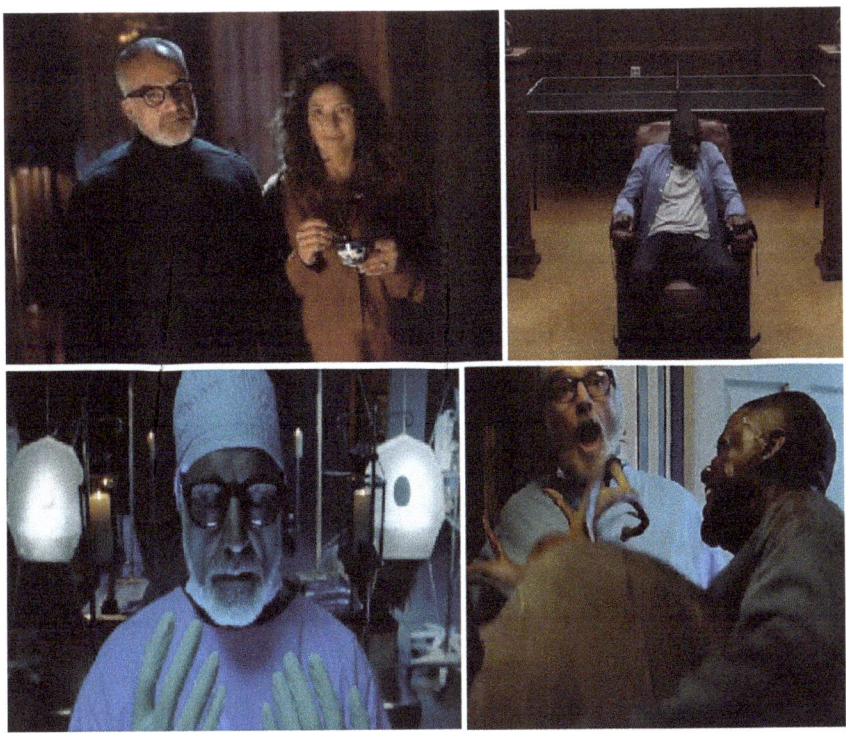

Figure 23. *Get Out* (Jordan Peele, 2017).

Classified as a horror film, Peele masterfully uses science fictional conventions such as the 'alien abduction' in the opening scene and body swapping via psycho-surgery. He blends such ideas with a contemporary slave auction, where affluent white folks bid to literally possess Chris's black body by transferring themselves, their minds and souls into it oddly reminiscent of the classic *Invasion of the Body Snatchers* (1956). Without doubt, white people bidding on black folks in this film calls to mind the horror of slave auctions like Solomon Northup experienced when he was abducted. Peele reminds us of science fiction's power to unsettle and provoke in his meta-commentary on race and racism. But the black guy wins at the end. Chris kills Rose's neurosurgeon father, hypnotherapist mother, and brother while burning down the house, and chokes her out before being rescued by his best friend who drives up in a police car and ignores the death pleas of Rose. That's an Afrofuturistic 'happy' ending if there ever was one (see Figure 24).

Figure 24. Chris (Daniel Kaluuya) and Rod (Lil Rel Howery) in *Get Out* (Jordan Peele, 2017).

Peele disrupts the repeating same of a science fictional blackness by initiating a *trans-historical feedback loop* previously generated by a *networked black consciousness* powered by the *hope impulse*. In popular black vernacular, we call this WOKE.

As a second more powerful cinematic example, *Black Panther* (2018), directed by African American Ryan Coogler, envisions what the entire African continent could have looked like (see Figure 25). For many the fictional country of Wakanda best symbolizes Afrofuturism by imagining a technologically and scientifically advanced black nation not disrupted by the Transatlantic slave trade or colonialism. Coogler and his cast manage to invert the lasting notion of Africa as the heart of darkness, a nineteenth-century white perception popularized by Joseph Conrad's novella *Heart of Darkness* (1899); a perception that still influences us with all kinds of negative associations regarding the African continent, its people, and their Diasporan descendants.

Figure 25. *Black Panther* (Ryan Coogler, 2018).

While Afrofuturism may have only been something scholars and artists were aware of at a particular moment in cultural history, the power of this film's vision has helped to make Afrofuturism a movement. *Get Out* and *Black Panther* demonstrate that audiences want to see complex images of race and racism and, more importantly, want to discuss the implications. Indeed, Afrofuturism enthrals so many people because it investigates the historical, cultural, and techno-scientific forces changing our planet.

Having become a significant buzzword in popular culture, the significance of sonic and visual avenues for Afrofuturism cannot be underestimated. But literature remains fundamental to understanding its full dimensions. In that respect, Martin R. Delany's serialized novel *Blake; or, the Huts of America* (1859–1862) is commonly acknowledged as the first work of black science fiction written nearly 160 years ago, followed by Sutton E. Griggs's *Imperium in Imperio* (1899), and Pauline Hopkins's *Of One Blood: Or, the Hidden Self* (1903). Delany, Griggs, and Hopkins provide future-oriented narratives of a budding slave revolution, the secret origin of a separate black American nation, and a lost-race tale returning to Africa respectively. Twenty-eight years later, George S. Schuyler writes *Black No More* (1931) which concerns a black doctor who invents a skin-whitening process causing a rapid depletion of negroes in America. Schuyler follows this novel with the serialized *Black Empire* (1936–1938), featuring a black genius who conquers the white world. Ralph Ellison writes the American classic *Invisible Man* (1952), concerning the identity quest and cultural blindness of a young nameless black man. Of course, there were other less regarded novels that might be considered science fiction,[5] but these seven novels represent the bedrock of Afrofuturism before the only black grandmaster of science fiction Samuel R. Delany, Jr first breaks into print in the early 1960s with his post-atomic future novel *The Jewels of Aptor* (1962), thirty-one years before Dery coins Afrofuturism. Delany's most important novels include *Babel-17* (1966), *The Einstein Intersection* (1967), *Nova* (1968), *Dahlgren* (1974), and *Stars in My Pocket like Grains of Sand* (1984). With this early historicizing in mind, the world owes a debt of gratitude to Sheree Renée Thomas for editing the ground-breaking anthologies *Dark Matter: A Century of Speculative Fiction from the African Diaspora* (2000) and *Dark Matter: Reading the Bones* (2004) and focusing attention on how blacks have envisioned futures for themselves in the past.

After Delany, Octavia E. Butler arrives as the first self-conscious African American woman to write science fiction with the publication of her first novel *Patternmaster* (1976). Set in the far future, *Patternmaster* concerns a master race of telepathic humans, selectively bred by a seemingly immortal being named Doro, at war with each other and at war with genetically mutated humans called clayarks. Though the first book written in the series, *Pattermaster* is the last book chronologically. The Patternist series begins with *Wild Seed* (1980), the fourth book written, and details the relationship between Doro and a shape-shifting healer named Anyanwu beginning when they first meet on the African continent in 1690. All of Butler's work promises a different tomorrow in the best Afrofuturist way, where the future, combined with science, technology, and black themes, demonstrates a maturing humanity overcoming manmade social obstacles like race, ethnicity, and gender. These two writers – Delany and Butler – represent a watershed moment for Afrofuturism because of the tremendous influence their writings have on the next wave of black speculative

---

5   See Mark Bould, 'Revolutionary African-American SF Before Black Power,' *Extrapolation* 51, no. 1 (2010), 53–81.

fiction writers to emerge in the 1980s and 1990s such as Steven Barnes, Charles Saunders, the virtually unknown John M. Faucette, Jewelle Gomez, Virginia Hamilton, and even Walter Mosley. In the 2000s Tananarive Due, Nalo Hopkinson, Tobias Buckell, Minister Faust, Andrea Hairston, Bill Campbell, Karen Lord, Nisi Shawl, Alaya Dawn Johnson, and Nnedi Okorafor come to the fore. And there are even newer voices such as Ayize Jama-Everett, Justina Ireland, Tomi Adeyemi, Kai Ashanti Wilson, Rivers Solomon, Nicky Drayden, Jennifer Marie Brissett, Sofia Samatar, and P. Djèlí Clark.

Figure 26. N. K. Jemisin. Photograph by Laura Hanifin, 2015 (<https://creativecommons.org/licenses/by-sa/3.0/deed.en>).

But none of these newest voices have yet made the impact that N. K. Jemisin has made (see Figure 26). Jemisin is the first black person to win the Hugo Award for Best Novel for *The Fifth Season* (2015) and the only author to ever win the Hugo Award for Best Novel three times straight with the sequels *The Obelisk Gate* (2016) and *The Stone Sky* (2017). *The Fifth Season*, first of the Broken Earth trilogy, introduces the world of The Stillness, a geologically unstable supercontinent that experiences catastrophic events on a frequent basis, and the magic of orogeny, the ability to manipulate seismic activity. The characters perilously traverse the unstable land seeking refuge from a xenophobic society and mastery of the orogeny earth science/magic. The sequel deals with the latest natural disaster's aftermath in the settlement of Castrima and further orogeny training in order to solve the mystery of the floating obelisks. And the concluding volume reveals whether or not humanity ultimately survives the post-apocalyptic rage of a father earth as two women must decide on catching the moon and returning it to orbit or crashing it. Jemisin traces systemic oppression throughout the trilogy and how it results in political tensions tinged by race as the protagonist Essun experiences racism caused by her difference as society attempts to control her magical ability. Consequently, Jemisin's trilogy offers an Afrofuturist critique on the abuses of power, privilege, and politics in our own world.

Using Afrofuturism to re-interpret black experience in combination with science fiction enables us to travel in time and across space to better understand this Afrotopian[6] pulsing, to create counter-narratives, to illustrate the many challenges we face. It shifts the power dynamics at work in analysing cultural history and popular culture. As De Witt Kilgore argues, 'Afrofuturism can be seen as less a marker of black authenticity and more a cultural force, an episteme that betokens a shift in our largely unconscious assumptions about what histories matter and how they may serve as a precondition for any future we may imagine' (2014: 564). As a combination of cultural history and science fiction, Afrofuturism intensifies black artistic production in such a way as to shift conversations on black experience.

---

6   See Wilson J. Moses, *Afrotopia: The Roots of African American Popular History* (Cambridge: Cambridge University Press, 1998).

Amy H. Sturgis

Indigenous Futurisms

> But I had forgotten that the Diné had already suffered their apocalypse over a century before. This wasn't our end. This was our rebirth.
> — Rebecca Roanhorse, *Trail of Lightning*[1]

The literature of Indigenous futurisms predates its label. During the bicentennial of the United States in 1976, for example, Standing Rock Sioux scholar and activist Vine Deloria, Jr offered 'Why the U.S. Never Fought the Indians', a bold work of science fiction recounting a remarkably different past and present for both Native Americans and the USA. Deloria's thought experiment challenges the inevitability of colonialism, Manifest Destiny, and (both cultural and literal) genocide, imagining instead a United States uplifted by a thriving 'Coalition of Indian Nations', a partnership that makes this might-have-been America 'the greatest demonstration of the vitality of human life that the world has ever seen' (1976: 12). While much of the tale reads like a lament for opportunities missed and lessons unlearned, at least part of this alternate present, Deloria implies, could yet be a very real future.

Decades after Deloria, inspired by the example of Afrofuturisms, Anishinaabe scholar Grace L. Dillon coined the term Indigenous futurisms and edited 2012's *Walking the Clouds: An Anthology of Indigenous Science Fiction*. In her introduction to the book, Dillon asks, 'Does SF have the capacity to envision Native futures, Indigenous hopes, and dreams recovered by rethinking the past in a new framework?' (2012: 2). Those Native creators who answer in the affirmative, she proposes, engage in/with Indigenous futurisms,

---

[1] Rebecca Roanhorse, *Trail of Lightning* (The Sixth World Book 1) (New York: Saga Press, 2018), 22.

and by doing so, they 'sometimes experiment, sometimes intentionally dislodge, sometimes merely accompany, but invariably *change* the perimeters of SF' (3).

Dillon's anthology served as a challenge of sorts for both creators and critics to claim earlier writers,[2] encourage new ones and devote critical attention to Indigenous science fiction. The genre now thrives, yielding story collections by single authors and anthologies with multiple contributors,[3] novels,[4] comics,[5] films[6] and critical conversations.[7] Furthermore, Indigenous

[2] Among these (re)claimed authors are award winners such as Anishinaabe author/scholar Gerald Vizenor and Cherokee author/editor William Sanders, both of whom are republished in *Walking the Clouds*.

[3] For example: Hope Nicholson, ed., *Love Beyond Body, Space & Time: An Indigenous LBGT Anthology* (Winnipeg: Bedside Press, 2016); Drew Hayden Taylor, *Take Us to Your Chief and Other Stories: Classic Science-Fiction with a Contemporary First Nations Outlook* (Vancouver: Douglas & McIntyre, 2016); Amy H. Sturgis, ed., 'A Celebration of Indigenous Fantasists' Double-Issue, *Apex Magazine*, Issue 99 (August 2017) <https://www.apex-magazine.com/issue-99-august-2017/> accessed 22 July 2018 and Joshua Whitehead, ed., *Love After the End: Two-Spirit Utopias and Dystopias* (Winnipeg: Bedside Press, 2019).

[4] For example: Daniel H. Wilson's *Robopocalypse* (New York: Doubleday, 2011) and *Robogenesis* (New York: Doubleday, 2014); Louise Erdrich, *Future Home of the Living God* (New York: Harper, 2017) and Roanhorse, *Trail of Lightning*.

[5] For example: Hope Nicholson, ed., *Moonshot: An Indigenous Comics Collection* (Toronto, Alternate History Comics Inc., 2015) and *Moonshot: An Indigenous Comics Collection* Volume 2 (Toronto, Alternate History Comics Inc., 2017) and Arigon Starr, ed., *Tales of the Mighty Code Talkers*, Volume 1 (Albuquerque, NM: Native Realities Press, 2016).

[6] For example: Charlene Agabao, Blackhorse Lowe, and Sydney Freeland, producers, Sydney Freeland, dir. *Hoverboard* (USA: 2012); Glen Wood, producer, Jordana Aarons, co-producer, Danis Goulet, dir., *Wakening* (Canada: 2013); Curtis Bridenstine, producer, Patricia Gnomes and Ian Skorodin, executive producers, Rodrick Pocowatchit, dir., *The Burden of Being* (USA: 2014) and Bryon Burkhead, co-producer, Deanie Eaton, Claudia LittleAxe, and Troy LittleAxe, executive producers, Rodrick Pocowatchit, producer and dir., *Red Hand* (USA: 2017).

[7] For example: Grace L. Dillon, ed., *Extrapolation*, Volume 57, No 1/2 (2016); Rebecca Roanhorse, Elizabeth LaPensee, Johnnie Jae, and Darcie Little Badger, 'Decolonizing Science Fiction and Imagining Futures: An Indigenous Futurisms Roundtable,' *Strange*

futurisms authors have received mainstream honours for their works. For example, Métis author Cherie Dimaline won the 2017 Governor General's Award for English-language children's literature and the 2017 Kirkus Prize in the young adult literature category, both for her novel *The Marrow Thieves*. In 2018, Ohkay Owingeh Pueblo author Rebecca Roanhorse won the Nebula Award and Hugo Award and was a finalist for the Theodore Sturgeon Memorial Award (and is currently nominated for the World Fantasy Award) for her short story 'Welcome to Your Authentic Indian Experience™', and she also won the John W. Campbell Award for Best New Writer in science fiction.

Dillon's vision of Indigenous futurisms includes Indigeneity in its widest context, and other editors, scholars, critics and creators also include storytellers of different global heritages (Aboriginal Australian, Native Hawaiian, Indigenous African, etc.) under the label. At the time of this writing, a survey of imaginative works, critical conversations and public appearances reveals that a majority of those who identify and/or are studied as part of the genre are Natives of the Americas. Works of Indigenous futurisms also transcend prose, poetry, and comics to include film and visual arts. The related flourishing of 'Indigenerds', as represented by such phenomena as the award-winning media platform A Tribe Called Geek (promising 'Indigenerdity for the Geeks at the Powwow')[8] and successive recent years of Indigenous Comic Cons (all thus far in the United States, with one planned for Australia),[9] also suggests that the project of Indigenous futurisms may be expressed in gaming, music, fashion, participatory fandom, and other areas of Native popular culture and experience (see Figure 27).

    Horizons, Issue 30 (January 2017) <http://strangehorizons.com/non-fiction/articles/decolonizing-science-fiction-and-imagining-futures-an-indigenous-futurisms-roundtable/> accessed 22 July 2018 and Daniel Heath Justice, *Why Indigenous Literatures Matter* (Waterloo: Wilfrid Laurier University Press, 2018).

8 *A Tribe Called Geek* <http://atribecalledgeek.com/> accessed 29 July 2018.
9 *Indigenous Comic Con* <https://www.indigenouscomiccon.com/> accessed 29 July 2018.

Figure 27. *Apex Magazine* #99 (August 2017), a special issue on Indigenous futurisms, featuring 'Welcome to Your Authentic Indian Experience™' by Rebecca Roanhorse.

The Projects of Indigenous Futurisms

The development of science fiction – a genre whose protagonists have so often been depicted as explorers, pioneers, and colonists – is closely tied to both the historical American west and its mythologizing in western fiction, film and television.[10] Of course, related notions of the frontier often either overlook the fact that the Americas were inhabited before European incursion, or offer tales of subjugation and conquest framed as 'winning' or 'taming' the west, a victory of the superior over the inferior, the civilized over the primitive. Cherokee scholar and author Daniel Heath Justice frames the challenge this way in *Why Indigenous Literatures Matter*: 'If the colonial imaginary is predicated on a fiction of Indigenous deficiency and absence, an empty frontier awaiting white supremacy to give it shape and substance, then what alternative does the escapist Indigenous imaginary offer to us as readers and bearers of story?' (2018: 152).

The answer is that Indigenous futurisms by their very nature push back against the legacy of colonialism and create new, sovereign narratives. Author Rebecca Roanhorse – whose Twitter profile photo as of the summer of 2018 shows her wearing a shirt quoting the description of Native Americans from the US Declaration of Independence: 'Merciless Indian Savages'[11] – defines the goal of Indigenous futurisms this way: 'to speak back to the colonialism tropes so prevalent in science fiction by reimagining space exploration from a non-colonial perspective and reclaiming our place in an imagined future in space, on earth, and everywhere in between'. Her 2018 debut novel, *Trail of Lightning*, clearly reclaims a place on earth; in a near-future post-apocalypse landscape, the Dinétah (the traditional name of the Navajo Nation) remains

---

10   See Gary K. Wolfe, 'Frontiers in Space' in *The Frontier Experience and the American Dream: Essays on American Literature*, eds David Mogen, Mark Busby, and Paul Bryant (College Station: Texas A&M University Press, 1989), 248–263; Carl Abbot, *Frontiers Past and Future: Science Fiction and the American West* (Lawrence: University Press of Kansas, 2006) and John Rieder, *Colonialism and the Emergence of Science Fiction* (Middletown, CT: Wesleyan University Press, 2008).

11   Rebecca Roanhorse Twitter Account <https://twitter.com/RoanhorseBex> accessed 30 July 2018.

'one of the last places standing' (2018: 69), renewed even as much of the United States is drowned or dying. Inverting both history and reader expectations, the Diné themselves erect walls around the 'rez' not only to protect their homes and resources, but also, in defiance of the Feds and multinationals and private armies, to 'remain Diné' (23).

Remaining Diné, or decolonizing the future, requires facing the legacy of past wrongs without succumbing to or becoming defined by them. Scholar David M. Higgins notes that postwar mainstream science fiction often represents a different colonialist message from the earlier one of subjugation and conquest; in contrast, 'victims are the ultimate heroes, and white men are often (astonishingly) the ultimate victims'. From *Star Wars* to *The Hunger Games*, 'Empires proliferate, and heroes liberate the oppressed minority'. What Higgins finds noteworthy is that Indigenous futurisms stories deny this 'imperial masochism' and reveal a 'consistent refusal to sanctify victimry' (2016: 53). As Dillon explains, the rejection of victimhood means that Indigenous futurisms tales are 'narratives of *biskaabiiyang*, an Ashininaaabemowin word connoting the process of "returning to ourselves", which involves discovering how personally one is affected by colonization, discarding the emotional and psychological baggage carried from its impact, and recovering ancestral traditions in order to adapt in our Post-Native Apocalypse world' (10).

Roanhorse agrees with the desire to discard the baggage of colonialism in order to recover and reclaim; in an interview with SyFyWire, she explains that she wanted 'to tell genre stories that didn't dwell on the effects of colonialism, but rather felt sovereign' (Krol 2018). In *Trail of Lightning*, Diné protagonist Maggie Hoskie, like her people, has experienced terrible things, but she is a survivor, not a victim – and certainly not anyone's stereotype. Maggie says, 'Some things are just bad. There's no redeeming value in suffering. All that noble savage shit is for suckers' (2018: 57). Maggie's story is the story of a woman returning to herself; in her Dinétah, old monsters once again roam the land, and so, infused by clan powers earned through tragedy, Maggie becomes a monster hunter.

Challenging colonialist tropes and providing new, sovereign stories in this case is an important task. As Rosebud Sioux author and educator Virginia Driving Hawk Sneve notes in her essay 'The Indians Are Alive', 'Eastern Abenaki author Joseph Bruchac has reported that many times he has gone into schools and children have asked him, "Are Indians still alive? I thought they all died a long time ago". Gayle Ross, Cherokee writer... had a five-year-old in Kansas City tell her that she couldn't be Indian, that the Indians were extinct, just like the dinosaurs' (2003: 298). In *Strange Horizon*'s January 2017 roundtable on Indigenous futurisms, Darcie Little Badger (Lipan Apache) explains how being 'pushed to the past tense' made her yearn for the corrective and positive lenses future-tense stories provide: 'I think that imagining a future, *period*, is a great start. ... The reality is, many Indigenous cultures in North America survived an apocalypse. The key word is *survived*. Any future with us in it, triumphant and flourishing, is a hopeful one.'[12]

In that same roundtable discussion, Little Badger, who is both an author of Indigenous futurisms stories and a professional scientist with a PhD in oceanography, joins Roanhorse, Elizabeth LaPensee (Anishinaabe and Métis) and Johnnie Jae (Otoe-Missouria and Choctaw) in emphasizing a point first made by Dillon; namely, that works of Indigenous futurisms allow creators to add diverse Native scientific insights and practices to the science in science fiction. Doing so serves as another act of decolonization, shedding mainstream assumptions that Indigenous equates to 'primitive' – and, equally problematic, non-Native 'awe-struck neoshamanism' (Dillon 2012: 8). Moreover, the many different Indigenous cultures and environments have yielded diverse knowledge and skills that promise contributions to science fiction conversations on topics from physics to pharmacology, sustainability studies to science pedagogy (7–8).

Scientific insights are not the only addition these works bring to science fiction; works of Indigenous futurisms also expand the ingredients available for science fictional thought experiments and world building. If science fiction truly explores what it means to be human, it follows that the more widely we understand the depth and variety of human individuals and cultures, the more angles from which we approach the question, then the more fruitful this

---

12 Rebecca Roanhorse, Elizabeth LaPensee, Johnnie Jae and Darcie Little Badger, 'Decolonizing Science Fiction and Imagining Futures: An Indigenous Futurisms Roundtable,' *Strange Horizons*, Issue 30 (January 2017) <http://strangehorizons.com/non-fiction/articles/decolonizing-science-fiction-and-imagining-futures-an-indigenous-futurisms-roundtable/> accessed 22 July 2018.

exploration will be. *Trail of Lightning* effectively draws on Navajo traditions, ancient and modern – from the centrality of the matriarchal clan system to the workings of the barter economy of the rez – to paint a nuanced portrait of the near-future Dinétah. What is more, Roanhorse does not frame the central conflict as one between whites and Natives; on the contrary, the Navajo Nation is wholly sufficient to provide all the tale requires, including heroes and villains and those in between (hence Roanhorse's stress on writing sovereign fiction). Perhaps most importantly, Roanhorse utilizes her knowledge of Navajo history and mythology to add substance and texture to her response to the science fictional question of 'What if?' Her use of dreams and visions, tricksters and monsters, big medicine and ancestral connection not only creates a compelling novel, but it also constitutes an act of survival, renewal and evolution for Indigenous storytelling and represents a rich infusion of imagination into the larger genre.

Works of Indigenous futurisms, then, challenge colonialist narratives and supply new, sovereign ones, claiming a space for Indigenous futures, and in the process they bring much to feed both the science and fiction of science fiction. They are, in true science fiction tradition, thought-provoking and imaginative agents of change. In *Why Indigenous Literatures Matter*, Justice considers Indigenous futurisms part of what he terms 'wonderworks', and he proposes that these stories matter very much indeed:

> They give us a future, even if it's only an imagined one. But without that imagined possibility, it's all too easy to believe we don't belong there. And that's a road to a very frightening place indeed.
>
> Indigenous writers continue to produce works that articulate and even anticipate our potential for transformative change, if only we bring to it the best of our imaginative selves. Freedom of love, of desire, of life, culture, and political survival – these are only realized through the linking of our courage to our imaginations. We can't possibly live otherwise until we first *imagine* otherwise. (2018: 156)

Figure 28. Whiter than white: the salvation of humanity in *Mad Max: Fury Road* (George Miller, 2015).

Christopher B. Menadue

George Miller's *Mad Max* (1979–2015) and Ryan Griffen's *Cleverman* (2016–2017)

In his documentary *White Fellas Dreaming: A Century of Australian Cinema*, also released as *40,000 Years of Dreaming: A Century of Australian Cinema* (Miller 1997), *Mad Max* director George Miller presented Australian film culture as a modern-day 'Dreamtime' for the white Australian public (see Figure 28). Miller's interpretation can be examined from the perspective of a colonial tradition that appropriates traditional indigenous culture, under the assumption that it has been expertly researched and understood by civilized, educated, white, authorities. This appears to be especially apt when applied to Miller's use of the term 'Dreaming' – the white terminology and interpretation of which approximates an indigenous phenomenological experience, presented from the cultural perspective of white writers and academics.

To use the expression 'White Fella Dreaming' is a clumsy analogical appropriation of an Australian Aboriginal cultural experience; and is an ironically 'white' undertaking in the Australian historical context. The background to Miller's *Mad Max* franchise is a postcolonial echo of the Australian settler ethos, which sought to obliterate Aboriginal Australians and subsume or destroy their culture. A more recent Australian science fiction offering, *Cleverman*, was conceived by an Australian Aboriginal, Ryan Griffen, and is steeped in contemporary culture, issues and traditional stories of the Australian Aborigine. *Cleverman* is a futuristic dystopian drama telling the story of the struggle for survival of the 'Hairypeople', a species of superhumans with roots in Australian Aboriginal mythology, who are persecuted and ghettoized by the dominant white culture. Their chances for survival are dependent upon the intervention of the legendary 'Cleverman' who is able to channel powers from the Australian Aboriginal Dreamtime.

The common underlying feature of these two representations of Australia is the impact and outcomes of colonialism. This is seen through the lens of the science fiction genre, demonstrating that SF is capable of providing a rich and nuanced commentary on social and cultural perspectives.

The *Mad Max* series at first sight might be thought of as the merging of the European SF tradition of the '*voyages extraordinaires*' of Jules Verne, and the cultural mythology of Australian colonization. The *voyage extraordinaire* pre-dates Mad Max by a century, and may appear similar due to common themes of exploration and discovery. But Verne's explorers encounter other races and species, and in contrast to Miller, Verne emphasized scientific discovery. We find anti-imperialist, and anti-colonial opinions, even satire, in some of his works (Cornick 2006; Dine 1997; Krobb 2016; Sandner 1998). Verne directly criticized the types of motives and outcomes portrayed in *Mad Max*, and has been described as his own 'Captain Nemo' (Freedman 2000: 51). Verne's anti-imperialist stance is especially clear in *De la terre a la lune*, which Adam Roberts has identified to be more of a critique of American imperialist and conquest-focused gun culture than a mere adventure story (2005: 133–135). Miller's fable is in reality an example of the worldview that Verne despises.

Australia is a land of demographic and environmental contrast – the majority (85 per cent) of the population live within 50 kilometres of the coast, while the inland regions maintain a remote, mythological status for the non-indigenous. This is the product of both colonization folklore and low population density – colonial settlements have been portrayed as islands of culture in a sea of wilderness (Khatun 2015). The history of the exploration of Australia was a series of speculative, often 'extraordinary', and generally ill-fated expeditions in a vast and forbidding continent in search of fertile lands and inland seas, disrupted by inconvenient encounters (some of them massacres) with Australian Aborigines. The consequent permeation of colonizing migrants as civilizers and gardeners of this ostensibly alien landscape was enforced by the assumptions that it was '*Terra Nullius*' – an empty land. Miller's vision of a future post-apocalyptic Australia is in perfect accord with this vision.

The doctrine of *Terra Nullius*, which was applied to claim Australia for early European settlers, stated that Australia had no inhabitants who could claim rights to title when the country was 'discovered' by Europeans. The existence of Aboriginal Australians was ignored, and Aboriginal Australian Ruby Langford-Ginibi describes how the whites saw her people as 'vermin to be cleared from the face of the earth' (Ginibi, cited in Brewster 1996: 2). The legal determination of *Terra Nullius* denied the very existence of Australian Aboriginal culture, and European settlers romanticized invasive colonization with their own mythology of taming and civilizing the new frontier (White 1981). Australian Aboriginal ontology was alien to the sensibilities of a colonial invader culture, and historically either interpreted from a European perspective, or ignored as an irrelevance – which has been carried forward into an imaginary future in SF film. In white Australian SF this is exemplified by the long-running tradition in the *Mad Max* franchise of white people inhabiting and exploring barren, ostensibly Australian, landscapes.

The adversarial colonists of the otherwise barren spaces of Miller's work are caricatures with sociopathic moral and ethical perspectives. The heroic protagonists, however, have human, white, virtues and appearance. The 'apocalyptic' portrayal of landscapes in the *Mad Max* films implies a sterile and alien environment in which the human actors are themselves islands of life and culture, and in this light, the portrayal of the beautiful white-clad fertile women in *Fury Road* as the only hope for the future of humanity emphasizes the assumption that life and growth can only occur through the direct intervention of the colonist. This simple and unashamed vision supports Lorenzo Veracini's observation that 'settler colonialism in many ways still goes without saying' (2011: 364). For the colonist, the indigenous population are to be subordinated, ignored, and quietly exterminated, and *Mad Max* presents a world in which this has been successfully completed. This is in direct opposition to the naturalistic, healthy, situatedness of place and time that we find for the Australian Aboriginal in *Cleverman*.

In the first film of Miller's series, *Mad Max* (1979), all the characters are white Australians – no Aboriginal Australians or Torres Strait Islanders were employed, and no indigenous people are visible in any background or passing shots. The urban areas are depicted as run-down, or industrial wastelands, and the landscape outside the cities is barren and devoid of life apart from police and roaming bandits. In contrast, we see Max experiencing his happiest times on a farm with his partner and child, living a pastoral idyll in an environment that has been civilized and transformed by the (beneficial) interventions of white settlers; this assumption of the improvement of wilderness by imposition of a systematically organized settler culture is a historical motif of SF writing (Menadue, 2017), which was only beginning to be replaced in print by more nuanced and culturally sensitive versions around the time that *Mad Max* was released. *Mad Max 2: The Road Warrior* (1981) is a similarly 'white' film. 'The Feral Kid' in *Mad Max 2* employs a boomerang as a weapon, but is a blond blue-eyed actor, not identifiable as an Australian Aboriginal, and the use of the boomerang suggests another cultural appropriation. In *Mad Max Beyond Thunderdome* (1985) there is added irony in the fact that the only non-white characters are played by African-Americans, with Tina Turner taking the joint lead with Mel Gibson. *Mad Max Fury Road* (2015), the latest instalment in the franchise, takes 'whitewashing' one, literal, step further – in the use of white body paint as an identifying characteristic for one of the factions portrayed. There are very few non-white actors in the film, and those present take minor supporting roles, are not Australian, or are only present in the crowd scene with which the film opens.

Considering the absence of an Aboriginal Australian presence in Miller's film, it is even more ironic that he appropriated the concept of 'Dreamtime' to describe the history of Australian cinema, equating the experiences of the descendants of white colonists with those of an indigenous population that was historically declared to not have any legal existence, and were not allowed to pursue legal rights over their historically occupied land until the 1992 Mabo case that determined the rights of native title and overturned the legal farce of *Terra Nullius* (Australian Bureau of Statistics, 2012). The majority, however, still do not have legal rights, as native title is extremely difficult to prove, given that it can be 'washed away' by the 'tide of history' as stated by Justice Howard Olney in response to the application for native title by the Yorta Yorta (Ritter 2004: 107). The use of 'Dreaming' is itself a colonial approximation of an Australian Aboriginal concept, and is a further appropriation of an indigenous culture through a white interpretation of that the values and beliefs of others who are outside their own experience. The significance and complexity of what is translated into English as 'Dreaming' or 'Dreamtime' is much broader and deeper than the limited frame of reference it is given by non-indigenous Australians (Wierzbicka and Goddard 2015), and is in some ways linguistically dependent upon specific language forms and physical locations that make it physically and linguistically inaccessible to outsiders such as Miller. It can be argued that Australian Aboriginals are the only people capable of telling these stories, which cannot be readily translated into the vernacular of the 'White Fella'.

Miller's films contrast with the contemporary postcolonial SF offering of *Cleverman* (Ford, 2017), which provides a more nuanced interpretation across both traditions, reflecting that indigenous culture is more visible in modern Australian society, and commenting on the prejudices that persist (Genzlinger, 2016). In *Cleverman* the settings are urban, multi-cultural and multi-racial. Most of the actors are Australian Aborigines, and the concepts that underlie the narrative are embedded in Australian Aboriginal legend and culture in a contemporary reimagining of traditional beliefs and expectations. Ryan Griffen, the driving force behind *Cleverman*, has been very conscious of his Aboriginal heritage in decisions regarding storylines: consulting with elders to ensure that material used does not contravene custom and belief. Reasons he gives for developing *Cleverman* include his personal experience with casual racism and the desire to provide a learning experience both for Australian Aboriginal people, but also for non-Aboriginal Australians (Griffen, 2016). In *Cleverman*, Griffen presents us with a perspective on Australian culture that is the polar opposite both in content and context to the cultural assumptions of the *Mad Max* franchise.

Cleverman is noteworthy both for the Australian Aboriginal focus and stewardship but also for the commentary it makes on contemporary and historic issues around cultural identity, prejudice and control. The physical ghettoization of the 'hairies' in the series by officials of a dominant Australian culture is a pointed reminder of a history of detention and abuse experienced by Australian Aborigines who suffer extraordinarily high levels of incarceration compared to their white Australian counterparts (Gray 2016), and it is also a commentary on the endemic treatment of 'undesirables' – the 'containment centres' bringing to mind Australian Border Force off-shore immigration detention, and associated degradation of basic human rights and obligations.

Cleverman is filmed in sites that are readily identifiable as being associated with modern Aboriginal Australian culture and life – Redfern, and La Perouse. Unlike *Mad Max*, the localization is celebrated – this is not a barren wasteland – and, as the star of the series, Hunter Page-Lochard, commented to Berlin Film Festival reporter Stephanie Bunbury: the Aboriginal inhabitants do not suffer the 'poor, troubled black kid who drinks' stereotypes that he had previously been employed to portray, and settings are accurately (and for the Aboriginal Australian, unremarkably) domestic (Bunbury, 2016; see Figure 29). This contrasts with the traditional white representations of

Figure 29. 'Not your average "poor, troubled black kid who drinks"...' Hunter Page-Lochard as Koen West, the titular Cleverman (Ryan Griffen, 2016–2017).

Aboriginal Australians associated with the bush, going walkabout and leading chaotic domestic lives.

Nevertheless, some mainstream Australian media sources have been critical of the series as over-hyped and heavy-handed (Quinn, 2016). This contrasts with reporting by *National Indigenous Times* that praised the series unreservedly (Caccetta, 2017), and Griffen's own more nuanced situating of the series as just one representative element of 60,000 years of hitherto untold Aboriginal stories (Griffen, 2017). Griffen has commented on the difficulties of achieving recognition in Australia, when international audiences have been more positive (Griffen, n.d.). Comparisons between the open reception given overseas and less sympathetic Australian reporting and commentary adds to the argument that the casual racism visible in the *Mad Max* series still underlies much of Australian culture. As Aboriginal Australian scholar Marcia Langton states: 'it is the challenge for settler Australians of recognizing that Aboriginal people are fully human beings' (2003: 82). This mixed reception is especially interesting given the flavour of the reporting – whereas Bunbury's report on the Berlin Film Festival and Griffen's own comments on international reception discover foreign viewers expressing interest in subjects of which they were previously unaware, Australian critics are without doubt aware of the existence of an Australian Aboriginal culture that has been denied in favour of an unsustainable white mythology of Australian settlement.

We can see in comparisons between *Mad Max* and *Cleverman* how the relationship between SF and human culture can illustrate genuine experiences and representations of human interactions, beliefs, and prejudices; a relationship that exists across a broad range of research interests (Menadue and Cheer, 2017). SF acts as an effective lens through which to observe our real-world social and cultural characteristics, and can tease out information about a range of human worldviews that conceal, ignore, or deny objective realities. The study of the changes in the fictional record over time provide insights into persistent and changing human attitudes and beliefs, and what can be radical differences in perspective between co-existing human populations. This is clearly visible in the comparative evaluation of those most Australian of SF stories: *Mad Max* and *Cleverman*.

Raffaella Baccolini

Margaret Atwood's *The Handmaid's Tale* (2017–present)

Utopian and dystopian science fiction written by women constitutes 'a continuous literary tradition in the West from the seventeenth century until the present day' (Donawerth and Kolmerten 1994: 1). Yet, in spite of that, SF has long been conceived as territory of the male. For example, 'between 1953 (the year of its inception) and 1967 there were no women winners of the Hugo award' (Lefanu 1988: 7). The 1970s, however, marked the beginning of an extraordinary relationship between feminism and utopian and dystopian SF, one that continues today.[1] And since 1968, there have been at least sixty winners in the four main categories of the Hugo (novel, novella, novelette, and short story). In fact, SF informed by feminist and radical politics has provided women writers with the ideal place to explore the construction of gender roles and subjectivities – a freedom that the constraints of realism do not always afford them. As Joanna Russ puts it, '*What If* literature [is] the perfect literary mode in which to explore (and explode) our assumptions about "innate" values and "natural" social arrangements, in short, our ideas about Human Nature, Which Never Changes' (1972: 80). If the radical optimism of the 1960s and 1970s saw a flourishing of feminist SF utopias (cf. Moylan), the return to conservativism of the past thirty-some years has seen a plethora of dystopian and, most recently, post-apocalyptic fiction by women (cf. Baccolini and Moylan). Today dystopian SF seems to be the preferred genre to give voice to a critique of present society and its gender roles. The enormous popularity of Suzanne Collins's *Hunger Games* trilogy and the revival of Margaret Atwood's

---

[1] Many studies have been devoted to post-1970s women's SF (e.g. Barr; Lefanu; Moylan); on the earlier period see, for example, Larbalestier.

The Handmaid's Tale, thanks to its TV serialization in 2017, are two of the main factors contributing to the flourishing of dystopian SF titles of recent years. Among them is Naomi Alderman's *The Power* (2016).

Feminism and SF have been 'intimately connected' for a long time, and Jane Donawerth traces this interconnection by identifying some recurring themes: women's rights to education, property, and voting as well as sexuality and self-expression (Donawerth 2009: 214). Feminist SF has allowed women writers to use the device of an imaginary society to affirm that 'women, deprived of civil rights in the real world, are fully capable of governance; and to demonstrate, with wit and ingenuity, that a world ruled by women would be a far more pleasant, peaceable, and ethical state' (Jones 2009: 484). Feminist dystopian SF, on the other hand, has concentrated on the attack against individual freedom by foregrounding, in particular, the issues of women's reproductive rights and the control of their bodies. If all-women utopias, for example, emphasize 'the essentially different nature of women' and represent 'models for a better society', feminist SF becomes 'a way of working out in narrative form central issues of 1970s and 1980s feminism' (Donawerth 2009: 216, 218). Joanna Russ's *The Female Man* (1975), Marge Piercy's *Woman on the Edge of Time* (1976), Vonda McIntyre's *Dreamsnake* (1978), Sally Miller Gearhart's *The Wanderground* (1979), Ursula K. Le Guin's *Always Coming Home* (1985), Joan Slonczewski's *A Door into Ocean* (1986), Pamela Sargent's *The Shore of Women* (1986), and Sherri Tepper's *The Gate to Women's Country* (1988) represent some of the extremely influential narratives that have shaped women's SF. These feminist utopian SF novels of the 1970s and 1980s highlight the creation of all-female communities that are supportive of women's agency. Some of the worlds depicted are places where women live harmoniously with the environment and where nature's wholeness becomes an expression of women's natural and moral development. Technology is not rejected but is considered subservient to social priorities; therefore, it is not used to master nature but to improve human life. Technology can then be reclaimed in women's utopian SF and becomes a means to free women from patriarchal constraints.

Women's bodies and sexuality have always been a central feature in dystopian SF narratives. In classical dystopias as well as in SF, for example, the bodies of certain female characters become disturbing elements for the male protagonists and, consequently, for the totalitarian regimes they inhabit.

Within the totalitarian societies conceived by Aldous Huxley or George Orwell, for example, whether sexuality is free (as in Huxley) or controlled (as in Orwell), the female body represents a powerful subversive element for the male protagonist who, stimulated by women's sexuality, is led to challenge the ideology of the hegemonic system. However, while these female characters serve the rebellion of the male protagonist, they remain passive instruments, incapable of self-consciousness and of actively subverting society on their own. Similarly, in the future societies described in SF classics such as Ray Bradbury's *Fahrenheit 451* (1953) and Harlan Ellison's 'A Boy and His Dog' (1969) the young women's bodies and sexualities act as dangerous awakenings for their male protagonists. The critique of the (patriarchal and totalitarian) societies of these dystopian texts does not address the relationship between gender and power, a theme that is present in many dystopian SF novels by women.

By setting their narratives in totalitarian future or past societies or hyper-technological worlds, women's dystopian SF identifies, in the critique and re-appropriation of sexuality and of women's bodies, a crucial means of emancipation from patriarchy. Such a revision is necessary in a critique of the patriarchal roots of totalitarianism and the abuse of technology, but also in the redefinition of women's agency and subjectivity. In dystopian SF novels like Katharine Burdekin's *Swastika Night* (1937), Suzy McKee Charnas's *Walk to the End of the World* (1974), Zoe Fairbairns's *Benefits* (1979), Octavia Butler's *Kindred* (1979), Suzette Haden Elgin's *Native Tongue* (1984), and Margaret Atwood's *The Handmaid's Tale* (1985), the authors describe oppressive societies where reproduction is controlled or compulsory, thus showing how gendered identities are the products of an androcentric, totalitarian discourse. The reduction of women to their biological function, even when performed in silence and passivity, is not an innate, essential quality; rather it is forced upon them through the use of institutionalized rape and violence, and it is constructed by the totalitarian discourse of male supremacy.

Central to women's dystopias – whether written in the 1930s and 1940s or in more recent years – are gender issues, such as violence against women and the exclusively reproductive function of women, which, in these texts, are seen as inextricably linked to the cult of virility and the idea of masculinity that underlie totalitarian regimes. These works expose the relationship between totalitarianism, violence, and gender discrimination, thus identifying in the climate, rituals, and mentality of the extreme right in Europe in the 1930s and 1940s, and of the fundamentalist and populist forces of today, which constitute some of the main threats to women's freedom and agency.

It is no surprise then, that Margaret Atwood's 1985 novel *The Handmaid's Tale* has enjoyed a revival in the past couple of years – years that have been characterized by a series of crises (Brexit; the election of Trump; the rise of populism; femicides; the migrant crisis; ongoing conflicts and wars; and ethnic and racial hatred) that have brought Atwood's future society extremely close to home (see Figure 30).[2] Set in a not-so-distant future in what was once the United States and is now a repressive theocracy where reproduction is compulsory, the novel describes a tragic and grotesque society (that takes the Book of Genesis at its word) from the perspective of one of the unfortunate Handmaids, Offred, who under the new regime is exploited as a surrogate mother. Rape is thus institutionalized in the new Republic of Gilead: a Handmaid is assigned to each household, consisting of an officially barren Wife and a Commander, who is also likely to be sterile (but officially only women can be fertile or not). Once a month, in the presence of his Wife, the Commander has sex with the Handmaid, in order to produce a child.

At once a dystopia and a work of speculative fiction, *The Handmaid's Tale* is a powerful feminist critique of patriarchal definitions of womanhood. In the novel, women are considered to be the property of the male-run State. They cannot work nor have possessions; reproduction is compulsory; and language – reading, writing, or speaking – is forbidden, with the exception of empty and trite religious phrases. Women are completely disempowered: they are reduced to their biological function, possess no proper name, and have no language, freedom or identity besides that defined by the State (see Figure 31). Their new names exemplify their new condition: they are forced to take a patronym composed of the possessive preposition 'of' and the first names of the Commanders who own them.

---

2   Cf. Atwood's own account on (re)reading her novel in the age of Trump.

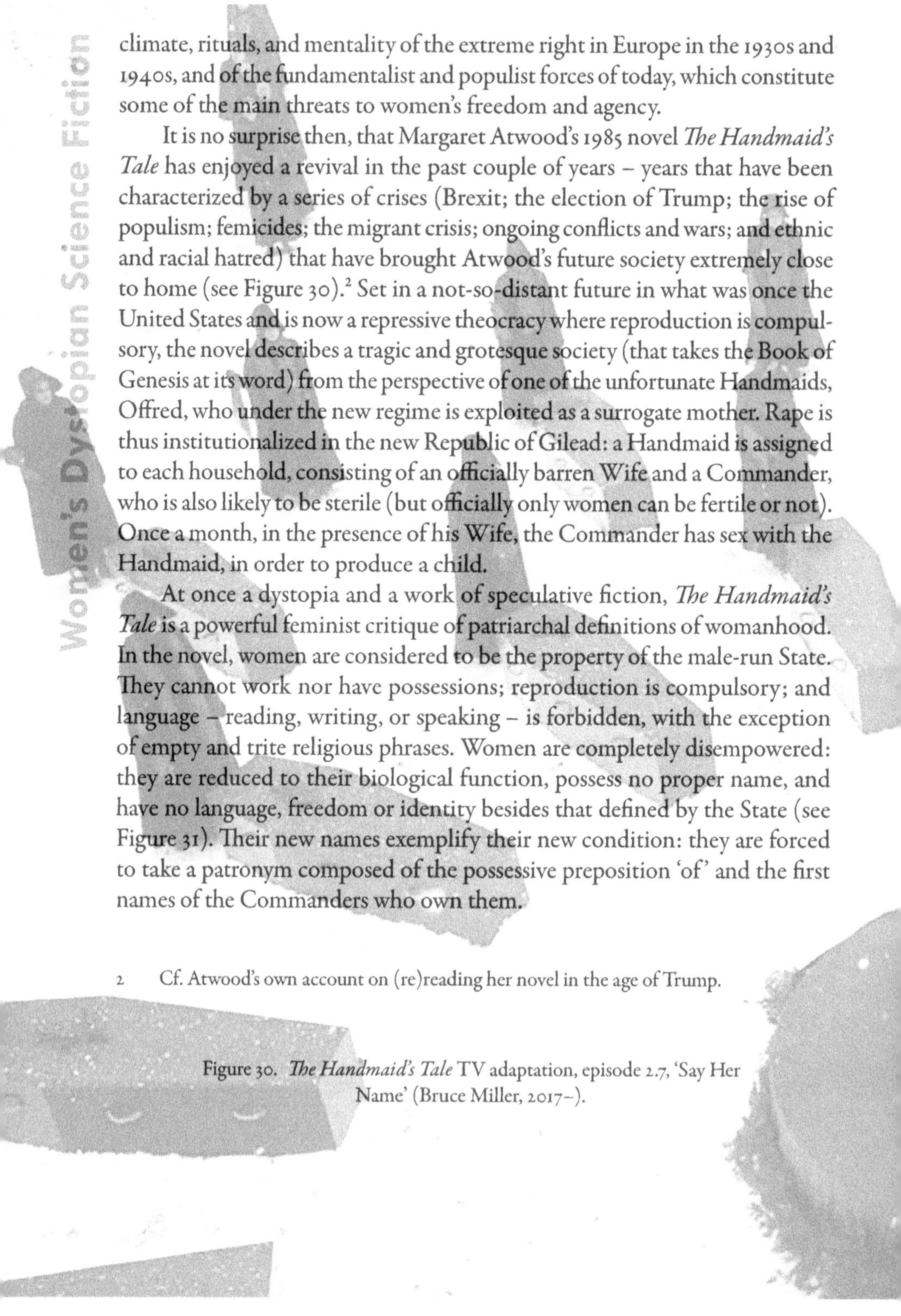

Figure 30.   *The Handmaid's Tale* TV adaptation, episode 2.7, 'Say Her Name' (Bruce Miller, 2017–).

Passivity and silence are not, however, innate qualities of women, and like other feminist authors of SF, Atwood demonstrates that these are forced upon the women of Gilead. Another recent dystopian SF work written by a woman, Naomi Alderman, can be and has been read in a direct dialogue with Atwood's text. Alderman's recent novel, *The Power*, is a battle of the sexes story, with a shocking sex-role reversal.[3] While at the heart of traditional battle-of-the-sexes texts 'is the struggle to restore male rule and the "natural order of things"' (Larbalastier 40), *The Power* presents a thought-provoking experiment about domination and violence, possibility and change.

Set some 5,000 years into the future, after a great event known as The Cataclysm that establishes women as the dominant sex, the novel is presented as a 'hybrid piece, ... a sort of "novelization" of what archaeologists agree is the most plausible narrative' (Alderman 2016: ix). The story, a manuscript written by a man (Neil Adam Armon, an anagram of the author's name) and sent to a woman fellow-writer (Naomi), is framed by the correspondence between the two. It begins when girls, all over the world, develop a 'skein', or a strip of muscles and nerves in their collarbones that conducts electricity, giving them the power to hurt, torture, and kill. Alderman therefore imagines the transition to an upside-down world, where men are afraid to walk alone at night and women's bodies become an instrument of power. Through the eyes of four different characters, she challenges traditional assumptions about gender and explores the ways power affects and changes relations at all levels. The result is a disturbing, thought-provoking dystopian SF novel: if, at first, the revolution may sound exhilarating, especially to female readers, Alderman makes sure to challenge our initial enthusiasm by showing that a (true) feminist revolution cannot just reproduce, in reverse, the values and norms of an androcentric society.

The various social, political, and religious developments produced by the simple overturning of hierarchies and gender relations show that the spread of female power rapidly degenerates from just retribution into gratuitous cruelty.

3   Daphne Patai (1982) has used the expression 'sex-role reversal,' while Joanna Russ and Justine Larbalestier have used the phrase 'battle of the sexes' to describe 'a body of stories explicitly about relations between men and women' (2002: 39). Alderman herself acknowledges Atwood's role as a mentor (340).

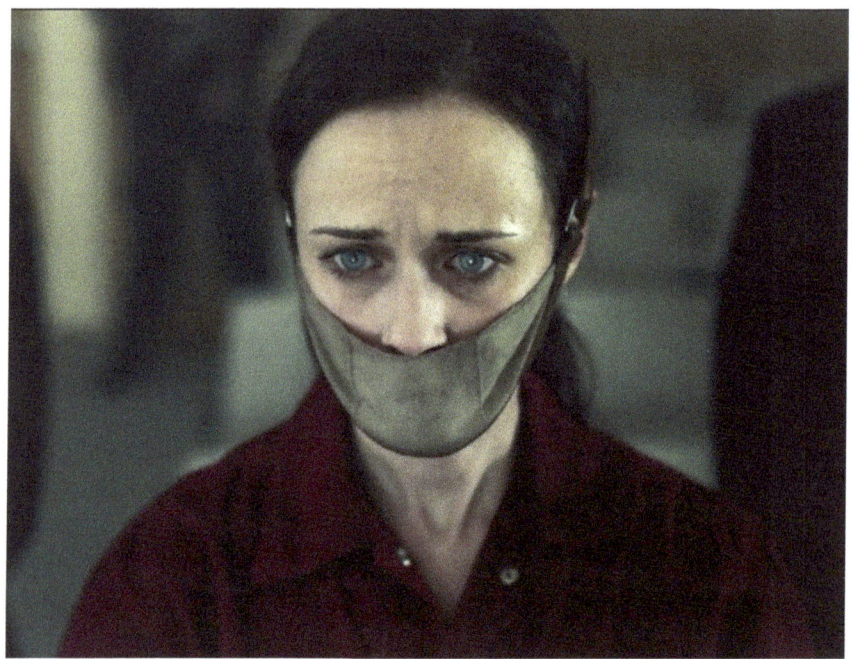

Figure 31. *The Handmaid's Tale*, episode 1.03, 'Late' (Bruce Miller, 2017–).

Women come to destroy, rape, torture, and kill, just as men did before them. Both societies – our patriarchal present and the dystopian future where women rule – are based on violence and the ruthless use of power. Why do people, regardless of gender or race, abuse power? 'They do it because they can', is the simple, yet disturbing answer (Alderman 2016: 283). Because in societies that thrive on inequality, impunity becomes the norm and accountability, even if demanded, can easily be ignored.

Can a universe ruled by women alone produce a better society? Not if the dynamics of power and the values at the basis of the new society remain the same, says Alderman. The sex-role reversal does not portray a utopian world run by women who rule with righteousness and justice. But Alderman does not call for a return to a natural order of things by showing only the reversal of sexism. Rather, by portraying the damages inflicted on women who become victims of the same system they are creating, she invites readers to reflect also on the damage that patriarchy does to males themselves. Alderman seems to evoke, then, Audre Lorde's famous claim that '*the master's tools will never dismantle the master's house*. They may allow us temporarily to beat him at his own game, but they will never enable us to bring about genuine change' (1984: 112, emphasis original). Feminism is not the simple reversal of the status quo. Likewise, the book suggests that gender is not 'natural' and invites us to go beyond traditional binaries:

> the world is the way it is now because of five thousand years of ingrained structures of power based on darker times when things were much more violent ... but we don't have to act that way now. We can think and imagine ourselves differently. (Alderman 2016: 338)

Some may think that by now, these are obvious ideas. But it is still useful to reflect on them. And it is certainly useful to recognize the similarities and parallelism with our present.

The recent publication of Alderman's novel as well as of Leni Zumas's *Red Clocks* (a disturbing meditation on motherhood, identity, women's rights, and freedom) and Louise Erdrich's *Future Home of the Living God* (a reflection on female agency, self-determination, biology, and natural rights) are signs of the exciting richness and variety of women's dystopian SF. Women's and feminist SF is still flourishing today 'in a way that would have been unthinkable before the 1970s, and the genre continues to be enriched by the alternative narratives of feminism' (Jones 2009: 488). Whether it speaks of dystopian future societies where women or man are enslaved, or it imagines future imperfect worlds where hybridity challenges and expands our understanding of gender, women's and feminist SF represents a still vital terrain for exploring and questioning injustice, inequality, and patriarchy.

Alec Charles

The Thirteenth Doctor, *Doctor Who* (2017–present)

Despite the genre's extensive associations with puerile entertainment, the most effective and enduring SF has always offered nuanced and complex perspectives on gender. As the works of such artists as Ursula K. Le Guin, Margaret Atwood, Joanna Russ, Rona Munro and Tanith Lee clearly attest, SF has never been the exclusive province of adolescent male geeks, nerds or 'fanboys', nor is it an unequivocally and irrevocably patriarchal genre. SF has long explored issues of gender, often influenced by the speculative complexities of feminism, post-structuralism and psychoanalysis. Now that popular screen SF is catching up with its literary antecedents, we are witnessing the suddenly strange and wonderful fruits of its ideological conflictedness Yet, perhaps surprisingly, this is a set of issues with which such franchises as *Star Trek* and *Doctor Who* have been engaging and wrestling, fruitfully, for some time.

    December 2017 saw the elevation of Daisy Ridley to the status of lead (and last surviving) Jedi (see Figure 32) and the accession of Jodie Whittaker to the role of lead (and once last surviving) Time Lord. *Star Wars* stalwart Mark Hamill had been reported as unhappy with the way his protagonist had been obliged to relinquish his lightsabre, as Ridley's Rey moved centre stage. On 22 December 2017 the *Daily Mail* quoted him asserting that his character in *The Last Jedi* was 'not [his] Luke Skywalker'. Many *Star Wars* devotees meanwhile expressed a similar dislike for what *BBC News* depicted as possibly 'the most divisive film ever'. Those hostile to the film included fans 'upset that the franchise's heroes now include women' (Watercutter 2017). In January 2018, one such enthusiast released online a pirate edit of the 210-minute film without its female leads. It ran to only forty-six minutes. It should be noted that Mark Hamill was one of the film's stars who unequivocally denounced this explicit misogyny (Belam 2017). *Doctor Who*'s outgoing star Peter Capaldi

Figure 32. Daisy Ridley as Rey in *Star Wars: The Force Awakens* (J. J. Abrams, 2015).

had, meanwhile, been vocally enthusiastic about surrendering his sonic screwdriver to his female successor: 'She's going to be brilliant' (Shephard 2017). The majority of the show's audiences appeared to share his enthusiasm. Indeed, many commentators considered this development long overdue (see Figure 33).

Mark Bould (2014: 267) has pointed out that there had been several precedents in the programme's history which allowed for regenerating Gallifreyans to change their gender. Lorna Jowett (2014: 88) has suggested that the relentless masculinity in the casting of the series' lead had prompted 'increasing criticism'. While John Tulloch and Henry Jenkins (1995: 100) observed that *Doctor Who* fans have celebrated its ability to explore such issues as 'gender relations', Mike Hernandez (2013: 47) had noted that for as long as the Doctor remained a 'white male' the programme's full potential was 'still to be realized'. This author had also argued that the casting of this role should be subject to a necessary alignment with the cultural zeitgeist (Charles 2017).

The Thirteenth Doctor, *Doctor Who* (2017–present)

Figure 33. Jodie Whittaker as the Thirteenth Doctor in *Doctor Who*.

Peter Capaldi's final episode of *Doctor Who*, broadcast on Christmas Day 2017, chose to rehearse the show's own historical misogyny and to anticipate any audience resistance to the introduction of a female lead by revisiting its central character's original incarnation in the form of a sexist old dinosaur who labours under the misapprehension that 'all ladies [are] made of glass'. Thus, before embarking upon the series' move towards a post-patriarchal era, it recalled the embarrassment of its own chauvinistic past. In doing so, it reminded us that SF, in those mediations with the past essential for its projections into future possibilities, must always look both ways. Steeped as it is in the present, SF gazes simultaneously forwards and back.

Fredric Jameson (2007: 211) has suggested that, far from being mere dalliances in otherworldly escapism, our literary and screen science fictions represent 'the projections of our own social moment and historical or subjective situation'. This mode of fantasy is steeped in urgent and concrete historicity. Thus, moving on from what Christine Cornea (2007: 146) has depicted as earlier screen SF's 'overwhelming concern with masculine identity and subjectivity', George Faithful (2016: 348) charts the evolution of such characters as Katniss Everdeen, Tris Prior and Imperator Furiosa from such female protagonists as Ellen Ripley and Sarah Connor who, in the Armageddon-aware worlds of late Cold War cinema, arose to combat monstrous and apocalyptic threats emerging from specifically 'man-made' (male-made) scenarios.

It may therefore seem appropriate that a world situation once more characterized by the macho posturings of male bombast (as epitomized by Donald Trump, Vladimir Putin, Kim Jong-un and the laddish lads of UKIP, ISIS and the KKK) would witness the return of the *Terminator* and *Alien* franchises, not to mention *Tomb Raider*, *Captain Marvel* and *Wonder Woman*, and would choose to reboot *Star Wars*, *Star Trek* and *Doctor Who* with female leads. The year in which a self-styled master of sexual assault became America's President was also the year in which the #MeToo movement emerged, a year whose most accomplished television series was, according to *The Guardian* newspaper (Nicholson 2017), Bruce Miller's adaptation of Margaret Atwood's *The Handmaid's Tale*, a narrative whose female servitors perform 'at the behest of a patriarchy that sees them in no other legitimate role' (Armitt 2000: 195).

Science Subjects

Joanna Russ (2017: 208) has pointed out that while 'there are plenty of images of women' in classical SF 'there are hardly any women' in the genre at all – hardly any real women, women as women, that is. Sarah Lefanu (1998: 14, 198) has added that though representations of women in such traditional texts 'reflect women only as seen by men' the genre also 'offers room' for feminist struggle. This site for feminist discourse encompasses both what Russ (1995: 58) depicts as 'room for female rage and female self-defence' and what Naomi Jacobs (1994: 202) calls 'a place where gender roles can drop away' – where the genre might 'explore the possibility of women's experience removed from patriarchal mores and oppression' (Moody 2002: 51). SF might therefore, in its essentially contemporary negotiation between an immediate reality and an imagined future, provide space not only for the articulation of utopian aspirations of gender equality and innumerability, but also for the deconstruction of the dystopian inequity of the present day.

Despite its often reactionary history, 'the shifting nature of the genre', according to Carlen Lavigne (2013: 177), allows SF to become 'a vehicle for serious feminist philosophical and political discussion'. Susan Thomas (1991: 111) witnesses SF's potential to allow the 'subversive female character' to operate 'outside the rules of masculine elitism' while Marleen Barr (1992: 227) observes that the genre's promotion of 'female versions of male-centred stories' may offer 'a springboard for subversive thought' which 'thwarts the typically masculine economy' of popular narratives. However, Elyce Rae Helford (2000: 3, 6) warns that, although such characters as *Star Trek*'s Nyota Uhura may have influentially projected 'a speculative representation of 'empowered' womanhood beyond the boundaries of domesticity', it nevertheless remains characteristic of the cinematic and televisual articulations of the genre that 'women's intellectual, technical and/or physical skills may pale in comparison to the way the wear their costumes'. This latter sentiment holds as true for Gal Gadot's Wonder Woman and Alicia Vikander's Lara Croft as it has for such classic objects of the male gaze as Uhura, Barbarella, Xena and Seven of Nine. Indeed, Brie Larson's first screen outing as Captain Marvel was remarkable not only for the fact that she was not defined by her relationship with a boyfriend or father (but by her resistance to a much more sinister figure of male authority) but also for her ability to remain fully clothed throughout.

Jane Donawerth (1997: 3) has observed that one of the problems of feminist SF is that 'almost no feminist science exists'. The history of science has promoted precious few roles or role models for women: 'science excludes women as agent-scientists and women's issues as worthy of examination' (Donawerth 1997: 178). The exclusion of women from science continues to be recognized as a significant issue. Stuart Allan (2002) cites a study which suggested that young women may be discouraged from careers in science because they perceive scientists as middle-aged males. In 2005 the UK's Equality Challenge Unit established the Scientific Women's Academic Network in order to enhance equality in the discipline. In 2017 the British company EDF Energy's 'Pretty Curious' campaign announced a partnership with Lucasfilm and Disney to exploit the popularity of *Star Wars: The Last Jedi* 'to inspire more girls to think about where a career in science [...] could take them' (EDF Energy). SF might therefore play a direct part in underpinning women's access to science itself, in re-appropriating the incongruity of the image of the female scientist as both a challenge and an opportunity.

In June 2015 the Nobel laureate Sir Tim Hunt caused consternation when he declared that women scientists cause problems because 'you fall in love with them, they fall in love with you and, when you criticise them, they cry' (Ratcliffe 2015). When *Doctor Who* began, in 1963, it demonstrated similar disdain for women in science. The series' two regular human characters were a pair of schoolteachers: a woman who taught history and a man who taught science. But, in a 1968 episode of the series, when a casually chauvinistic soldier asks a female scientist what a girl like her is doing in a job like hers, she responds: 'When I was a little girl I thought I'd like to be a scientist. So I became a scientist'.

Later that same year, the Doctor was joined in his travels by a brilliant female astrophysicist; two years later, she was replaced by another female scientist. This progressive trend was, however, halted in its tracks by the Doctor's next companion, Jo Grant (Katy Manning) – one who fulfilled his need (as her employer put it) for someone to pass him his test tubes and tell him how brilliant he was. The shift towards a normalization of the image of the woman scientist had been reversed and the lazy sexism of the 1970s continued to alienate women from science. (But we may note, at least, that by the end of the decade another female scientist had taken on another significant role in the UK – as its Prime Minister).

Loving the Alien

Donawerth (1997: 43) has observed that the 'experience of woman-as-other' may powerfully be captured in the representation of the female alien. The incongruous alien female scientist – a striking and authoritative figure unlikely to shed her clothes at the behest of the male gaze – might offer particularly inspirational opportunities in this field ... when, for example, as former *Doctor Who* star Colin Baker wrote in *The Guardian* on 17 July 2017, 'it's not just little boys in the playground [...] saying: "I want to be the Doctor one day."'

Figure 34. The Doctor in episode 11.1, 'The Woman Who Fell To Earth'.

The day before, a talented young actor from Huddersfield had, as they say, broken both the internet and Gallifrey's glass sky (see Figure 34). The BBC reported that the announcement that Jodie Whittaker had been cast as the new Doctor Who not only prompted a response from the UK's latest female Prime Minister (who was said to be 'pleased' by the news) but also 'sent social media into a frenzy'. As the *Huffington Post* suggested, 'man babies' were unable to cope with this traumatic development (Demlanyk 2017). That publication offered 'little sympathy for the broflakes' who had expressed their outrage at the lunacy of the notion that a body-morphing alien who travels the universe of space and time in an old British police telephone box, saving diverse civilizations from the threats of living statues, killer snowmen and clockwork robots, might also be able to change her outward gender. Yet it appeared for the most part that the online neanderthalisms of those who objected to a female Time Lord ('he's a doctor not a nurse ... what's next, Jane Bond?'), as to women Ghostbusters, or to the female leads of *The Force Awakens*, *Rogue One* or *Star Trek: Discovery* (without a gold bikini or a miniskirt in sight), were precisely that: the last gasps of a forgotten species, a dying strain.

Some outposts of the media continued, of course, to fight these reactionary rear-guard actions. The pertinence of Helford's earlier warnings as to the scanty cladding of SF's female leads (an offence of which *Doctor Who* in its earlier incarnations was hardly itself innocent) was borne out when a pair of tabloid newspapers chose to use Whittaker's casting as an excuse to print pictures of her unclothed in previous acting roles (Ruddick 2017).

However, these were the exceptions. Emma Saunders and Lauren Turner (2017) saw the Doctor's transformation as part of a trend whereby 'male-dominated franchises could be reinvented for the modern day with women taking a leading role'. Zoe Williams (2017), meanwhile, described Jodie Whittaker's Time Lord as 'the revolutionary feminist we need right now' – 'a heroine who is not only preternaturally strong, but also can talk' – adding that 'it is exhilarating to think how many clichés a woman in this role will tear down'. This modest development might not only reflect the evolution of social attitudes but also offer revolutionary opportunities in relation to gender equalities, fluidities and transitions in what Riley Silverman (2017) has described as this simultaneously inspirational and alienated character's 'strange journey through self-identity and finding one's place in the world'.

The teaser trailer for Whittaker's first season saw her (quite literally) shattering the glass ceiling. It was therefore somewhat disappointing when – despite her evident capacities to portray quiet strength, moral courage and dazzling wit – her early episodes tended to present an infantilized version of the Doctor, a character dressed in oversized children's clothes who seemed panicky and 'wet' and whose role was too often overshadowed by her male companions (Elledge 2019). Yet the episode which played best to those capacities – her third episode – was notably also one which focused upon another iconic female role model, Rosa Parks; and it was here that the series' latest incarnation most clearly demonstrated its potential as a progressive instrument of social reinvention (see Figure 35).

Figure 35. Doctor Who, episode 11.1, 'The Woman Who Fell to Earth'.

Michel Foucault (1998: 101) observed that, though discourse reinforces power, 'it also undermines and exposes it, renders it fragile and makes it possible to thwart it'. The innate gender conservativism of this genre's traditions may thereby be reimagined to promote the modes of subversion envisioned by Thomas and Barr. The heroines of speculative fiction offer a timely and much-needed antidote to a resurgent politics of chauvinism; and the possibilities advanced by these transformations in popular screen SF might one day be seen, as the thirteenth Doctor herself put it in the opening words of her own first scene, as simply, radically and earth-shatteringly *brilliant*.

Thomas Connolly

Disability in Science Fiction

'The genre of science fiction', writes Michael Bérubé, 'is as obsessed with disability as it is with space travel and alien contact' (568). Initially, this might seem like a hyperbolic statement – yet a quick glance through some key works of SF soon reveals the ubiquity of disability in the genre. Luke Skywalker has his hand severed in *A New Hope* and replaced with a bionic substitute (see Figure 36). Professor X makes use of a wheelchair, while several other X-Men possess powers that can easily be read as analogues for disability. Philip K. Dick's *Do Androids Dream of Electric Sheep?* features 'specials', individuals with (implied) 'low' cognitive capabilities. Case, the protagonist of William Gibson's *Neuromancer*, has his central nervous system medically impaired in order to prevent him from interfacing with cyberspace. John Wyndham's *The Day of the Triffids* depicts a cosmic event in which the population of the Earth is rendered blind. Even Mary Shelley's *Frankenstein* can be read as a coded commentary on disability: the physical appearance of the Creature is prejudged by a society conditioned to accept certain kinds of bodies as 'normal', while James Whale's reimagining of the Creature in the 1930s reimagines the Creature as a socially maligned individual with non-normative cognitive abilities.

Thus it appears that, once you begin looking for it, disability can indeed be found throughout SF. Alongside its ubiquity, however, what is equally remarkable about disability in SF is its *invisibility*. How many readers (or viewers) of *Frankenstein* – a text that has been read extensively in relation to other areas of critical literary enquiry, such as gender, race and colonialism – have read it through the lens of disability? This is not unique to SF as a genre: as Ria Cheyne notes, '[the] general lack of critical engagement with disability in fields that it could so obviously enrich is a familiar story' (118). In this chapter, we will examine some key concepts in disability studies before turning briefly to a well-known SF story, James Tiptree, Jr's 'The Girl Who Was Plugged In' (1973), to consider how disability can be productively explored in SF works.

Figure 36. The changing aesthetics of prosthesis in *Star Wars*: in *The Empire Strikes Back* (1980) and *Return of the Jedi* (1983), Luke Skywalker's replacement hand is indistinguishable from the one he lost; in *The Force Awakens* (2015) and *The Last Jedi* (2017), an older, more jaded Skywalker has a much more obvious robotic substitute.

To begin with, we will spend some time considering disability as a social phenomenon. Even to think of disability in these terms – as a social, rather than an individual, phenomenon – is to challenge the conventional view of disability as an isolated 'condition' that 'afflicts' particular individuals. This conventional view of disability is generally termed the 'medical model': a view of disability that considers it only from the perspective of the individual whom it directly affects, and which considers how such individuals may adapt their behaviours or their bodies in order to better get along in society. The issue with such conceptions of disability is their implied assumption that there exists a particular range of bodily or psychological experiences that can be characterized as 'normal', with disability thus understood as a problem to be 'fixed' so as to re-situate individuals with 'abnormal' minds and bodies within those accepted parameters.

As Lennard J. Davis argues, disability activists and scholars take issue with such conceptions of disability: 'the "problem,"' Davis writes, 'is not the person with disabilities; the problem is the way that normalcy is constructed to create the "problem" of the disabled person' (3). Such conceptions of normalcy, and the way that societies are built around the assumption of a 'normal' human mind and body, have been termed 'ableism' – a form of discrimination and oppression that sits alongside racism, sexism, classism and speciesism (among others) as reifying a certain kind of bodily and cognitive experience as the social 'ideal' at the expense of others. The movement from a medical to a social model of disability thus changes the question from one of how the individual can be made to fit into society, to how societies can be adapted in order to better cater for non-normative bodies and minds.

One of the key concerns raised in such debates concerning the experiences of disabled people, and one that highlights the relationship between disability and SF, is the question of technology. Technology can be understood in the context of both medical and social models of disability. The notion of individualized technological innovations for 'fixing' disabled bodies is a fairly common one: we need only think of the symbol of the wheelchair, perhaps the archetypal technology of disability, often used as cultural shorthand for representing disabled bodies. Yet the most common location of such symbols – on the doors of public bathrooms designed for use by disabled people – also points to the *social* contexts in which such technologies are situated, and of the presence (or absence) of social technologies that aid or hinder the ability of the disabled individual to participate in social life. A consideration of such technologies, as Vasilis Galis suggests, requires a grasp of 'the lived experience of impaired, gendered, ethnic bodies interacting with the configuration of the built environment and its materiality' (827).

The blurring of individual and social technologies, highlighted in the wheelchair symbol on the public bathroom door, also highlights the double-edged nature of technology in its relationship to disability. Although developments in technology have brought about substantial changes in the individual experience of disability by 'making life with serious and chronic impairments increasingly feasible' (Albrecht et al., 1), such uses of technology also contribute towards a perception of disability as something that can or should be 'cured' through technological innovation on an individual level, thus obscuring the way that social or infrastructural technologies actually contribute to the creation of disability.

So common is this understanding of technology as a 'cure' for disability that it forms the subtitle of the (thus far) only edited collection of essays focusing on disability in SF works. As Kathryn Allen notes in her introduction to that collection, 'SF narratives involving people with disabilities inevitably also feature technology as either curing or attempting to contain their unruly bodies'; the aim, when reading SF through the lens of disability, is thus to 'discover not only the ways in which disability is socially constructed today but how we might approach conceiving disabled embodiments in the future' (2). SF texts offer productive spaces in which to imaginatively engage with a whole host of concerns that can be related to disability: alternative social formations, non-normative forms of embodiments, and new technologies – both individual and social – to 'cure' or, in a more radical vein, rethink the experience of disability.

James Tiptree, Jr's 'The Girl Who Was Plugged In', set in a near-future American society, features a disabled character, P. Burke. The exact nature of P. Burke's disability is never quite disclosed: she is described as 'a tall monument to pituitary dystrophy', and the narrator is at pains to stress the 'abnormal' nature of Burke's body – 'her jaw, it's half purple, almost bites her left eye out [...] her mismatched legs [...] a pumped-out hulk' (Tiptree, 44–46). The narrative of the story follows Burke's 'rebirth' in the form of 'Delphi', a mechano-biological body that is controlled remotely by Burke. Delphi is the property of a multinational corporation, who capitalize on her sexual appeal in order to promote consumer products.

Tiptree's story invokes and critiques the 'technology as cure' narrative. Such narratives often take a Cartesian view of the body as a mechanistic structure with parts that can be 'replaced' or 'upgraded' – such a narrative assumes, as N. Katherine Hayles puts it, that 'the liberal subject' of post-Enlightenment thought, although it *'possesse[s]* a body', is not 'usually represented as *being* a body' (1999: 4). Luke Skywalker, for instance, is not depicted as being much impacted by the sudden replacement of his biological hand with a prosthetic replacement. Yet for disabled people, the phenomenological experience of the body is often intrinsic to the way that the world is negotiated and experienced – indeed, one of the major criticisms that has been aimed at the social model of disability is its downplaying of impairment as a mere social construction, rather than a lived material reality (see Shakespeare).

In the way that Burke transfers her consciousness to the body of Delphi, Tiptree's story seems to endorse a dematerialized view of the mind as capable of being moved from one bodily 'vessel' to another – yet the story also undercuts such a view by emphasizing the phenomenological experience implied in the process of gaining a 'new' body. Hence, for example, Burke must spend time learning how 'to walk, sit, eat, speak, blow her nose, how to stumble, to urinate, to hiccup – DELICIOUSLY' (47). It is not a simple matter of stepping into a new set of body parts – Burke must relearn basic physical actions in order to make her way through the world, a consequence of her newly altered material embodiment. Similarly, it is significant that Burke does not actually 'leave behind' her own body: at the climax of the story, Burke's true identity is discovered by Paul, a radical who has become infatuated with Delphi, but who viciously rejects Burke when she tries to explain the truth behind Delphi. Paul's rejection epitomizes the wider social rejection of Burke as a disabled 'monster' (76), while also literally, and ironically, disabling Delphi herself by causing the death of Burke.

The story thus dramatizes the processes of normalization that contribute to disability as a social phenomenon. Burke's body, viciously described by the ironic narrator as an aberration in this future society, is literally hidden away from public view, while in her place appears Delphi, whose body achieves a level of apparent physical perfection sought after by ableist societies. Delphi possesses the 'ideal' body, valued for its conformity to a set of socially prescribed standards as to what bodies 'should' be. The overlap with feminist readings here is clear: Burke is trapped in a double bind, situated at an intersection of distinct but related oppressive social stigmas, and is subsequently punished for failing to meet cultural expectations for both female beauty and bodily autonomy.

Hence, like feminism, disability studies, as Rosemarie Garland-Thompson suggests, aims to 'show […] that disability – similar to race and gender – is a system of representation that marks bodies as subordinate, rather than an essential property of bodies that supposedly have something wrong with them' (1557–1558). At the same time, we can question to what extent such SF narratives engage *productively* with questions of disability, as opposed to simply deploying disability as a signifier of physical 'deformity' or, more commonly, as a sign of moral degeneracy. David T. Mitchell and Sharon Snyder have described the use of disability as a 'narrative prostheses': 'both a destabilizing sign of cultural prescriptions about the body *and* a deterministic vehicle of characterization for characters constructed as disabled' (50). Disability, in other words, can be read in such a work as 'The Girl' as both a means of troubling conventional attitudes towards the body *and*, less positively, as a determining quality that delimits the character of P. Burke by designating her specifically as a 'disabled character' (as opposed to a fully rounded character who also happens to have a disability). Such opportunistic uses of disability can also be seen throughout SF: in H. G. Well's 'The Country of the Blind' (1911), for instance, in which blindness becomes a metaphor for stubborn conservatism.

This chapter barely scratches the surface of the potential for disability studies to throw new light on SF works (I have focused mainly on physical disability, for instance, without going into great detail on other forms). But it has hopefully demonstrated both the relevance of disability studies as a lens for usefully reading SF texts, and the need for greater attention to this field of enquiry if disability is ever to become as visible as it is widespread in SF works.

Andrew Milner

Science Fiction and Climate Change

Climate fiction has increasingly become a matter for public commentary in both scholarly and popular circles. In academia, Amitav Ghosh's 2015 Berlin Family Lectures at the University of Chicago mounted a very strong case for the necessity of climate fiction and an equally strong indictment of 'literary fiction' for its failure to rise to this challenge. In the media, the Taiwan-based blogger and activist Daniel Bloom has been an indefatigable propagandist on behalf of 'cli-fi', a term he coined in 2007 (Merchant). For Ghosh and Bloom contemporary climate fiction is essentially 'about' the kind of climate change described as *anthropogenic* or human induced. For Ghosh it is cause for regret that such fiction has been banished from the literary mainstream into the 'generic outhouse' of SF (2016: 24); for Bloom, it is cause for celebration that cli-fi has begun to emerge as a new genre in its own right. But contemporary cli-fi is actually most plausibly understood as a sub-genre of SF. Certainly, its texts normally satisfy the criteria stipulated in Darko Suvin's famous definition of the genre as '*distinguished by the narrative dominance or hegemony of a fictional "novum" (novelty, innovation) validated by cognitive logic*' (1979: 63).

Cli-fi in this sense is a comparatively recent SF sub-genre by no means co-extensive with the older tradition of climate fiction that stretches back to the stories of Ūta-napišti in the *Sha naqba īmuru* [*Epic of Gilgamesh*] and Noah in *Bereshith* [*Genesis*]. Extreme climate change is the novum driving these narratives, but their logic is strictly theological, the causes of their great floods not anthropogenic, but rather *theogenic*. Prior to the emergence of modern SF, extreme climate change was normally represented as either theogenic or the result of terrestrial natural causes, that is, *geogenic*. The second motif, though not the first, persists into contemporary SF, especially by way of 'new ice age' fictions. But with the emergence of modern SF as a genre centred on the consequences, negative or positive, of human mastery of nature by science and

Figure 37. NOAA/NASA image of Cyclone Debbie, which killed fourteen people and caused A$3.5 billion in damages when it made landfall in Australia in March 2017.

technology, it became possible to imagine properly anthropogenic variants of extreme climate change. And, once humanity had itself been imagined as capable of transforming a planet's climate, it was only a small step to imagine alien species capable of producing what we might call *xenogenic* climate change.

Treatments of catastrophic climate change in SF have tended to be organized around three main tropes: the drowned world, the freezing world, and the warming or burning world. Only the first has a deep history in the Western mythos. When modern SF began to take shape in the early nineteenth century, it inherited this preoccupation with the great flood from its parent cultures: witness the drowned cities in Mary Shelley's 1826 novel *The Last Man* and Richard Jefferies's 1885 *After London*. These texts – and many others – tell of floods that destroy or damage human civilization, but are never strictly anthropogenic. There is, however, a limit text, published only four years after *After London*, where anthropogenically produced rising sea levels are anticipated, but nevertheless not actually realized, Jules Verne's *Sans dessus dessous* [*Topsy*

Turvy] (1889). Hugo Gernsback published a complete English translation of *Sans dessus dessous*, under its British title *The Purchase of the North Pole* in the September and October 1926 issues of *Amazing Stories* and thereafter catastrophic floods became a pulp staple.

These American pulp fictions were clearly indebted to *Genesis* and some also to *Sans dessus dessous*, but none seem closely related to scientific concerns about the real possibilities for global warming. Much the same is true of the two main British SF flood narratives of the 1950s and early 1960s, John Wyndham's *The Kraken Wakes* (1953) and J. G. Ballard's *The Drowned World* (1962). In *The Kraken Wakes*, perhaps the most famous of all stories of xenogenic climate change, floods are part of an alien invasion by sea creatures; in *The Drowned World*, they are the effect of persistent solar flares. Ballard made the connection between warming and flooding, but neither novel was interested in scientifically plausible models of global warming. This tradition of *Genesis*-inspired flood narratives divorced from scientific concerns over climate change, continues into the twenty-first century, for example in Stephen Baxter's *Flood* (2008) and Roland Emmerich's *2012* (2008). If none of these countenanced the possibility of anthropogenically produced rising sea levels, the same cannot be said of Japanese writer Kōbō Abe's novel *Dai-Yon Kampyōki* [*Inter Ice Age 4*] (1958–1959), often claimed as the foundational text of postwar Japanese SF. The primary concerns in *Dai-Yon Kampyōki* are nonetheless not with climate change, but with government plans to genetically engineer gilled humans. With Abe, then, we reach yet another limit text, which acknowledges the possibility of anthropogenically induced global flooding, only so as to set it aside.

Cooling and warming are more recent preoccupations than flooding. For most of the twentieth century both science and SF were more interested in cooling than in warming. In geological terms the period we inhabit, the 'Holocene', is an 'interglacial', that is, a comparatively warm period within the longer, colder 'ice age' defined by the 'Quaternary period'. So the most likely future climate change was widely anticipated to be a return to the ice age. This motif recurs throughout the SF of the period, from American pulp SF, for example Robert Silverberg's *Time of the Great Freeze* (1964), through John Christopher's *The World in Winter* (1968) to Michael Moorcock's *The Ice Schooner* (1966), Douglas Orgill and John Gribbin's *The Sixth Winter* (1979) and Jean-Marc Rochette and Jacques Lob's graphic novel *Le Transperceneige* (1984). Pulp SF borrowed the ice motif from climate science, but normally without much interest in or understanding of ice age theory. *The World in Winter* and *The Sixth Winter*, by contrast, both engage with plausible science. But in *The Ice Schooner* and *Le Transperceneige* the ice age is not a natural-cyclical development, rather the effect of military weapons. Bong Joon-ho's 2013 Korean film adaptation of the latter depicts its new ice age as the result of a spectacularly over-effective attempt to counter global warming, but there is no such suggestion in the original novel.

Warming – as distinct from flooding – seems only rarely to have engaged the genre before the last quarter of the twentieth century. The obvious contrary instance is Ballard's 1964 *The Burning World*, but here, as in *The Drowned World*, his main concerns are not so much with climate science and climate change as with reverse-evolution to the primeval lizard brain. Widespread scientific concern that anthropogenic warming might more than offset longer-term cooling dates primarily from the 1970s and the 1980s. In 1979 the US National Research Council and the World Meteorological Organization published predictions that then current levels of CO_2 emission would result in increases in average global temperature. In 1988 the World Meteorological Organization and the United Nations Environmental Program combined to establish the Intergovernmental Panel on Climate Change (IPCC); and in 1990 it completed its *First Assessment Report*, concluding that, if emissions proceeded on a 'business as usual' basis, the result would be levels of global warming greater than those seen in the previous 10,000 years (xi). Where science had led SF would follow. In 1977, the American Arthur Herzog explored the fictional possibilities of a runaway greenhouse effect in his novel *Heat*. A decade later, the Australian George Turner's *The Sea and Summer* depicted a world of mass unemployment and social polarization, in which global warming had produced rising sea levels and consequent inundation of the city of Melbourne's Bayside suburbs.

The novelty of this latest stage in the history of climate fiction is its comparative fidelity to the findings of the relevant sciences. The range of imaginative responses to global warming runs roughly parallel to the options available in real-world discourse. Climate policy distinguishes between mitigation and adaptation strategies and between positive and negative variants of adaptation, the former seeking possible advantages to be seized upon, the latter disadvantages to be minimized. Mitigation strategies in the strict sense are simply strategies to reduce emissions, but these are rarely the stuff of SF narrative. Insofar as climate fiction does contemplate mitigating the effects of global warming, it typically does so through the kind of technological fix implied in climate engineering. Mitigation and climate engineering can thus be considered more or less the same trope. To these three responses we can add as a fourth option various forms of climate change denial; as a fifth, the kind of deep ecological anti-humanism sometimes associated with Lovelock's 'Gaia hypothesis' (1979); and, as a sixth, the kind of pessimistic fatalism that seems very common in the real world, but less so in SF.

Instances of all six kinds of response – denial, mitigation as engineering, positive adaptation, negative adaptation, deep ecology, fatalism – can be observed in climate fiction. Good examples of denial include Michael Crichton's *State of Fear* (2004) and Nele Neuhaus's *Wer Wind sät* (2011); of the special kind of denial that calls into question the scientists rather than the science, Ian McEwan's *Solar* (2010) and Sven Böttcher's *Prophezeiung* (2011); of mitigation as engineering, Herzog's *Heat* (1977) and Kim Stanley Robinson's *2312* (2012); of positive adaptation, Margaret Atwood's *Oryx and Crake* (2003), Bernard Besson's *Groenland* (2011) and Paolo Bacigalupi's *The Water Knife* (2015); of negative adaptation, Turner's *The Sea and Summer* (1987), Atwood's *The Year of the Flood* (2009), Robinson's *Science in the Capital* trilogy (2004–2007) and its 2015 omnibus edition *Green Earth*, Jean-Marc Ligny's *AquaTM* (2006), Bacigalupi's *The Windup Girl* (2009) and Dirk C. Fleck's *MAEVA!* trilogy (2008–2015); of deep ecology, Brian Aldiss's *Helliconia* trilogy (1982–1985), Frank Schätzing's *Der Schwarm* (2004), Ligny's *Exodes* (2012) and *Semences* (2015); of fatalism, Jeanette Winterson's *The Stone Gods* (2007), Alexis Wright's *The Swan Book* (2013) and James Bradley's *Clade* (2015).

There seem to be far fewer climate utopias than climate dystopias. There is a case to be made, nonetheless, that these are likely to become more culturally significant as the climate crisis develops. As Robinson observed in a recent article: 'Climate change is inevitable ... It has become a case of utopia or catastrophe, and utopia has gone from being a somewhat minor literary problem to a necessary survival strategy' ('Remarks' 9). *New York 2140* (2017) is the latest in his attempts at utopia and climate fiction, the first to combine the two to

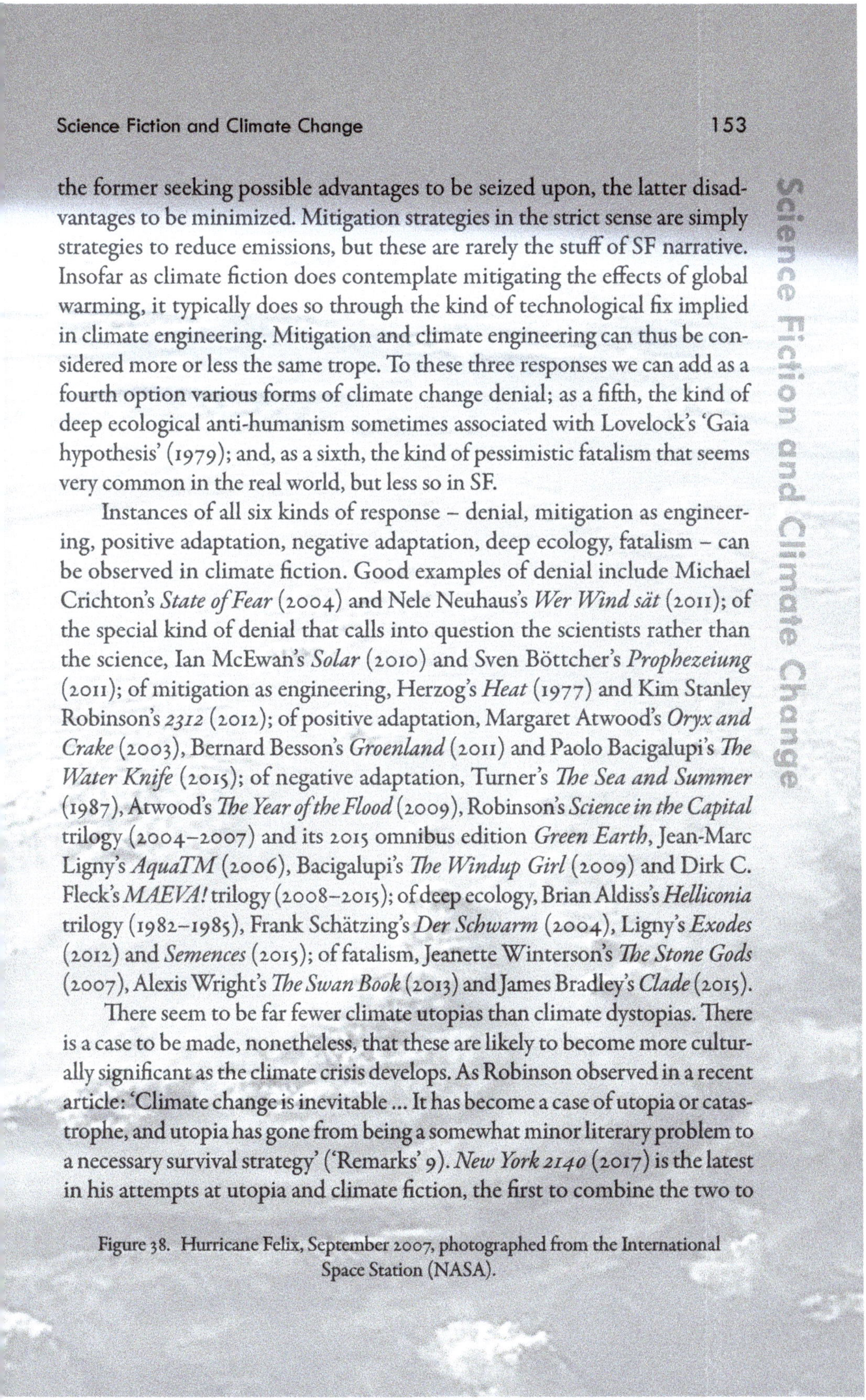

Figure 38. Hurricane Felix, September 2007, photographed from the International Space Station (NASA).

depict a specifically utopian outcome from global climate crisis. Initially, climate change appears to function in the novel as its dystopian mise en scène: by the early to mid-twenty-second century sea levels have risen by 50 feet so that the whole of Lower Manhattan has long since been flooded. The main plot seems at first to be a detective mystery about the disappearance of two coders, Mutt and Jeff, from their temporary home in the Met Life tower on Madison Square. But this turns out to be the trigger for a more important political narrative, which moves the novel towards its utopian climax, when 'Hurricane Fyodor' batters the city so badly as to prompt a popular constitutional revolution. Charlotte Armstrong, the radical lawyer who alerted the NYPD to the coders' disappearance, persuades her ex-husband, now head of the Federal Reserve, that bank nationalization should be the price for a financial bailout, and runs for Congress campaigning against the banks (554). She is elected, the banks are nationalized, Congress passes a 'Picketty tax' on income and capital assets, and 'a leftward flurry of legislation' is 'LBJed through Congress' (574, 601, 602, 604). Robinson himself feels that his first utopian novel, *Pacific Edge*, 'dodged the necessity of revolution' (2016: 4). But so too do his later climate fictions: in *Green Earth* a charismatic Democratic President saves the world; in *New York 2140* that task falls to a radical Democratic Congresswoman and the chance that the Federal Reserve might be headed by her ex-husband. Such hopes are 'utopian' in the pejorative sense of being hopelessly unrealistic. Ultimately, then, the novel's utopia is betrayed by its own utopianism.

Mark Bould

Science Fiction and the Anthropocene

Somewhere in the African veldt, a hominid ape uplifted into sentience by an alien monolith hurls a bone into the air; 4 million years later, in 2001, a nuclear weapons platform orbits the Earth. The entire Anthropocene (apart from its final couple of years, in which humans again encounter the alien technology and are uplifted into posthumanity) is to be found between the frames on either side of Stanley Kubrick's celebrated match cut. Of course, *2001: A Space Odyssey* (1968) is not the only SF text to be interested in the origins and ends of humankind (the *anthropos*). Numerous novels, from Jack London's *Before Adam* (1907) to Stephen Baxter's *Evolution* (2003), explore the emergence of *Homo sapiens* as a species, and others, from H. G. Wells' *The Time Machine* (1895) to Octavia Butler's *Lilith's Brood* trilogy (1987–1989), contemplate our further evolution into posthuman daughter species.

However, the 'Anthropocene' designates not the era of *Homo sapiens* but the period in which human activity has altered significant geological conditions and processes. The term has not yet been recognized as a geological epoch by either the International Union of Geological Sciences or the International Commission on Stratigraphy, and its precise parameters are still open to debate. But it has taken on a life of its own outside of official ruminations as a way of talking about the devastating impact on the biosphere of burning fossil fuels; it often functions as a kind of euphemism for anthropogenic climate destabilization.

While no one would date the Anthropocene as far back as Kubrick's 'Dawn of Man', writers such as Alfred W. Crosby and Mark Lynas imply that it can be traced to humans discovering fire. J.-H. Rosny's *La Guerre du feu* [*Quest for Fire*] (1909), which features a tribe of early humans threatened by the loss of the lightning-ignited flames they have learned to sustain and use in multiple ways, gives some sense of the radical transformation to human being and community wrought by mastery of fire. However, to suggest that learning to control fire – tens or perhaps hundreds of thousands of years ago – somehow made a carbon economy inevitable is merely an ideological sleight-of-hand. To insinuate that somewhere in our evolution it became human nature to increase the atmospheric concentration of carbon dioxide is to redistribute responsibility for the global consequences of burning fossil fuels onto all humans equally.

A more common, but equally ideological, starting point for a 'long' Anthropocene is the Neolithic or Agricultural revolution of 12,000–15,000 years ago, making it more or less synonymous with the entire Holocene epoch. Various prehistoric fictions – from Claude Anet's *La Fin d'un monde* [*The End of a World*] (1925) to John Tempest's *Vision of the Hunter* (1989) – focus on this transformation. J. Leslie Mitchell's more overtly science fictional *Three Go Back* (1932) depicts it as a big mistake, but this comes from a romantic attachment to the imagined anarchistic – and nudist – communalism of hunter-gathering folk rather than any concern with the ecological impact of settlement, agriculture and the domestication of farm animals (agricultural livestock are now responsible for significant proportions of three greenhouses gases: nitrous oxide, methane and carbon dioxide).

Popular discourse most commonly dates the Anthropocene to the industrial revolution or, more precisely, the late eighteenth-century turn to coal and steam-power, which in turn led to the oil economy, the pollutants from which have left discernible traces in the geological record. The collision of geological and human timescales has long occupied the SF imagination. Jules Verne's *Voyage au centre de la Terre* [*Journey to the Centre of the Earth*] (1864) takes its subterranean explorers back down into prehistoric times, transforming the fossil record and geological time into an immersive spatial experience, while in HP Lovecraft's *At the Mountains of Madness* (1936) such scientific endeavours turn irrational as its explorers encounter not dinosaurs but a deadly shoggoth – a semi-sentient, archaic and suspiciously oil-like protoplasmic slime.

The period of the industrial revolution, particularly Victorian Britain, is central to steampunk, which coalesced in the 1970s, the decade of OPEC's most serious challenge to the neo-colonialism of the global oil economy. While steampunk has tended to prefer technological fantasia – mechanical computers, dirigibles, steam-driven superscience – and swashbuckling adventures, Iain R. MacLeod's *The Light Ages* (2003) also imagines a new fuel source and thinks through some of its consequences. Powered by 'aether', its alternative England has developed a rigidly stratified structure designed to further concentrate vast new wealth in the hands of the capitalist class – not unlike the way in which the real-world transition from water-power to more costly and less efficient coal-burning energy systems was driven, argues Andreas Malm, by a desire to undermine worker organization, suppress wages and to otherwise avoid the costs involved in the social reproduction of labour. (Jason W. Moore argues that the Anthropocene should more properly – and even less euphoniously – be called the 'Capitalocene', and be dated from capitalism's first emergence in roughly 1450 CE.)

China Miéville's steampunk-inflected YA novels move the consequences of fossil fuel extractionism centre stage: in *Un Lun Dun* (2007), both London and its mirror version are threatened by The Smog, a malevolent radioactive cloud that evolved from particulates in the city's air and functions as a metaphor for reckless consumerism, while *Railsea* (2012) is set in the blighted post-apocalypse created by carbon-capitalist competition. Post-carbon futures are imagined – with varying degrees of ambivalence – in Andrew Marvell's *Three Men Make a World* (1939), Gwyneth Jones's *Bold as Love* cycle (2001–2014) and Robert Charles Wilson's *Julian Comstock* (2009); more positive visions can be found in such solarpunk anthologies as Phoebe Wagner and Brontë Christopher Wieland's *Sunvault* (2017) and Claudie Arseneault and Brenda J. Pierson's *Wings of Renewal* (2017).

A final start date that is often proposed for Anthropocene is 1945, when the 16 July Trinity test began the global spread of radioactive isotopes from atomic weapons, and when the end of the Second World War inaugurated a new consumer capitalism, ramping up the consumption of fossil fuels through increased car-ownership and, even more significantly, the mass production of plastics. At the 1939 New York World's Fair, General Motors' Futurama exhibition/ride, designed by Norman Bel Geddes, which imagined a 1959 dominated by sprawling suburbs and multilane expressways, presaged the conscious reconstruction of the American landscape in favour of privately owned automobiles, and atomic anxieties prevalent in 1950s America gave rise to all manner of monsters and apocalyptic fantasies. Two texts which capture the interrelations of postwar capitalism, petroculture and atomic culture are Ray Bradbury's *Fahrenheit 451* (1953) and Robert Aldrich's SF-tinted film noir *Kiss*

Me Deadly (1955). In the former, plastic-sheathed suburban houses are occasionally dowsed in kerosene and set alight by book-burning firemen, while the latter is obsessed with automobiles and the other commodity-accoutrements of the *Playboy* bachelor; both end in nuclear fireballs. In the neoliberal era, such critical concerns are revived in the opening narration of *Mad Max 2: Road Warrior* (Miller 1981), *Repo Man* (Cox 1984) and *Southland Tales* (Kelly 2006). J. G. Ballard's *Crash* (1973) digs deep into our psychosexual investments in cars, while Heathcote Williams's *Autogeddon* (1991) treats the short but devastating history of the car as the progress of an incurable metastasizing cancer.

SF has a well-established repertoire of catastrophic imagery with which to depict anthropogenic climate destabilization: tides and/or temperatures rise in Sydney Fowler Wright's *Deluge* (1927), Karel Čapek's *War with the Newts* (1936), Storm Jameson's *World's End* (1937), John Wyndham's *The Kraken Wakes* (1953), *The Day the Earth Caught Fire* (Guest 1961), Ballard's *The Drowned World* (1962) and *Night of the Big Heat* (Fisher 1967). Although the greenhouse effect was discovered in the mid-nineteenth century (by Joseph Fourier, Claude Pouillet and John Tyndall), with Svante Arrhenius in 1896 predicting the effects of doubling atmospheric carbon dioxide, the science of global warming did not really register in public consciousness until the 1980s. Climate change – as an element of near-future world-building and as a driver of narratives – began to feature regularly in SF with George Turner's *The Sea and Summer* (1987), Octavia Butler's *Parable* novels (1993–1998), John Barnes's *Mother of Storms* (1994), Bruce Sterling's *Heavy Weather* (1994) and Norman Spinrad's *Greenhouse Summer* (1999). In parallel, authors not usually or only occasionally associated with the genre also turned to 'climate fiction' or 'cli-fi', such as Margaret Atwood's *Maddadam* trilogy (2003–2013), Maggie Gee's *The Flood* (2004), Saci Lloyd's *The Carbon Diaries* series (2008–2011) and Nathaniel Rich's *Odds Against Tomorrow* (2013).

More recently, Paolo Bacigalupi's *Pump Six and Other Stories* (2008), *The Windup Girl* (2009), *The Water Knife* (2015) and YA *Shipbreaker* series (2010–2017) suggest that anthropogenic climate destabilization has become an unavoidable current and imminent reality for SF. The pre-eminent author of the Anthropocene in this sense is Kim Stanley Robinson. Engineering and maintenance of closed biospheres, which if untended generally find an equilibrium unfavourable to human needs, let alone desires, feature in *Icehenge* (1984), *2312* (2012) and *Aurora* (2015), as well as the *Mars* trilogy (1992–1996), which is centrally concerned with terraforming the red planet and subsequently areoforming – making habitable again – of an Earth wracked by the rising tides and extreme weather. Similar debates about the nature and extent of acceptable intervention into environments which precede us can be found in *Pacific Edge* (1990) and *Galileo's Dream* (2009), and rather more urgently in the *Science in the Capital* trilogy (2004–2007), later condensed as *Green Earth* (2015), in which a senator, duly elected US President, and his science advisor drive efforts to mitigate and adapt to climate change. *New York 2140* (2017), set among the skyscrapers and canals of Manhattan after two catastrophic icecap collapses have seen the sea-level rise fifty feet, is unabashed in identifying capitalism – especially unregulated finance capital – as the primary cause and proposes reining it in through vigorous Keynesian reforms.

In addition to fiction that is overtly about anthropogenic climate destabilization, a wide range of contemporary cultural productions register an Anthropocene unconscious – although precisely how intentional this might be is difficult to determine. For example, China Miéville's 'Polynia' (2014), in which icebergs suddenly appear floating in the sky above London and hint at a weird realm beyond human perception, depicts an encounter with what Timothy Morton describes as a 'hyperobject' – a phenomenon so massively distributed in time and space that it cannot be apprehended directly. For Miéville, this is a way to think about climate (rather than the more readily perceptible weather) without mentioning it. At the other extreme, entries in the new millennium's global cycle of zombie movies rarely evoke climate change directly, but at this conjuncture any text that demonizes massive mobile – and unwanted – populations cannot not be in some way about climate refugees, of which it is commonly estimated there will be 150–200 million by 2050. That such films typically rework old colonial fictions of settlers under siege by to-be-slaughtered indigenes, focus on the violent defence of resources, and feature turn-on-a-dime willingness to kill former allies, friends and family, does not bode well. Somewhere between these poles lie *Pacific Rim* (del Toro 2013), Nnedi Okorafor's *Lagoon* (2014), Tade Thompson's *Rosewater* (2016) and *Arrival* (Villeneuve 2016), in which weird alien visitors are not presented as metaphors of climate change; however, their intrusions and actions – and their world-changing consequences – are readily understood as hyperobjects and as parapraxes that reveal an Anthropocene unconscious.

Chris Pak

Animals in Science Fiction

Societies depend on animals as an essential part of the planet's ecosystems, as food, subjects for experimentation, pets, entertainment, and as a way to think about what it means to be human (DeMello 2012; Herzog 2010; Ingold 1988). Research in human–animal studies has become increasingly urgent in the light of the extinction events of the twentieth and twenty-first centuries, particularly Earth's sixth and ongoing mass extinction event, which can be traced to society's exploitation of resources and the increasing severity of the effects of climate change (Ceballos et al. 2015; Kolbert 2014; Leakey and Lewin 1996). These events point to significant shifts in our cultural understanding of human–animal relationships over the course of the nineteenth and twentieth centuries. The growth of the urban population, the decline of the rural, and the expansion of science and technology as ways to mediate between culture and nature involve new institutions and practices that influence our relationships with animals. These developments are rooted in the seventeenth and eighteenth centuries, but the exponential growth of scientific knowledge and technological capabilities transformed these influences in the late nineteenth and twentieth centuries.

Science fiction is not popularly associated with inquiries into the animal relationship to individual humans or to societies, nor is it thought of as a locus of critique regarding the attitudes, stances and orientations toward different animals or classes of animals. Yet SF does take the question of the animal to be crucial to its engagement with ideas of human nature, evolution, social change and ethics. SF's entanglement with science, technology and society has played its role in constructing, sustaining and transforming cultural representations of animals. It has informed the ways animals have been regarded and treated, and has been instrumental in developing new modes of interaction with animals and nature. SF has offered a nexus for fictional, scientific and philosophic conceptions of human–animal relationships and continues to exert a considerable influence on how individuals and groups position themselves with regard to animals (see Figure 39).

Figure 39. The animal Other abounds in early twentieth-century pulp fiction.

The thematic primacy of the Other and of engagements with Otherness in SF invites reflection on the irreducible Otherness of the animal subject. Sherryl Vint argues that the emergence of SF at a time when the rise of industrial capitalism alienated people from their historic and economic relationship with animals 'might thus be understood as at least in part a desire to re-establish a world shared with other beings. Animals thus "haunt" SF, always there in the shadows behind the alien or the android with whom we fantasise exchange' (2010: 12). While animals have thus shaped the development of SF icons, SF has also directly engaged with animal themes.

SF's interest in the animal makes it a valuable source for thinking about contemporary issues in human–animal studies. Indeed, this complementarity has prompted Rob Latham to describe the discourse of human–animal studies as science fictional (2014: 17). The scholar who best exemplifies the connection between SF and human–animal studies is Donna Haraway, whose foundational essay, 'A Cyborg Manifesto', drew together the figure of the cyborg and feminism to offer 'an ironic political myth faithful to feminism, socialism, and materialism' (1991: 149). Centrally, Haraway's cyborgs are 'creatures simultaneously animal and machine, who populate worlds ambiguously natural and crafted' (149). Extending this concern with fuzzy boundaries and the synthesis of the human and non-human, Haraway questions the status of the human–animal relationship in *When Species Meet* to ask what it means to become *worldly* with other species. Becoming worldly requires a recognition of the complex histories of animals and the ecological communities that they evolve within. 'The point', Haraway explains, 'is not to celebrate complexity but to become worldly and to respond' (2008: 41). Haraway's *Staying with the Trouble: Making Kin in the Chthulucene* continues to extend this concern with developing relationships with animal Others to become worldly, and to re-create our contexts for living during an age dominated by the human capacity to dramatically reshape the global climate. It is a project at odds with centuries of Western political thought.

Francis Bacon's scientific utopia, *The New Atlantis* (1627), proposes a scheme for the improvement of humankind that is based on the domination and exploitation of animals. It positions control over nature as the source of technological innovations in medicine, a central arena for instituting improvements to society. The narrator points to the 'parks, and enclosures of all sorts, of beasts and birds', all of which are kept for aesthetic reasons but, more importantly, for medical research – 'for dissections and trials'. Control over animals enable these utopians to affect miraculous and strange cures and to exert mastery over nature's development. *The New Atlantis* has been influential on the development of SF, particularly in SF's incorporation of the Baconian scheme for imagining science and technology's ability to improve society and to harness nature for humankind's benefit.

H. G. Wells' *The Island of Doctor Moreau* (1896) takes the possibilities for reshaping animal life as its central theme. Dr Moreau's project, to transform the animal body according to the human model and to invest animals with consciousness, is informed by eighteenth-century debates surrounding vivisection: Dr Moreau's goal, he tells the narrator Prendick, is 'to find out the extreme limit of plasticity in a living shape' (online at Project Gutenberg). The implications of evolution's slow transformation of bodies informed views of the plasticity of the body and encouraged experiments into the reshaping of the animal, conceived of as a technologically accelerated evolutionary process. The perception of the vivisectionist as supplanting God's role finds expression in the beast-people's ritual chants about the 'Law', a reference to evolution with Moreau positioned as a Creator-figure. This chant, with the regular refrain 'Are we not Men?', highlights an anxiety regarding the policing of the boundaries between the human and animal that has shaped how animals have historically been positioned in European and Anglo-American cultures. Giorgio Agamben accounts for how European traditions of science and philosophy constructed an 'anthropological machine', a way of demarcating the boundary between the human and the non-human animal that relies on the abstraction of qualities that reside only in the human, and which thus make the human exceptional in some way (Agamben 2004). In *Moreau*, the Beast People illustrate the operations of the anthropological machine such as to subvert notions of human exceptionalism, leading Prendick to reflect pessimistically on his fellow citizens upon returning to London: 'I could not persuade myself that the men and women I met were not also another Beast People, animals half wrought into the outward image of human souls, and that they would presently begin to revert, to show first this bestial mark and then that' (Wells 2004).

Animal consciousness has been a prevalent theme in SF. Influenced by Wells' oeuvre, Olaf Stapledon's *Sirius: A Fantasy of Love and Discord* (2000 [1944]) tells of a modified sheepdog able to reason and to communicate telepathically. Frederik Pohl's wartime novel *Slave Ship* (1963 [1956]) similarly involves modifications to animals which allow them to communicate telepathically and to contribute to war efforts against an enemy aligned with Vietnam. Frank Herbert's 'Greenslaves' (1965) describes animals that have attained consciousness, although in this case it is insects that have surpassed a threshold enabling a communal consciousness to develop in response to pressures instigated by humankind. In this story they cluster to mimic human bodies and attempt to intervene to preserve the ecological integrity of their habitat from human encroachment. Like the animals of Cordwainer Smith's Instrumentality stories, in which animals known as Underpeople are granted human consciousness and form (see *Norstrilia* 1988 [1975]), animals in these stories are often imagined as slaves to humankind, creatures that are subjugated to human desires and prerogatives and who either learn to adapt to their new capacities by following human models, or who contest these boundaries in favour of behaviours appropriate to their own modes of existence. David Brin coined 'uplift' to describe the process of imbuing animals with consciousness in his series of novels beginning with *Sundiver* (1996 [1980]), and the term has subsequently been used by other writers such as Adrian Tchaikovsky in *Children of Time* (2015).

Another tradition that examines relationships between humankind and non-human animals centres on stories of apes and ape intelligence: Franz Kafka's 'A Report to an Academy' (2018 [1917]) takes the form of an address to a scientific establishment regarding the narrators' own uplift. Karen Joy Fowler's 'What I Didn't See' (2006 [2002]) reframes James Tiptree Jr's short story, 'The Women Men Don't See' (1973), to comment on the imposition of motivations onto both women and animals from a normative male subjectivity. Haraway explains in *Primate Visions* that Carl Akeley, the leader of an expedition to hunt and photograph gorillas, believed that '[t]he best thing to reduce the potency of game for heroic hunting is to demonstrate that inexperienced women could safely do the same thing. Science had already penetrated; women could follow' (Haraway 1989: 34). Tiptree's mother, Mary Hastings Bradley, was the woman selected to accomplish this task, and Tiptree herself was present at the expedition. These resonances link the incorporation of the natural world into a scientific scheme to questions of gender and subjectivity, thus questioning the knowledge generated about animals and women when the capacity to appropriately respond to the other fails. Fowler's *We Are All Completely Beside Ourselves* (2014 [2013]) takes up the question of appropriate responses to non-human animals: the narrator, Rosemary Cooke, reflects on her experience growing up in a close relationship with a chimpanzee named Fern.

This chapter has necessarily focused on only a small sample of SF's engagement with animals. Works such as Anne McCaffrey's *Catteni* sequence (beginning with *Freedom's Landing*, 1996 [1995]) and Michel Faber's *Under the Skin* (2014 [2000]) examine industrial meat production by positioning humankind as meat animals. Brian Aldiss' *Helliconia* trilogy (beginning *Helliconia Spring* 1982) and Joan Slonczewski's *A Door Into Ocean* (1986) imagine extra-terrestrial ecologies and the modes of adaptation to those systems, while stories such as 'Victor and the Fish' (2016) and Kim Stanley Robinson's *New York 2140* (2017) explore animal conservation in the context of climate change. As Earth's ecosystems continue to be diminished, SF can be expected to continue to extend its investigation into the human relationship to animal others and the consequences to life and wellbeing of animal exploitation and extinction.

Jeremy Brett

Science Fiction Archives

Libraries and archives are institutions representative of their particular historical and social moment. That is to say, as Terry Cook and Joan M. Schwartz once noted, they 'are not passive storehouses of old stuff, but active sites where social power is negotiated, contested, confirmed' (2002). By extension, memory is not something found or collected in archives, but something that is made, and continually re-made'. There has always been a great power in libraries and archives to shape the historical narrative simply by virtue of what they collect – or, in many cases, refuse or neglect to collect. Although traditionally archivists' and librarians' views of themselves hold that we are neutral distributors of information, objective professionals who exercise no prejudice or subjective decisions in choosing what we preserve, that is far from the case in reality. No library outside the pages of a Borges story will be able to collect absolutely everything ever published or created, no matter what the subject. No information management system yet exists that could arrange, describe, and make accessible all possible material on virtually any topic.

As a result of these physical and technological limits, every library and every archive makes conscious decisions about the kinds of materials it will collect. This necessary subjectivity has serious and lasting impact on the creation of historical memory. Libraries and archives that collect SF and fantasy-related materials have the same influence on future generations' understanding of and access to the history of the genres. Therefore, they have a responsibility to SF&F research to ensure as complete a record of the development of SF and fantasy over time as they might, both through individual collection development and through cooperation, collaboration, and information sharing with other institutions that collect in those genres.

This piece is geared towards, first and foremost, the small number of institutions that specifically collect SF&F materials as part of their institutional missions. Entities such as the University of California, Riverside, Texas A&M University (see Figure 40), the University of Iowa, the University of Kansas, the University of Liverpool, and the Toronto Public Library (see Figure 41), to name some of the most prominent, that collect in this manner, have a special duty to the SF&F genres because they construct such significant permanent parts of the SF&F documentary record. Future scholars and researchers rely on these large-scale collections for primary source research materials as well as more obscure or hidden examples of published or broadcast media products that make up the genres in the scholarly and popular imaginations.

Figure 40. Cushing Memorial Library and Archives, Texas A&M University.

Figure 41. Toronto Public Library, home to the Merrill Collection of Science Fiction, Speculation and Fantasy, the largest collection of its kind in Canada.

However, it applies broadly also to any library or archives in which SF and fantasy materials are collected. After all, every library, every archives, every cultural institution that collects on any topic is a gateway to access for that topic to multiple audiences. People come to many different subjects through their availability at these institutions, and their perceptions of those subjects are seen through the lens of collection limits and access. In other words, people understand things based on the information they have available to them. A library or archival collection has the power to influence how a patron understands the history and extent of SF: for example, if a library makes the decision to collect only, say, the works that win or are nominated for Hugo Awards in any given year, they will build a superlative and compact collection of quality literature. However, they are also excluding a wide array of creative voices. (Of course, the institution may have perfectly valid reasons for this decision: available funding, shelf space, the decision not to collect materials outside the existing collection development policy, and so forth. And, as mentioned above, no institution could practically collect everything on a particular subject.) Therefore, patrons are only getting a limited exposure to the complexity and breadth of the SF&F genres. This ultimately does a disservice to the genres and their rich and diverse histories. As scholar and spokesman for archival advocacy Randall C. Jimerson points out,

> archivists have only recently begun to re-examine their assumptions about the neutrality and objectivity of archives. In the 'information age', knowledge is power. This power gives those who determine what records will be preserved for future generations a significant degree of influence. Archivists must embrace this power, rather than continuing to deny its existence. In addition to protecting the rights and interests of all citizens, archives preserve vital aspects of cultural heritage. (Jimerson 2007)

This mandate applies equally to libraries, circulating and special alike.

The SF and fantasy genres, for the longest time, were dominated in the popular imagination by a narrow corpus of 'the Greats': people like H. G. Wells, Jules Verne, Isaac Asimov, Ray Bradbury, Arthur C. Clarke, Robert Heinlein, J. R. R. Tolkien, H. P. Lovecraft. The vast majority of the creators that readers and scholars thought worth considering tended to be, as is so often the case, white Anglo-American males, comprising a small and limited choir of voices. True, a few others managed to pass the barricades from time to time: writers such as Ursula K. Le Guin, Leigh Brackett, Samuel Delany, Marion Zimmer Bradley, or Octavia Butler. But by and large the true diversity of SF and fantasy – in race, gender, sexual orientation, religion, ethnic origin, and other diversities in both creator and theme – have been eschewed in many library and archival collections; this fallout from the persistence of the dominant narrative of SF and fantasy's creation and development, results in a poorer understanding of the genres in the popular (and even scholarly) understanding.

Collecting institutions can help alleviate this imaginative poverty by broadening the scope of their SF&F collecting strategies. SF&F librarians and archivists must be proactive in identifying authors, publishers, and other creators beyond the traditional narrative of white males (though certainly that narrative is a strand in the overall history of the genres and should also be documented). Notable collecting efforts such as the University of Oregon's work to collect papers and other materials relating to feminist SF help to counteract the traditional collecting scope. The limits to acquisition resources for any single institution, of course, dictate that institutions should cooperate on preserving the history and development of SF and fantasy. There exists now a Science Fiction Collections Consortium, populated by most of the institutions that collect SF&F materials systematically. These kinds of alliances allow for information- and resource-sharing opportunities. They create a network in which collegial institutions might observe each other's collecting practices and strengths, and design their own collecting accordingly.

In this way, one institution that might be focusing primarily on materials relating to the golden age of science fiction (1930s–1940s), can identify a sister repository that collects more in the area of New Wave (1960s–1970s) novels and stories, or one that specializes in modern media fanworks. The first institution can then make conscious collecting decisions to not spend resources on New Wave materials, but instead to focus on its own chosen area, and in fact might direct donors of New Wave collections towards the repository that specializes in that subject. Thus, can SF&F collecting repositories maximize their available resources, eliminate unnecessary or unwanted duplication of effort, and better assist researchers in their work by concentrating in a smaller network the institutions relevant to their needs.

Libraries and archives can also help deepen our understanding of SF and fantasy by realizing that their story resembles a triangle: the record of the voices that produce the traditional creative products of the genre describes one side – the novels, the stories, the films, the television shows, the comic books, and so forth. It also includes the primary archival materials produced by those voices documenting their lives and careers and how those products were constructed: materials such as manuscripts, drafts, story notes, correspondence, and diaries.

Another side consists of the scholarly corpus of research from generations of researchers, academics, students, and others who have deepened our understanding of the SF and fantasy genres with their scholarship – monographs, articles, theses, and documentaries (see Figure 42).

Figure 42. The Thomas Rivera Library at the University of California, Riverside, home to the Eaton Collection of Science Fiction and Fantasy – the largest research collection of its kind in the world.

The third side of the triangle is comprised of the products created as popular responses to creative works, that is, fanworks: fanzines, filksong, fanvids, fan art, and so forth. The history and development of SF and fantasy cannot be realistically extricated from fans' reactions; this relationship stretches back at least as far as the 1920s, when American fans began using the letter columns of pulp magazines as forums for the exchange of views, opinions, and information. Since that time, SF and fantasy have been shaped by fans' responses, their criticisms, and even their headcanon, which can bleed over into and alter the canonical narratives established by the product creators. (One example of this would be fans of the 1990s television fantasy show *Xena: Warrior Princess*, who promulgated and championed a lesbian relationship between the title character and her sidekick Gabrielle, to the point where the show's creators decided to adopt it – subtly – as part of the show's canon.)

Should their resources permit, SF libraries and archives would do well to consider all sides of the triangle and to collect accordingly. The rich and diverse history of SF and fantasy is inherently incomplete without consideration of all its facets; to understand it in full (to the extent that such a thing is possible), the repositories on which scholars and students rely for their work must strive to ensure the collections they curate accurately reflect the diversity of the genres. Libraries and archives, as noted above, have a special responsibility to ensuring that future generations of scholars, fans, and others have full access to every part of the far-flung, endlessly fascinating evolutionary chronicle of these most interesting genres of fiction.

Part IV

Science Fiction Media

Dan Byrne-Smith

Science Fiction Comics

Contemporary comics offer some of the most vibrant, dynamic, adventurous, subversive and inventive examples of SF as a visual form today. This field is global, demonstrating variations in formats, cultural traditions and histories. This short overview of SF comics will focus on some of the dominant histories of the field, discussing the United States, Japan, France and the UK.

USA

The best case for the first clearly recognizable SF comic is offered by the daily newspaper strip *Buck Rogers in the 25th Century AD*.[1] The story focused on the adventures of a former pilot accidentally preserved for centuries, to awaken in a future war. First published across the USA in January 1929, the strip was adapted from a story by Philip Nowlan, with illustrations by Frank R. Paul, published in the September 1928 edition of Hugo Gernsback's *Amazing Stories* magazine. Changing the protagonist's name from Anthony to Buck, Nowlan wrote the script, while artist Dick Chalkins drew it, basing his designs on Paul's work. The strip emphasized adventure and advanced technology, was read by an audience of millions (Benton 1992: 10) and was adapted as a radio

---

1. In the United States, science fiction comics were preceded by the outlandishly inventive work of Winsor McCay. His full-page weekly newspaper strip *Little Nemo in Slumberland* (1905–1911) depicted a child's dreams, where technologies of industrial modernity overlapped with the impossible. McCay's dreamscapes point to influences further back, including graphic works from France, such as Jean Jacques Grandville and Albert Robida, as well as the Swiss artist Rodolphe Töpffer.

show in 1932. Among the numerous imitations, serious competition entered the field in 1934 with the debut of *Flash Gordon*, written and drawn by Alex Raymond.² The popular *Flash Gordon* newspaper strips inspired a movie serial (1936) which prompted a similar treatment for *Buck Rogers* (see Figure 43).

The 1930s saw a change in how comics were read. No longer were they exclusively found in newspapers. Strips were collected in small publications and sold as comic books. Initially these were reprinted from newspaper strips. The first of these newsstand comic books, *Famous Funnies*, included reprints of *Buck Rogers* newspaper stories but original SF material was soon being generated.³ SF proliferated in the early comic books, although most stories were unremarkably formulaic, filled with ray guns, rocket ships and sexualized depictions of women.⁴ In 1938, the expanding field of comic books was joined by the first issue of *Action Comics*, featuring the debut of cover star Superman, an alien from the planet Krypton who is dedicated to doing good on Earth (see Figure 44). Created by Jerry Siegel and Joe Shuster, *Superman* saw the beginning of a new SF trope that proved popular over the next decade. This first era of superhero comics in the United States, between 1938 and around 1950, is generally referred to as the golden age.

Figure 43. *Buck Rogers* #1 (Eastern Color Printing, Winter 1940). Cover art by Dick Calkins.

The waning popularity of superhero comics was reflected by a demand for other genres, including romance, crime, war, horror, westerns and SF. These genres were all catered for by the publisher EC, run by William M. Gaines.

---

2   Visually, Raymond's work was distinct from the look of *Buck Rogers*, more reliant on a stylized and dynamic sense of realism.
3   Gernsback moved into comics in 1940, publishing three issues of *Superworld Comics* drawn by Frank R. Paul. Many science fiction writers, including Theodore Sturgeon and Alfred Bester were also involved in writing science fiction comics.
4   A notable anomaly among them is *Spacehawk*, written and drawn by Basil Wolverton, which reads as a bizarre, darkly surreal take on familiar tropes.

Figure 44. *Action Comics* # 1 (June 1938), featuring the first appearance of Superman. Art by Joe Shuster, colours by Jack Adler.

Harvey Kurtzman, who wrote, drew and edited for EC, is clear about the importance of the company during this time:

> The early 1950s were in many ways the most extraordinary period in the comic book's history. At no time in the preceding fifteen years had so much pure artistic talent been unleashed with such intensity. For the first time, a publisher brought out a whole line of comic could hold an adult reader's interest. (Kurtzman 1991: 28)

EC's SF comics, *Weird Science* and *Weird Fantasy*, both ran from 1950 to 1953, before poor sales led to the titles combining as *Weird Science-Fantasy* in 1954.[5] EC's SF may not have sold as well as their horror titles but they followed a similar formal approach, favouring short tales with a twist or shock ending. However, this was SF with a sense of the form's ability to unsettle and ask questions: Wally Wood's adaptation of Ray Bradbury's story *There Will Come Soft Rains*, published in issue 17 of *Weird Fantasy* in 1953, reads as a powerful and resonant work of SF in any context.

The comic book industry in the United States was transformed in 1954, when a self-imposed set of restrictions dramatically changed the tone and content of comics.[6] Distributors would

---

[5] There was a short-lived relaunch in 1955 as *Incredible Science Fiction* which lasted only four issues.

[6] The moral panic generated by psychiatrist Fredric Wertham and his popular book *Seduction of the Innocent* (1954) transformed the production of comics in the USA. Wertham's belief that comics could be directly responsible for violent acts of juvenile delinquency, and for encouraging abhorrent or perverted behaviour, sparked a Senate Hearing in 1954. This in turn led to the establishing of the Comics Code Authority soon after. It was a self-imposed form of regulation to ensure that the industry survived. For further reading see David Hajdu (2008), *The Ten Cent Plague: The Great Comic Book Scare and How it Changed America*, New York: Farrar, Strauss and Giroux, Bart Beaty (2005), *Fredric Wertham and the Critique of Mass Culture*, and Dan Byrne-Smith (2018),

only handle and display comics that presented the seal of the Comics Code Authority on their covers. The content would have to be free of material that could be interpreted as immoral, unsavoury or generally disrespectful to authority. This effectively brought an end to EC's successful titles, out of which only the humour comic *Mad* survived, changing format into a magazine. However, other SF comics survived under the Code, such as DC's *Strange Adventures*,[7] and new titles continued to appear as the atomic age became the space age. At a struggling company, then known as Atlas comics, editor and writer Stan Lee began a period of collaboration with artist Jack Kirby which began on existing title *Strange Tales* but led to many new publications with covers and lead stories drawn by Kirby, with an emphasis on monsters from space.[8]

In 1961, by which time Atlas had become Marvel, Lee was tasked with providing a response to DC's popular comic featuring a superhero team, *The Justice League of America*. Lee and Kirby's *Fantastic Four*, published in November 1961, gave readers a team that behaved like a dysfunctional family, who had gained special powers through exposure to cosmic rays. These were SF stories, with aliens, cyborgs, inter-dimensional beings, whilst the superhero characters themselves were engagingly flawed. *Fantastic Four* ushered in a new era of superhero comics, followed by an expanding range of Marvel characters who all inhabited the same fictional universe. Although focusing on New York City, Marvel Comics embraced the cosmic. As rival publishers Marvel and DC continued to dominate mainstream comics with superheroes, more explicitly science fictional elements were often a significant part of the stories.

Both publishers would also experiment in SF projects beyond the territory of traditional superhero stories. For example, in the 1980s, Marvel's *Epic Illustrated* SF and fantasy magazine and the subsequent Epic imprint, or DC's

---

'Harvey Kurtzman and the Influence of Mad Magazine', in Jan Baetens, Hugo Frey and Stephen E. Tabachnick (eds), *The Cambridge History of the Graphic Novel*.

7   It may be odd to note, but for some reason *Strange Adventures* sold particularly well whenever the cover featured a gorilla.

8   Issue 13 of *Tales to Astonished* featured a cover monster called Groot, a massive tree monster, who in a very different incarnation would return to Marvel as a character in *Guardians of the Galaxy*.

commissioning of *Ronin*, a six-issue series written and drawn by Frank Miller, reflected an interest in SF stories beyond superheroes.⁹

Since first appearing in 2012, the ongoing comic series *Saga*, written by Brian K. Vaughn and drawn by Fiona Staples, has achieved critical and commercial success (see Figure 45). It is published by *Image*, a company that after Marvel and DC is one of the dominant publishers of comics in the USA. Founded on the principle of creator-owned properties, Image's SF output has been prodigious in recent years, including the following titles: *Prism Stalker*, *Low*, *Tokyo Ghost*, *Black Science*, *Descender*, *Bitch Planet*, *ODY-C* and *Paper Girls*. These and many others offer a broad range of SF narratives and formal approaches.

Figure 45. *Saga* (2012–). Written by Brian K. Vaughn, art by Fiona Staples

Japan

Postwar Japan saw the emergence of a comics tradition in which SF was to feature heavily. Comics were an area of print culture that fell outside of the censorship of occupying US forces.¹⁰ Despite connections to existing pictorial traditions, modern manga emerged in a period of US and European influences. Osamu Tezuka's *Metropolis*, published in 1949, is a SF story partly inspired by images of Fritz Lang's film, set in a fictional city that resembled New York and Chicago. Tezuka then created *Mighty Atom*, known internationally as *Astro Boy* (see Figure 46). The story

---

9 It is also worth noting that a large amount of science fiction comic production, including from Marvel and DC, from the 1960s to the present has been dedicated to stories that relate to movies and TV shows.

10 A useful and concise history of the emergence of printed comics in this period can be found in Helen McCarthy (2014).

of a powerful android who resembles the dead son of its creator, it was serialized weekly and collected in paperback volumes, the original stories running between 1950 and 1968. Adaption into animated form, or anime, made this an international success.

In 1982, anime director Hayao Miyazaki began writing and drawing *Nausicaä of the Valley of the Wind*, which ran for twelve years. Set in a distant post-apocalyptic future, the story focuses on a young female protagonist exploring her toxic world and having to address the legacy of the destruction. The same year also saw the beginning of *Akira* by Katsuhiro Otomo, set in Neo Tokyo, a city rebuilt after World War Three, and destined to be destroyed again. The series was reprinted in the USA by Marvel's imprint Epic after the international release of the film adaptation (1988) and helped to popularize manga outside of Japan. Masamune Shirow's *Ghost in the Shell*, first serialized in 1989 (see Figure 47), was also adapted into an internationally released film in 1995, taking posthumanist themes to a wide audience, while Shirow's *Appleseed* (1985–1989) is an example of a series making use of the *mecha* trope of piloted armoured suits that resemble robots. Contemporary SF manga continue to be popular in Japan and globally, often reaching audiences through anime adaptations, as has been the case with *Attack on Titan* by Hajime Isayama (2009–).

Figure 46. Osamu Tezuka's *Astro Boy – Long Adventure*, Vol. 1 (Kobunsha Publishers Ltd, 1956–1957).

France/Belgium

Barbarella, written and drawn by Jean-Claude Forest, took familiar SF adventure story elements but reconfigured them. First serialized in 1962, the stories rejected the trope of passive women in SF comics, instead presenting a sexually liberated female protagonist who openly pursues sex during her adventures.

The more conventional *Valérian: Spatio-Temporal Agent* (or *Valerian and Laureline* as it is now known) ran in serialized form in the Franco-Belgian comics magazine *Pilote* from 1967. Reprinted in large format albums, the last of these was published in 2010.[11] Perhaps the most influential of all European SF comics is the anthology magazine *Métal Hurlant*, first published in 1974 (see Figure 48).[12] It became a space for experimenting with non-linear narratives, sex, eroticism and various degrees of weirdness.[13] *Metal Hurlant* ceased publication in 1987 but resumed in 2002. The magazine's publishing company, Les Humanoïdes Associés, continues to publish new material as Humanoids.[14]

Britain

Figure 47. Masamune Shirow's *Ghost in the Shell*, Vol. 1 (Kodansha, 1989).

SF comics in postwar Britain were dominated by *The Eagle*, first published in 1950 (see Figure 49). Initially conceived by Marcus Morris, an Anglican vicar, as a tool for the promotion of edifying Christian values, this weekly anthology comic is best known for the SF story *Dan Dare: Pilot of the Future*, created by the comic's co-founder Frank Hampson. *Dan Dare* stories were long-running serialized narratives, populated by tropes from war adventure stories, painted in a meticulously detailed form that took advantage of the expensive printing methods used to produce *The Eagle*. Overlapping with the latter years of *The Eagle*, *Century 21* was launched in 1965, featuring characters and vehicles created for television by Gerry and Sylvia Anderson.

---

11   The comic had been adapted in Luc Besson's movie *Valerian* (2017).
12   Metal Hurlant's co-founders include Moebius (Jean Giraud) and Philippe Druillet.
13   A US version appeared in 1977.
14   As of 2013 Humanoids has moved headquarters from Paris to Los Angeles.

Figure 48. *Métal Hurlant* # 74 (Les Humanoides Associés, 1982). Cover art by Philippe 'Caza' Cazaumayou.

Figure 49. *Eagle* # 1 (14 April 1950). Art by Frank Hampson.

Figure 50. *2000AD* # 1854 (16 October 2013). Cover art by Cliff Robinson.

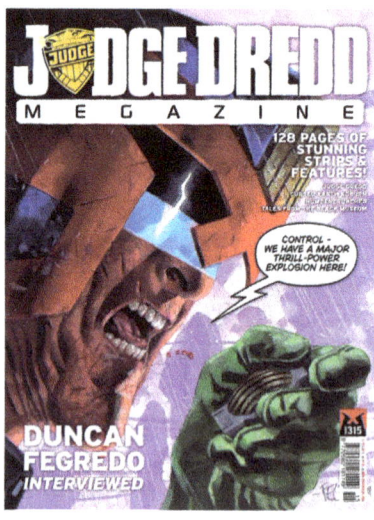

Figure 51. *Judge Dredd Megazine* # 315 (15 September 2011). Cover art by Duncan Fegredo.

The publication of *2000AD* in 1977 deliberately pre-empted the release of a number of Hollywood SF films, including *Star Wars* (see Figure 50). However, for founding editor Pat Mills, the model for this weekly anthology comic was *Métal Hurlant*. Mills looked to European comics as examples of sophisticated and adult-orientated SF. He aimed to translate something of their approach into stylized and violent stories, with an anti-establishment tone, aimed at a youth audience. Early issues of *2000AD* also made use of artists based outside of the UK, particularly in Spain, who had a profound influence on the visual sensibility of the comic. The early years of *2000AD*, in the late 1970s and early 1980s, were a period of high sales and creative innovation. Writer Alan Moore's contribution to *2000AD* in the early 1980s led to unusual and engaging SF stories. *The Ballad of Halo Jones*, created with artist Ian Gibson, is a subtle and resonant piece of storytelling. *Skizz*, drawn by Jim Bakie, is a take on *ET* set in Birmingham. *2000AD* is still in print as a weekly title, with a monthly counterpart, the *Judge Dredd Megazine* (see Figure 51).

These ongoing traditions of SF comics contain a rich history of visual and conceptual innovation, reflecting and shaping the visual and textual cultures of the genre, which in turn have fed back into wider culture,[15] visualizing possible futures and SF's visual languages on a global scale. Contemporary SF comics are read widely across sexual divisions and age groups, while the diversity of creators continues to expand.

---

15   Stories published in *Metal Hurlant*, such as *The Long Tomorrow* by Dan O'Bannon and oebius, have had a profound influence on Hollywood cinema, as have Japanese Manga.

Mariano Martín Rodríguez

Science Fiction Metafiction

'Science fiction' is, obviously, composed of two substantial elements: 'science' and 'fiction'. In literature, fiction is constituted by any text that generates a possible world where imaginary events take place or imaginary objects exist; it operates as a construct of an artistic nature not expected to be factually true.[1] Fictional worlds are created through language, and often through pre-existing rhetorical macro-devices, or formal genres such as the novel or drama, which are prevalent vehicles for literary fiction today. Fiction can be expressed, however, through non-novelistic, and even non-narrative devices. There are fictional works entirely written using diverse prescriptive discourses, from legal codes to directions (Martín Rodríguez 2015), and there are also texts written as mock advertising (Martín Rodríguez 2016). In both cases, they may posit alternate or futuristic imaginary worlds, thus taking on the conventions of SF and/or speculative texts and fulfilling the above semantic criterion for fiction.

The main way in which fiction writing masquerades as non-fiction is related, however, to the first element of the SF linguistic formula: science. This is not the place to discuss what science is, or which sciences are, indeed, 'scientific'. However, both the human, or 'soft' sciences (such as historiography,

---

[1] 'Entscheidend für die Bestimmung eines dargestellten Geschehens als real oder fiktiv ist die Referenz, nämlich die Frage, ob der im Text dargestellte Sachverhalt in der außersprachlichen Realität tatsächlich der Fall war/ist oder nicht' [when determining if a represented event is real or fictitious, the frame of reference is decisive, namely the question of whether the facts presented in the text had/have actually occurred in the extralinguistic reality or not] (Klein and Martínez 2009: 2). Moreover, 'ist die Fiktionalität der Erzählung durch die Phantastik der Geschichte für den Leser deutlich, obwohl die Erzählstruktur keine Fiktionalitätshinweise enthlt' [thanks to the fantastic features of the story, the fictionality of the narration is clear to the reader, even if the narrative structure has no indication of such fictionality] (Zipfel 2001: 134). All translations are mine.

ethnology or philology), and the experimental and highly mathematized 'hard' sciences (such as physics or chemistry), are commonly associated with scientific and academic status in our society. More importantly for us here, their textual expression has been well-established from the nineteenth century onwards, and it is readily recognizable by any reader exposed to the discursive features used to communicate knowledge to the public. Although the manner in which findings, theories and facts are presented in books and journals devoted to science is not fully uniform, a purely expository kind of discourse is now prevalent in most sciences, even though the argumentative discourse, as well as contain a greater degree of rhetorical variety and stylistic ornamentation, may also be important in the so-called human ones. In all of them, however, the scientific text must be seen as devoid of any subjectivity, as well as of any literary self-referentiality, ideally being only a transparent linguistic vehicle for a description of pure factuality.[2] Indeed, drawings, graphs and formulae abound in modern scientific texts, as well as the footnotes and bibliographical information more prevalent in traditional human sciences, in order to enhance the objective tone required, as well as to suggest the objective and extra-textual nature of the phenomena described. These textual devices underline that the reported facts do not result from any form of personal fancy and invention, but are based on documentation and true evidence – this is to say, that they

---

2   'Zusammenfassend zu nennen sind eine kodifierte Argumentation, ein reduzierte Wortschaft, ein hochstandardisiertes Format, ... eine grammatikalisch weitgehend ausgestrichene Autorschaft und insbesondere die Eliminierung jeglicher Orts- und Zeitangaben... Dies trägt erheblich dazu bei, das Forschungslabor als einen Ort der Produktion von zeitloser Erkenntnis zu inszenieren. Im Forschungsbericht wird also nicht über individuelle, zeitlich und räumlich verankerte Experimente berichtet, sondern das Experiment wird als ein zeitloser, da prinzipiell immer wiederholbarer Handlungsakt erzählt' [to name a few in short, there are a codified sequence of reasoning, a limited terminological domain, a highly standardized format, a grammatically largely suppressed authorship, and in particular the elimination of any place and time... This significantly contributes to stage the research laboratory as a place of production of timeless knowledge. Therefore, individual experiments in a concrete time and place are not identified in a research report, but the experiment is portrayed as a timeless and in principle always reproducible event] (Brandt 2009: 104). Although these features are related here to the natural sciences, if we replace 'experiment' by 'observed or documented facts,' they are also applicable to the social sciences, including historiography.

have a scientific basis and, therefore, that the text portrays and expresses 'science'. Even when the facts are false, the text which reports them does so in such a discursive way that the reader is invited to see them as 'factually' sound, as well as 'scientific'. Their textual discourse supposes their 'factuality', or, in other terms, 'non-fictionality'. In short, when reading a novel, its fictionality is taken for granted, whereas when reading a scientific report, we assume its factuality.

This reading effect caused by factuality, however, can be used for fictional purposes. We would have then a particular kind of 'fictional non-fiction' that could be named 'scientific fictional non-fiction'. This encompasses all works where a fantastical content is infused into a text that methodically and consistently presents, in its entirety, as a formally independent written work, the standard rhetorical features of scientific discourses usual in real-world scientific practice. This fantastic content can be of a science fictional nature (it can include Suvinian *nova*), and a great number of fictional texts which use factual discourses actually feature contents that can safely be labelled 'sf'. The content is, however, of little relevance for a taxonomy of scientific fictional non-fiction. The main criterion to define the genre and its major subgenres is, actually, formal. In all of them, literariness is achieved mostly through the fictionalization of their contents, while their language imitates the highly formalized, uniform, descriptive, seemingly objective, and un-literary tone commonly used in current natural, formal or social sciences.[3] Each science, however, has its own jargon which in turn generates various discursive subgenres.

Fiction in the natural sciences has brought about a whole genre, the spoof paper, of which examples abound (Lewin 1983). Many of them are often intended as humorous hoaxes or practical jokes by actual scientists. Others have appeared, however, in literary venues, and they should be studied as literary

---

3   Scientific fictional non-fiction achieves then literariness through an opposite procedure to that used, for example, in didactic and science poetry (Fusil 1918), where factually 'true' contents are expressed through a highly literary discourse, featuring numerous figures of speech and, primarily, a clear mark of literariness such as the use of verse. A borderline genre between science poetry and scientific fictional non-fiction is the cosmological poem describing the alleged origins and evolution of the universe, Earth and its inhabitants from a secular perspective, such as Louis Bouilhet's *Les Fossiles* (1854), where 'the poet envisages a new creation, born of yet another terrestrial revolution which has submerged the old world and cast up new continents' (Hunt 1941: 275).

fiction. Since both the natural and the formal sciences employ a highly formalized prose, fictional non-fiction of this kind leaves little room for rhetorical embellishment. Their literary interest is to be found elsewhere, in the altered views on science and society brought about by their confrontation within the text. A strict adherence to the dry styles of Mathematics or Linguistics can highlight the potential inhumanity of scientific objectivity; for example, George Orwell's semiotically independent appendix on 'The Principles of Newspeak' is 'an epitome of Orwell's techniques of parody' (Fink 1971: 163) that tacitly suppresses all suffering from the terrible events just narrated in *Nineteen Eighty-Four* (1949). Also in the natural sciences, the coldness of 'hard' scientific discourse can be adroitly imitated to undermine it, as it happens in the two papers collectively entitled 'The Marvellous Properties of Thiotimoline' (1948–1952; collected in *Only a Trillion*, 1957) by Isaac Asimov. These not only demonstrate the linguistic and rhetorical skill of the author, but also 'allow for readings deconstructing the way in which truth presents itself as absolute, as well as instrumental, at least through the linguistic expression common in the natural sciences' (Martín Rodríguez 2018b). Regarding 'softer' sciences, such as Biology, the descriptions of imaginary beings and of their habitats are usually devoid of the irony pervasive in the fictional use of 'hard' scientific discourse, often implying attempts at renovating, through the biological discourse as well as through the pure invention of the animals and plants described, the traditional genre of the bestiary, for example, in J. K. Rowling's textbook *Fantastic Beasts and Where to Find Them* (2001).

Perhaps because the high formalism of written expression in the natural and formal sciences imposes a rhetorical discipline that many writers are unwilling or unable to adopt, spoof scientific papers constitute only a small part of scientific fictional non-fiction, at least if compared to the high number of imitations of human/social sciences discourse. Among them, historiography has provided the discourse most extensively used in the formal macro-genre here studied, from the nineteenth century onwards (Martín Rodríguez 2013, 2014). Imaginary history written in the historiographic style has three main varieties, according to the chosen time frame: past, present or future. If set in the past, the historiographic narrative may describe events that had occurred in an imaginary country or civilization, such as the ancient Eurasia described by Robert E. Howard in 'The Hyborian Age' (1938). Alternate history initially employed a true historiographical form, in Louis Geoffroy's *Napoléon et la conquête du monde. 1812 à 1832. Histoire de la monarchie universelle* [*Napoléon and the Conquest of the World, 1812–1832: A Fictional History*] (1836), before being replaced more recently by alternate history in the form of mostly novelistic 'stories'. What Ostrowski called 'anticipated history' in the very first survey on historiographical fictional non-fiction (1960) is a narrative usually by a future historian which uses the verbal past tenses of past events to present readers with future events that we know to be imaginary. Among fictional historiographical works of anticipation, some are classics of scientific romance, such as Gabriel Tarde's *Fragment d'histoire future* (1896), whose English translation appeared in 1905 as *Underground Man* with a preface by H. G. Wells; to this we may add Olaf Stapledon's history of the successor species to humankind along many millennia *Last and First Men* (1930), and Wells' socio-political history of *The Shape of Things to Come* (1933). Anticipatory history, which is the kind of fictional historiography closer to SF proper, has been relatively popular among speculative writers for both intellectual and formal reasons. Imagining future history as if it were past has allowed them to directly show, with the persuasive power of the factual 'true' discourse, the evolution of human societies had any particular trend prevailed, from the 'yellow peril' in Jack London's 'The Unparalleled Invasion' (1910; collected in *The Strength of the Strong*, 1911) to technocracy in Michael Young's *The Rise of the Meritocracy* (1958). Moreover, although its narrative is of a descriptive nature,[4] historiography also tells a story, which can be expanded in time and detail until it reaches novelistic proportions. The same applies to mythopoeias such as Lord Dunsany's *The Gods of Pegāna* (1905).

Both the discourses of narrative historiography and of mythography are, therefore, less alien to the usual patterns of the readers' novelistic consumption than other subgenres of fictional non-fiction based on plain descriptive social sciences, such as Geography and its sibling discipline Ethnography. These are

---

4 'In weitesten Sinne ist die historiographische Erzählung also nach der [...] Differenzierung zwischen deskriptiver, normativer oder voraussagender Erzählung eine deskriptive Erzählung' [based on a [...] differentiation between descriptive, normative or predictive narrative, in the broadest sense, the historiographic narrative is, then, a descriptive one] (Jaeger 2009: 110–111).

often combined in fictional works on the conditions and customs of imaginary peoples – in the present, on Earth or otherwise, or in the past, when the borrowed scientific discourse is that of Archaeology, such as Andrew Lang's 'The Great Gladstone Myth' (1886; collected in the same year in the volume *In the Wrong Paradise and Other Stories*). True geographic/ethnographic accounts have offered a rhetorical model for world-building in the descriptive mode such as the famous tongue-in-cheek study on reverse anthropology entitled 'Body Ritual Among the Nacirema' (1956) by Horace Mitchell Miner, as well as Jorge Luis Borges' description of the workings of social groups in 'La secta de los treinta' [The Sect of the Thirty] (collected in *El libro de arena* [*The Book of Sand*], 1975). This latter 'fiction' could also be considered an example of fictional Philology, since it is presented as the translation of an ancient text with a short introductory note. Philology is, unsurprisingly, an academic discipline also quite popular among literary writers. As readers at least, many of them must be familiar with the presentation features of critical editions of classics, and some have imitated them in reviews and studies on imaginary works, such as 'A prophetic account of a grand national epic poem, to be entitled *The Wellingtoniad*, and to be published A. D. 2824' (1824) by historian Thomas Babington Macaulay, and the 'History of the *Necronomicon*' (1938) by H. P. Lovecraft. The latter has inspired a number of alternative, but equally philologically oriented histories of that mythic grimoire (Martín Rodríguez, 2018a).

A superbly representative example of science fictional non-fiction is Ursula K. Le Guin's '"The Author of the Acacia Seeds" and Other Extracts from the *Journal of the Association of Therolinguistics*' (1974; collected in *The Compass Rose*, 1982). This work conflates the concepts and rhetoric of the three main groups of sciences (formal, natural and social) into the framework of a model scientific paper, endowed with all the intellectual and rhetorical features that make this genre culturally and literarily significant. Divided in three parts, the first one offers a version of a text written by an ant, the second explores languages written by groups in moving media, and the third speculates about the possibilities of plant languages and literatures. Le Guin's fictional science 'Therolinguistics' combines linguistics, literary criticism and biology in order to invite readers to consider the almost infinite possibilities of both nature and culture beyond any limiting human-centred perspective. In doing so, Le Guin 'casts the future as a heroic exploration of the non-human world: but it casts this exploration in philological terms' (Willis 2014: 499). As scientific fictional non-fiction usually does, this fully academic text shows how fictionalizing science can be used to expand both our minds and our literary sensibilities, thus increasing our awareness of the literary potential of any kind of written discourse, including the scientific one through the fusion of scientific discourse and fictional contents – this is to say, science and fiction, 'science fiction.'

Ian Farnell

Alistair McDowall's X (2016)

The point of first contact between SF and the theatre is difficult to determine – an oft-cited example is Karel Čapek's *R. U. R.* (1920), primarily remembered for introducing the word 'robot' to the world. However, the SF plays of the twentieth century have been considered unremarkable, even something of a failure,[1] aside from a few notable exceptions, such as the opening of the Cottesloe (now Dorfman) stage in London's National Theatre with an eight-hour, five-part production of *Illuminatus!* (1977) by Ken Campbell's Science Fiction Theatre of Liverpool (Coveney 2008). By contrast, the twenty-first century has already delivered several critically acclaimed plays which examine contemporary issues via the lens of SF. The inception of this new wave may be found in Caryl Churchill's *A Number* (2002), which explored fatherhood and masculinity via futuristic human cloning, and demonstrated a technology-conscious reflexivity that saw it dubbed 'the first true play of the 21st century' (de Jongh 2002). Numerous others have since followed – from the post-apocalyptic world of *Mr Burns* (2012) where *The Simpsons* is reimagined as classical drama, to the post-pandemic re-imagining of Brontë's *Villette* by Linda Marshall Griffiths (2016); from the West End run of Jennifer Haley's virtual reality drama *The Nether* (2014) to London's annual Vault Festival of new plays, which in 2017 found itself with enough material to curate a mini-programme of SF dramas (Wilson 2017). If, as Kim Stanley Robinson argues, SF has become the new realism (Lea 2015), then British playmaking is flexing its muscles in the genre.

---

1   Ralph Willingham's *Science Fiction and the Theatre* (1994), to date the only book on the subject, documents the history of science fiction on stage from the late nineteenth century to the 1980s. Highlighting the varying approaches towards its depiction, he ultimately concludes that 'most playwrights who have explored science fiction have usually failed' (147).

This is most evident in the work of the young playwright Alistair McDowall. A graduate of Manchester University and the influential Royal Court Theatre's scriptwriting group, his work has been described by the playwright Simon Stephens, McDowall's friend and mentor, as a fusion of 'economic socio-naturalism and science fiction [...] with more honesty and commitment to the form than any other playwright this millennium' (Stephens 2016). He won the prestigious Bruntwood New Writing Prize with *Brilliant Adventures* (2014), which interrogated inner-city poverty via time travel and was hailed for its 'sizzling exuberance and imagination' (Brennan 2013). His dystopian crime thriller *Pomona* (2014) enjoyed a critically acclaimed run at the National, while his latest play *X* (2016) opened at the Royal Court, and has been hailed as the exemplar SF play (Foley 2017; see Figure 52). It remains memorable for its confident and surprising theatricality, with McDowall incorporating the themes and imagery of SF as a destabilizing agent to test the boundaries of realism and live performance, thus raising unique questions about the representation of time, language and meaning in typical theatrical practice.

Figure 52. Alistair McDowall's *X* at the Royal Court Theatre, London, March 2016. Photograph by Manuel Harlan. Reproduced with permission of the photographer.

X is set on Pluto, where a team of British scientists – captain Ray, deputy Gilda, and researchers Clarke, Mattie and Cole – are awaiting their overdue relief shuttle to take them home. The base supports their continued presence as it designed to sustain, in Ray's words, 'Multiple missions. Indefinite timescale' (McDowall 2016: 35). However, some unknown glitch (or unthinkable catastrophe) has caused the crew to lose communication with Earth, which has fallen silent. The first act is predominantly occupied with exploring the crew's claustrophobia and paranoia, which is rendered both humorously and with mounting dread – while Cole obstinately refuses to work because his contract has technically expired, the panic-stricken Gilda listens to audio recordings taken on the planet surface, which she believes offers a deeper and more meaningful silence to counteract the constant background noise of the station's systems. Ray, the oldest member of the crew, considers their mission a tax write-off, and reflects bitterly on the effects of exploitative profiteering and overwhelming global ecological disaster:

> RAY   There's nothing left back there. Trees. Birds. Animals. Countries gone.
> Everyone crammed too close together on what's left of the land.
> It's a shadow.

The varying attitudes of the crew add political and cultural resonance to McDowall's future world, as issues of ownership, economy and class are extrapolated to the edge of the solar system. However, the drama's early naturalistic configuration – represented in the airport-like layout of the base, the mundanity of the crew's day and their use of board games and exercise bikes to pass the time – is gradually abandoned as horrifying events overwhelm the action, fracturing the play into what the critic Dominic Cavendish labelled as 'fifty per cent sitcom, fifty per cent archetypal sci-fi nightmare' (Cavendish 2016). Gilda's silent recordings become corrupted, spooling out the voice of a child. Ray kills himself after seeing a young girl on the lifeless surface of the planet and later within the walls of the base itself – he slashes his throat and smears a giant, bloody X on the window, which disappears and reappears as scenes begin to occur non-chronologically. Most disturbingly, Cole discovers that the base's clocks, which are configured to Earth's twenty-four-hour cycle, have malfunctioned and are now leaping backwards at random:

> *They watch the clock*
> *[...]*
> *The display stutters, faults,*
> *then snaps backwards one hour and forty-three minutes.*

With no way to measure time, the crew loses track of the days, weeks and even years of their isolation. As the second act begins, they attempt to piece together their recollections of recent events, by turns interrogating, rejecting and restructuring their collective memories. This extended discussion, occupying the majority of the second act, seemingly moves in a linear fashion as if it were a normal conversation in real time, yet as the scene plays out, any notion of time becomes distorted. When Cole and Clark demand that Gilda retell her experience – asking 'Tell it again. Tell us. Start again' – they forget their own part in the episode and come to rely on her (equally uncertain) interpretation:

> COLE   And *what* do we ask.
> GILDA You were there –
> COLE   Tell me. You tell me what I asked.

Past and present tenses interchange, and personal stories shared in the first act are here repeated by someone else, only to be angrily reclaimed or retold. The very existence of one crewmember is questioned. Cole develops a limp which worsens exponentially in just a few moments:

> CLARK Let her scan it so you can shut up about it.
> COLE   No...
> GILDA It's a tumour.
> COLE   Stop it –
> GILDA I'm sorry.
> CLARK You forgot again –
> COLE   Stop doing this – Stop it –
> GILDA I'm sorry. Do you remember?
> CLARK We scanned you mate, remember?

Within a couple of pages, the tumour has moved from being wrapped around the lower vertebrae, to consuming the entirety of Cole's spine. It is now clear that the narrative of the play and its moment-by-moment depiction have become unfixed and are occurring at vastly opposing rates – the physical has detached itself from the temporal. The text is stripped of structural features such as scenic breaks, which ordinarily signal the passage of time, and instead the dialogue becomes quite literally spaced out, with large gaps on the page that suggest both a speeding-up and a dragging-out of time. Stage directions disappear, as if the action can no longer keep up with, or attempt to represent, the speed with which time is moving. Even the act and scene numbers on each page are stripped out and replaced with the hollow symbol of empty square brackets.

Figure 53. McDowall's *X*, March 2016. Photograph by Manuel Harlan. Reproduced with permission of the photographer.

McDowall utilizes this loss of measured time to not only corrupt the narrative of the play, but to act as a metatheatrical deconstruction of the perception of time in live performance (see Figure 53). Compressing the events of an unknowable span of time into just a few moments of stage time, McDowall confounds the natural experience and naturalistic depiction of linear temporal existence. Ordinarily, stage-time runs parallel to the real time of the audience, at least within each scene if not scene-by-scene – but in *X*, the action surpasses real time, with the actors (whose bodies are caught in the real time of the audience) unable to physically recreate the debilitating effects of time experienced by their characters. This creates a rift between the narrative-as-occurred and the action-as-performed, leaving the audience caught between these two increasingly oppositional states.

Yet even this is not the end of the play's tumultuous assault on conventional theatricality – after Cole's death, as time continues to disintegrate, so too does language. Lines lose focus, and an X symbol soon begins to erupt and multiply within the dialogue:

GILDA	X
CLARK	X
GILDA	And the algorithm –
CLARK	Watch
GILDA	Rain
CLARK	Rain
GILDA	Rail
CLARK	X

Soon the names of Gilda and Clark disappear, and the formal structure of the text is lost as the X replicates itself, virus-like, across nearly four pages, like so:

```
XXXXXXXXXXXXXXXXXXXXXXXXXXXXXXXXXXXXXXXXXXXXXX
XXXXXXXXXXXXXXXXXXXXXXXXXXXXXXXXXXXXXXXXXXXXXX
XXXXXXXXXXXXXXXXXXXXXXXXXXXXXXXXXXXXXXXXXXXXXX
XXXXXXXXX
```

This single symbol, normally redolent with connotation – mathematical character, buried treasure, kiss – now cannibalizes the text to render it impenetrable and meaningless; it becomes the play's event horizon. This total abandonment of the normative rules and restrictions of live performance positions X as 'a pioneering provocation [that] fires up the cylinders of debate' (Cavendish 2016), with its science fictional narrative cleverly employed to help stage the seemingly impossible.

As troublesome as it is imaginative, viewing *X* can be a frustrating experience. Some critics were keen to spot the flaws in McDowall's speculative world, pointing out the dissonance between this decidedly British, low-key interpretation of space exploration and its usual, big-budget depiction in other media (Shenton 2016), or even questioning the play's entire premise (McDougall 2016). Inevitably, this reaction stems partially from a kind of background theatrical mistrust towards the genre (Haydon 2008), and while the continuing emergence of SF in theatre is gradually shifting perceptions, there remains a high/low art dialectic which preferentially views theatre as a product of the former, and SF as the latter[2] – as Andrzej Lukowski writes in his review, *X* is 'so unabashedly other that I suspect it'll be heavily misunderstood by folk suspicious of something that's as influenced by *2001* and *Event Horizon* as any of the theatre canon' (Lukowski 2016). Yet while *X* may contain echoes of, say, Ridley Scott's *Alien*, it is a play first and foremost, and thus has more in common with Shakespeare's *King Lear* or Beckett's *Waiting for Godot*, two plays that explore frailty in the wilderness, which tell us that 'nothing will come of nothing' and there is 'nothing to be done'. McDowall's own rendition of this nothingness is made literal in the emptiness of space, and in the X symbol which comes to dominate and brutalize the text. More importantly, *X* remains a unique product of live performance, placing the living human body in front of an audience. Composed of both the live and the science fictional, *X* strives to be 'aggressively theatrical' (Williams 2016), as McDowall himself puts it – by incorporating the imagery of SF within the structures of the theatre, he proceeds to tear down that same architecture, rejecting the conventions of temporality and space in a medium which by its very nature is limited by time and location. In doing so, *X* challenges the entire orthodoxy of theatrical practice.

2   A recurrent theme in some critical reviews is a reluctance to discuss, or outright rejection of, the science fiction label. Churchill's *A Number*, while utilizing the science fictional image of human cloning, is rarely discussed as a work of the genre. Similarly, Anne Washburn's *Mr Burns*, which explored post-apocalyptic communal storytelling via *The Simpsons*, received as much derision for this concept as it did praise. Moreover, the growing number of science fiction plays belies an abiding misunderstanding of the terms, imagery and key concepts of science fiction, which may hopefully be addressed as scholarly attention grows.

Future productions of *X* will doubtless reveal alternate interpretations – premiering amongst the tumultuous cultural and political events of 2016, the play's focus on social alienation and the nihilistic, wholesale destruction of natural life felt like the inescapable sci-fi endgame of nationalism, climate change and capitalism, writ large across space. However, that same production has been read as an intervention on mental health (Haydon 2016), an examination of memory (*Culture Whisper* 2016) and a rumination on mathematics (Pringle 2016). This is a uniquely theatrical quality – while a novel or film remains a fixed cultural product open to interpretation, each subsequent staging of a play employs its own design, direction and performance choices to offer an entirely new reformulation of that initial text. As the theatre continues to embrace SF, McDowall's play functions as the standard-bearer for infusing the imagination of the genre with this singular potential of the dramatic form, to resonate with the most urgent preoccupations of both our present and future.

Bibliography

12 Years a Slave, dir. Steve McQueen (Fox Searchlight Pictures, 2013).
2012, dir. Roland Emmerich (Columbia, 2008).
Abbot, Carl, *Frontiers Past and Future: Science Fiction and the American West* (Lawrence: University Press of Kansas, 2006).
Abe, Kōbō, *Dai-Yon Kampyōki* (Tokyo: Hayakawa Shobo, 1964 [1959]).
Abraham, Nicolas, and Maria Török, *The Shell and the Kerne*, trans. Nicholas T. Rand (Chicago: University of Chicago Press, 1994).
Adams, Gretchen, *The Specter of Salem. Remembering the Witch Trials in Nineteenth-Century America* (Chicago: The University of Chicago Press, 2008).
Agamben, Giorgio, *The Open: Man and Animal* (Palo Alto, CA: Stanford University Press, 2004).
Albrecht, Gary L., Michael Bury and Katherine D. Seelman, eds, *Handbook of Disability Studies* (Thousand Oaks, CA: Sage Publications, 2001).
Alderman, Naomi, *The Power* (London: Viking, 2016).
Aldiss, Brian W., *Billion Year Spree: The True History of Science Fiction* (Garden City, NY: Doubleday, 1973).
——, *Helliconia Spring* (New York: Atheneum, 1982; New York: Collier, 1992).
——, *Helliconia Summer* (New York: Atheneum, 1983).
——, *Helliconia Winter* (New York: Atheneum, 1985).
—— (ed.), *Space Opera: Science Fiction from the Golden Age* (London: Futura; Weidenfeld & Nicolson, 1974).
Alien, dir. Ridley Scott (20th Century Fox, 1979).
Alien: Covenant, dir. Ridley Scott (Brandywine Productions, 2017).
Alien Resurrection, dir. Jean-Pierre Jeunet (Brandywine Productions, 1997).
Alien3, dir. David Fincher (Brandywine Productions, 1992).
Aliens, dir. James Cameron (Brandywine Productions, 1986).
Allan, Stuart, *Media, Risk and Science* (Buckingham: Open University Press, 2002).
Allen, Kathryn, ed., *Disability in Science Fiction: representations of technology as cure* (London: Palgrave Macmillan, 2013).
Anderson, Reynaldo, and Charles E. Jones, eds, *Afrofuturism 2.0: The Rise of Astro-Blackness* (Lanham, MD: Lexington Books, 2016).
Armitt, Lucie, *Contemporary Women's Fiction and the Fantastic* (Basingstoke: Macmillan, 2000).

Asimov, Isaac, 'Robbie'. In *Super Science Stories* (September 1940, entitled 'Strange Playfellow'). Revised and reprinted in *I, Robot* (1950), *The Complete Robot* (New York: Doubleday, 1982), and *Robot Visions* (New York: Roc, 1990).

——, 'Runaround'. *Astounding Science Fiction* (March 1942). Reprinted in *I, Robot* (1950), *The Complete Robot* (New York: Doubleday, 1982), and *Robot Visions* (New York: Roc, 1990).

——, 'Little Lost Robot'. *Astounding Science Fiction* (March 1947). Reprinted in *I, Robot* (1950), *The Complete Robot* (New York: Doubleday, 1982), *Robot Dreams* (1986), and *Robot Visions* (New York: Roc, 1990).

——, 'The Evitable Conflict'. *Astounding Science Fiction* (June 1950). Reprinted in *I, Robot* (1950), *The Complete Robot* (New York: Doubleday, 1982), and *Robot Visions* (New York: Roc, 1990).

——, 'A Boy's Best Friend'. *Boys' Life* (March 1975). Reprinted in *The Complete Robot* (New York: Doubleday, 1982).

——, 'The Bicentennial Man'. *Stellar-2* (February 1976). Revised and Republished in *The Bicentennial Man and Other Stories* (New York: Doubleday, 1976).

——, ed., *Isaac Asimov Presents the Best Science Fiction Firsts* (New York: Barnes and Noble Inc., 1984).

Atwood, Margaret, *The Handmaid's Tale* (Boston, MA: Houghton, 1985).

——, *Oryx and Crake* (London: Bloomsbury, 2003).

——, *The Year of the Flood* (London: Bloomsbury, 2009).

——, 'What *The Handmaid's Tale* Means in the Age of Trump', *The New York Times* 10 March 2017 <https://www.nytimes.com/2017/03/10/books/review/margaret-atwood-handmaids-tale-age-of-trump.html> accessed 9 August 2018.

Australian Bureau of Statistics (2012), 'The Mabo case and the Native Title Act'. Retrieved from <http://www.abs.gov.au/Ausstats/abs@.nsf/Previousproducts/1301.0Feature Article21995> accessed 3 April 2018.

Babatunde, Mark, 'High-Tech Racism: Soap Dispenser Designed Only for White Skin', *Face 2 Face Africa*, 24 August 2017 <https://face2faceafrica.com/article/high-tech-racism-soap-dispenser-designed-white-skin> accessed 21 March 2018.

Baccolini, Raffaella and Tom Moylan, eds, *Dark Horizons: Science Fiction and the Dystopian Imagination* (New York: Routledge, 2003).

Bacigalupi, Paolo, *The Windup Girl* (San Francisco, CA: Night Shade Books, 2009).

——, *The Water Knife* (London: Orbit, 2015).

Bacon, Francis. *The New Atlantis*. 1627. Project Gutenberg (2000) <https://www.gutenberg.org/files/2434/2434-h/2434-h.htm> accessed 31 January 2018.

Bailey, Hilary, 'Dr. Gelabius', *New Worlds Magazine* 181 (April 1968), 4–5.

Baker, Colin (2017) 'I was the Doctor and I'm over the moon that at last we have a female lead' in *The Guardian*, 17 July <https://www.theguardian.com/commentisfree/2017/jul/17/colin-baker-doctor-who-female-lead-doctor-jodie-whittaker-inspire-fans> accessed 2 February 2018.

Baker, Emerson W., *A Storm of Witchcraft. The Salem Trials and the American Experience* (Oxford: Oxford University Press, 2015).
Ballard, J. G, 'Prima Belladona'. *Science Fantasy* 7/20 (December 1956), 63–75.
——, *The Drowned World* (London: Fourth Estate, 2012 [1962]).
——, 'Which Way to Inner Space?' *New Worlds Magazine* 40/118 (May 1962), 2–3.
——, *The Drought* [US title of *The Burning World*] (New York: Liveright Publishing, 2012 [1964]).
Banks, Iain M., *Consider Phlebas* (London: Orbit, 1987; 2008).
——, 'A Few Notes on the Culture' (1994), <http://www.vavatch.co.uk/books/banks/cultnote.htm> accessed 24 January 2018.
Barclay, William, 'Obituary', ed. Charles Platt, *New Worlds Magazine* 197 (January 1970), 33.
Barr, Marleen, *Future Females: A Critical Anthology* (Bowling Green, CT: State University Popular Press, 1981).
——, *Feminist Fabulation: Space/Postmodern Fiction* (Iowa City: University of Iowa Press, 1992).
——, ed., *Afro-Future Females: Black Writers Chart Science Fiction's Newest New-Wave Trajectory* (Columbus: Ohio State University Press, 2008).
Baxter, Stephen, *Flood* (London: Victor Gollancz, 2008).
Belam, Martin, '*Star Wars* Actors Mock Fan Who Recut Film to Remove Women', *The Guardian* (17 January 2018).
Benner, Jeff A,. *Hebrew Text and Lexicon of Genesis* (College Station, TX: Virtualbookworm.com, 2007).
Benton, Mike, *The Illustrated History of Science Fiction Comics* (Dallas: Taylor, 1992).
Bérubé, Michael, 'Disability and Narrative', *PMLA* 120/2 (2005), 568–576.
Besson, Bernard, *Groenland* (Paris: Odile Jacob, 2011).
Black Panther, dir. Ryan Coogler (Walt Disney Studios, 2018).
Blade Runner, dir. Ridley Scott (Warner Brothers, 1982).
Blanchot, Maurice, *The Unavowable Community*, trans. Pierre Joris (Barrytown, NY: Station Hill Press, 1988).
Borges, Jorge Luis, 'The Immortal'. In *Labyrinths* (London: Penguin, 1962), 135–149.
Bostrom, Nick, 'In Defense of Posthuman Dignity', *Bioethics* 19/3 (2005), 202–214. Web. <http://www.nickbostrom.com/ethics/dignity.html> accessed 20 March 2018.
Böttcher, Sven, *Prophezeiung* (Cologne: Kiepenheuer & Witsch, 2011).
Bould, Mark, 'Revolutionary African-American SF Before Black Power', *Extrapolation* 51/1 (2010), 53–81.
——, 'Bigger on the Inside, Or Maybe on the Outside', *Science Fiction Film and Television* 7/2 (2014), 265–285.
——, Andrew M. Butler, Adam Roberts, and Sherryl Vint, eds, *The Routledge Companion to Science Fiction* (New York: Routledge, 2009).
Bradley, James, *Clade* (Melbourne: Penguin, 2015).

Brandt, Christina, 'Narrative Strukturen im naturwissenschaftlichen Diskurs' in Christian Klein and Matías Martínez, eds, *Wirklichheitserzählungen. Felder, Formen und Funktionen nicht-literarischen Erzählens* (Stuttgart – Weimar: J. B. Metzler, 2009), 81–109.

Brantlinger, Patrick, 'The Gothic Origins of Science Fiction', *NOVEL: A Forum on Fiction* 14/1 (1980), 30–43.

Brennan, Clare, 'Brilliant Adventures – review'. *Observer*, 19 May 2013. <https://www.theguardian.com/stage/2013/may/19/brilliant-adventures-review-alistair-mcdowall> accessed 1 April 2018.

Brewster, Anne, *Reading Aboriginal women's autobiography* (Melbourne: Sydney University Press in association with Oxford University Press, 1996).

Brin, David, *Sundiver* (London: Orbit, 1996).

Brittain, David, *Eduardo Paolozzi at New Worlds* (Manchester: Savoy Books, 2013).

Broderick, Damien, 'New Wave and Backwash', in Edward James and Farah Mendelsohn, eds, *The Cambridge Companion to Science Fiction* (Cambridge: Cambridge University Press, 2003), 48–63.

Brooks, Kinitra D., *Searching for Sycorax: Black Women's Hauntings of Contemporary Horror* (New Brunswick, NJ: Rutgers University Press, 2018).

Bunbury, Stephen, 'ABC TV Indigenous series *Cleverman* provokes curiosity at Berlin Film Festival'. *Sydney Morning Herald* 23 February 2016, <https://www.smh.com.au/entertainment/movies/abc-tv-indigenous-series-cleverman-provokes-curiosity-at-berlin-film-festival-20160223-gn14q3.html> accessed 3 April 2018.

The Burden of Being, dir. Rodrick Pocowatchit (Producers: Curtis Bridenstine, Patricia Gnomes and Ian Skorodin, 2014).

Butler, Octavia E., *Patternmaster* (New York: Doubleday, 1976).

——, *Wild Seed* (New York: Doubleday, 1980).

Caccetta, W., 'Ryan Griffen's TV creation is very clever, man'. *National Indigenous Times*, 5 April 2017 <https://nit.com.au/ryan-griffens-tv-creation-clever-man/> accessed 2 April 2018.

Calinescu, Matei, 'Secrecy in Fiction: Textual and Intertextual Secrets in Hawthorne and Updike', *Poetics Today* 15/3 (Autumn, 1994), 443–465.

Callus, Ivan, and Stefan Herbrechter, 'What's Wrong with Posthumanism?' *Rhizomes* 7 (2003). Web. <http://www.rhizomes.net/issue7/callus.htm> accessed 20 March 2018.

Canavan, Gerry, *Octavia E. Butler* (Urbana: University of Illinois Press, 2016).

Čapek, Karel, *R. U. R.: Rossum's Universal Robots* (Play, 1920).

Caroti, Simone. *The Generation Starship in Science Fiction* (Jefferson, NC: McFarland, 2011).

——, *The Culture Series of Iain M. Banks: A Critical Introduction* (Jefferson, NC: McFarland, 2015).

Carrington, André M., *Speculative Blackness: The Future of Race in Science Fiction* (Minneapolis: University of Minnesota Press, 2016).

Cavendish, Dominic, 'X rivetingly marks the birth of the sly-fi genre'. *Telegraph*, 6 April 2016 <http://www.telegraph.co.uk/theatre/what-to-see/the-royal-courts-x-sees-the-birth-of-a-new-genre-sly-fi---review/> accessed 1 May 2018.

Ceballos, Gerardo, et al., 'Accelerated Modern Human–Induced Species Losses: Entering the Sixth Mass Extinction'. *Science Advances* 1/5 (2015) <http://advances.sciencemag.org/content/1/5/e1400253> accessed 31 January 2018.

Chan, Edward K., *The Racial Horizon of Utopia: Unthinking the Future of Race in Late Twentieth-Century American Utopian Novels* (New York: Peter Lang, 2015).

Charles, Alec, 'What the casting of the next Doctor Who will tell us about the BBC' in *The Conversation*, 13 April 2017. <https://theconversation.com/what-the-casting-of-the-next-doctor-who-will-tell-us-about-the-bbc-76162> accessed 2 February 2018.

Cheyne, Ria, 'Introduction: popular genres and disability representation', *Journal of Literary and Cultural Disability Studies* 6/2 (2012), 117–123.

Chiang, Ted, *The Lifecycle of Software Objects* (Subterranean Press, 2010).

Christopher, John. *The Long Winter* [US title of *The World in Winter*] (Greenwich, CT: Fawcett, 1968).

Chude-Sokei, Louis, *The Sound of Culture: Diaspora and Black Technpoetics* (Middletown, CT: Wesleyan University Press, 2015).

Cleverman, created by Ryan Griffen (Goalpost Pictures, Pukeko Pictures, Red Arrow International, ABC TV and Sundance Studios, 2016–2017).

Colvin, James, 'Introduction', in Michael Moorcock and Langdon Jones, eds, *The Nature of the Catastrophe* (London: Hutchinson & Co., 1971), vii–viii.

Conrad, Joseph, *Heart of Darkness* (New York: Dover, 1990 [1899]).

Cook, Terry, and Joan H. Schwartz, 'Archives, Records, and Power: From (Postmodern) Theory to (Archival) Performance', *Archival Science* 2 (2002), 172.

Cornea, Christine, *Science Fiction Cinema: Between Fantasy and Reality* (Edinburgh: Edinburgh University Press, 2007).

Cornick, Martyn, 'Representations of Britain and British Colonialism in French Adventure Fiction, 1870–1914'. *French Cultural Studies* 17/2 (2006), 137–154.

Coveney, Michael, 'Ken Campbell obituary'. *Guardian*, 1 September 2008 <https://www.theguardian.com/stage/2008/sep/01/obituary.ken.campbell> accessed 4 January 2018.

Crichton, Michael, *State of Fear* (London: HarperCollins, 2004).

Crosby, Alfred W., *Children of the Sun: A History of Humanity's Unappeasable Appetite for Energy* (New York: WW Norton, 2006).

Csicsery-Ronay, Istvan, Jr, 'Marxist Theory and Science Fiction', in Edward James and Farah Mendlesohn, eds, *The Cambridge Companion to Science Fiction* (Cambridge: Cambridge University Press, 2003), 113–124.

Culture Whisper (uncredited contributor), '*X*, Royal Court Theatre review'. *Culture Whisper* 7 April 2016 <https://www.culturewhisper.com/r/theatre/x_royal_court_theatre/5826> accessed 2 September 2018.
Davis, Lennard J., *The Disability Studies Reader*, 5th edn (New York: Routledge, 2017 [1997]).
Davison, Carol Margaret, *Gothic Literature 1764–1824* (Cardiff: University of Wales, Press, 2009).
de Jongh, Nicholas, 'Tears of a Clown'. *Evening Standard*, 27 September 2002 <https://www.standard.co.uk/go/london/theatre/tears-of-a-clown-7382551.html> accessed 4 November 2018.
Delany, Martin R., *Blake; or, the Huts of America* (Boston, MA: Beacon Press, 1989 [1859–1862]).
Delany, Samuel R., *The Jewels of Aptor* (New York: Ace Books, 1962).
——, *Babel-17* (New York: Ace Books, 1966).
——, *The Einstein Intersection* (New York: Ace Books, 1967).
——, *Nova* (New York: Doubleday, 1968).
——, *Dhalgren* (New York: Bantam Books, 1974).
——, *Stars in My Pocket like Grains of Sand* (New York: Bantam Books, 1984).
——, *Silent Interviews* (Hanover, NH: Wesleyan University Press, 1994).
Deloria, Vine, Jr, 'Why the U.S. Never Fought the Indians', *Christian Century* 93 (7–14 January 1976), 9–12.
DeMello, Margo, *Animals and Society: An Introduction to Human-Animal Studies* (New York: Columbia University Press, 2012).
Demlanyk, Graeme, 'New Doctor Who: "man babies" cannot cope with Jodie Whittaker as the first female in lead role' in *The Huffington Post*, 17 July 2017 <http://www.huffingtonpost.co.uk/entry/doctor-who-menbabies-jodie-whittaker-first-female_uk_596b9412e4b017418628374d> accessed 2 February 2018.
Demos, John, *The Enemy Within. 2,000 Years or Witch-Hunting in the Western World* (London: Penguin Viking, 2008).
Derrida, Jacques, *On the name*, trans. David Wood et al. (Palo Alto, CA: Stanford University Press, 1995).
——, and Maurizio Ferraris, *A Taste for the Secret*, trans. Giacomo Donis (Cambridge: Polity Press, 2001).
Dery, Mark, 'Black to the Future: Interviews with Samuel R. Delany, Greg Tate, and Tricia Rose', *South Atlantic Quarterly* 92/4 (1993), 735–778.
Deutsch, David, and Michael Lockwood, 'The Quantum Physics of Time Travel', in Susan Schneider, ed., *Science Fiction and Philosophy. From Time Travel to Superintelligence* (Hoboken, NJ: Blackwell, 2016), 370–383.

Dillon, Grace L., 'Imagining Indigenous Futurisms' in Grace L. Dillon, ed., *Walking the Clouds: An Anthology of Indigenous Science Fiction* (Tucson: The University of Arizona Press, 2012), 1–12.
——, ed., *Extrapolation* 57/1–2 (2016).
Dillon, Tom, '"Jerry Cornelius Was Oscillating Badly."' *Science Fiction Studies* 45 (2018), 161–176.
Dimaline, Cherie, *The Marrow Thieves* (Toronto: DCB, 2017).
Dine, Philip, 'The French Colonial Empire in Juvenile Fiction: From Jules Verne to Tintin', *Historical Reflections / Réflexions Historiques* 23/2 (1997), 177–203.
Disch, Thomas M., *The Dreams Our Stuff Is Made Of* (New York: The Free Press, 1998).
Donawerth, Jane, *Frankenstein's Daughters: Women Writing Science Fiction* (Syracuse, NY: Syracuse University Press, 1997).
——, 'Feminisms', in Mark Bould et al., *The Routledge Companion to Science Fiction* (London: Routledge, 2009), 214–224.
——, and Carol Kolmerten, 'Introduction', in Jane Donaweth and Carol Kolmerten, *Utopian and Science Fiction by Women: Worlds of Difference* (Liverpool: Liverpool University Press, 1994), 1–14.
Doyle, Arthur Conan, *The Lost World* (Oxford: Oxford University Press, 1998 [1912]).
EDF Energy, 'Pretty Curious' Campaign. 2017. <https://www.edfenergy.com/prettycurious> accessed 4 November 2018.
Elledge, Jonn, 'Why isn't Jodie Whittaker's Doctor Who the lead character in her own damn show?' in *New Statesman*, 7 January 2019 <https://www.newstatesman.com/culture/tv-radio/2019/01/why-isn-t-jodie-whittaker-s-doctor-who-lead-character-her-own-damn-show> accessed 26 March 2019.
Ellison, Ralph, *Invisible Man* (New York: Vintage Press, 1990 [1952]).
Erdrich, Louise, *Future Home of the Living God* (New York: Harper Collins, 2017).
Eshun, Kodwo, *More Brilliant than the Sun: Adventures in Sonic Fiction* (London: Quartet, 1998).
——, 'Further Considerations of Afrofuturism'. *CR: The New Centennial Review* 3, no. 2 (2003), 287–302.
Espronceda, José de, *Obras completas* (Madrid: Cátedra, 2006).
Evans, Richard J., *In Defence of History*, 2nd edn (London: Granta Publications, 2000).
Eve of Destruction, dir. Duncan Gibbons (Orion Pictures and Metro-Goldwyn-Mayer, 1991).
Faber, Michel, *Under the Skin* (Edinburgh: Canongate, 2014).
Faithful, George, 'Survivor, warrior, mother, saviour: the evolution of the female hero in apocalyptic science fiction film of the late Cold War' in *Implicit Religion* 19:3 (2016), 347–371.

Farscape, created by Rockne S. O'Bannon (Jim Henson Company, Nine Films and Hallmark Entertainment, 1999–2003).

Ferreira, Rachel H., *The Emergence of Latino American Science Fiction* (Middletown, CT: Wesleyan University Press, 2011).

Fink, Howard, 'Newspeak: The Epitome of Parody Techniques in *Nineteenth Eighty-Four*'. *Critical Survey* 5/2 (1971), 155–163.

Fleck, Dirk C., *Das Tahiti-Projekt* (Munich: Pendo Verlag, 2008).

——, *Das Südsee-Virus: Öko-Thriller* (Munich: Piper, 2013 [2011].

——, *Feuer am Fuss* (Murnau am Staffelsee: pMachinery, 2015).

Foley, Tim, 'Sci-fi Theatre: why it's time to embrace the weird'. *Exeunt Magazine*, 30 January 2017 <https://www.google.co.uk/search?q=tim+foley+embrace+weird&oq=tim+foley&aqs=chrome.1.69i57j69i59j35i39j0l3.2854j0j4&sourceid=chrome&ie=UTF-8> accessed 4 November 2018.

Ford, Felicity, 'Screen Dreaming in *Cleverman*: Reimagining indigenous identities', *Screen Education* 85 (June 2017), 26–35.

Foucault, Michel, *The Will to Knowledge*, trans. Robert Hurley (London: Penguin, 1988)

Fowler, Karen Joy, 'What I Didn't See' in Justine Larbalestier, ed., *Daughters of Earth: Feminist Science Fiction in the Twentieth Century* (Middletown, CT: Wesleyan University Press, 2006), 340–355.

——, *We Are All Completely Beside Ourselves* (London Serpent's Tail, 2014).

Franklin, John, *Narrative of a Journey to the Shores of the Polar Sea, in the Years 1819, 20, 21, and 22* (London: John Murray, 1823).

Frasca, Gonzalo, 'Simulation Versus Narrative: Introduction to Ludology', in Mark J. P. Wolf and Bernard Perron, eds, *The Video Game Theory Reader* (New York: Routledge, 2003), 221–236.

Freedman, Carl, *Critical Theory and Science Fiction* (Middletown, CT: Wesleyan University Press, 2000).

——, 'Hail Mary: On the Author of "Frankenstein" and the Origins of Science Fiction', *Science Fiction Studies* 29/2 (2002), 253–264.

Fusil, Casimir-Alexandre, *La Poésie scientifique en France de 1750 à nos jours* (Paris: Scientifica, 1918).

Galis, Vasilis, 'Enacting Disability: how can science and technology studies inform disability studies?', *Disability & Society* 26/7 (2011), 825–838.

Galloway, Alexander, *Gaming: Essays on Algorithmic Culture* (Minneapolis: University of Minnesota Press, 2006).

Garland-Thompson, Rosemarie, 'Feminist disability studies', *Signs* 30/2 (2005), 1557–1587.

Genzlinger, Neil, '*Cleverman* is Sci-Fi With a Social Conscience'. *New York Times* (26 May 2016).

George, Andrew R., ed., *The Babylonian Gilgamesh Epic: Introduction, Critical Edition and Cuneiform Texts*. Vol. I (Oxford: Oxford University Press, 2003).

Get Out, dir. Jordan Peele (Universal Pictures, 2017).

Ghosh, Amitav, *The Great Derangement: Climate Change and the Unthinkable* (Chicago: University of Chicago Press, 2016).

Gray, Stephen, 'Scoring the intervention: Fail grades on closing the gap, human rights', *Indigenous Law Bulletin* 8/23 (2016), 10–14.

Greenland, Colin, *The Entropy Exhibition* (London: Routledge & Kegan Paul, 1983).

Griffen, Ryan, 'We need more Aboriginal superheroes, so I created *Cleverman* for my son'. *The Guardian*, 27 May 2016 <https://www.theguardian.com/tv-and-radio/2016/may/27/i-created-cleverman-for-my-son-because-we-need-more-aboriginal-super-heroes> accessed 21 August 2018.

——, 'Imagine the untold stories we'll find with more people of colour on television'. *The Guardian*, 13 July 2017 <https://www.theguardian.com/commentisfree/2017/jul/13/imagine-the-untold-stories-well-find-with-more-people-of-colour-on-television> accessed 10 August 2018.

——, *Cleverman: Ryan Griffen*. Create NSW Arts, Screen & Culture, New South Wales Government, Sydney.

Griggs, Sutton E., *Imperium in Imperio* (New York: Modern Library, 2003 [1899]).

Guess Who's Coming to Dinner, dir. Stanley Kramer (Columbia Pictures, 1967).

Gutiérrez Rodríguez, Marta María, 'Reescrituras de los procesos por brujería de Salem en la literatura popular actual'. *El futuro del pasado,* vol. 7, 2016, pp. 85–126.

Haggard, H. Rider, *King Solomon's Mines* (Oxford: Oxford University Press, 1998 [1885]).

——, *She* (Oxford: Oxford University Press, 1998 [1886]).

Hampton, Gregory J., *Changing Bodies in the Fiction of Octavia Butler: Slaves, Aliens, and Vampires* (Lanham, MD: Lexington, 2010).

——, *Imagining Slaves and Robots in Literature, Film, and Popular Culture: Reinventing Yesterday's Slave with Tomorrow's Robot* (Lanham, MD: Lexington, 2015).

Haraway, Donna, *Primate Visions: Gender, Race, and Nature in the World of Modern Science* (New York: Routledge, 1989).

——, 'A Cyborg Manifesto: Science, Technology, and Socialist-Feminism in the Late Twentieth Century', in *Simians, Cyborgs, and Women: The Reinvention of Nature* (New York: Routledge, 1991), 149–181.

——, *Modest_Witness@Second_Millennium.FemaleMan©_Meets_OncoMouse™: Feminism and Technoscience* (New York: Routledge, 1997).

——, *When Species Meet* (Minneapolis: University of Minnesota Press, 2008).

——, 'Sowing Worlds: A Seed Bag for Terraforming with Earth Others', in Margret Grebowicz and Helen Merrick, eds, *Beyond the Cyborg: Adventures with Donna Haraway* (New York: Columbia University Press, 2013), 137–146.

———, *Staying with the Trouble: Making Kin in the Chthulucene* (Durham, NC: Duke University Press, 2016).
Hardesty, William, 'Space Opera without the Space: The Culture Novels of Iain M. Banks', in Gary Westfahl, ed., *Space and Beyond: The Frontier Theme in Science Fiction* (Westport, CT: Greenwood, 2000), 115–122.
Harrison, M John, 'The Flesh Circle', in Michael Moorcock and Langdon Jones, eds, *The Nature of the Catastrophe* (London: Hutchinson & Co., 1971), 149–164.
Hartwell, David G., and Kathryn Cramer, 'Introduction: How Shit Became Shinola: Definition and Redefinition of Space Opera', in David G. Hartwell and Kathryn Cramer, eds, *The Space Opera Renaissance* (New York: Tom Doherty Associates, 2006), 9–20.
Hassan, Ihab, 'Prometheus as Performer: Toward a Posthumanist Culture?' in Michel Benamou and Charles Caramello, eds, *Performance in Postmodern Culture* (Madison, WI: Coda, 1977), 201–220.
Hawthorne, Nathaniel, *Nathaniel Hawthorne's Tales* (New York: Norton, 2012).
Haydon, Andrew, 'Is sci-fi theatre's final frontier?' *Guardian*, 1 April 2008. <https://www.theguardian.com/stage/theatreblog/2008/apr/01/istheatrescifisfinalfrontier> accessed 7 February 2018.
———, 'X – Royal Court, London'. *Postcards from the Gods* blog, 11 April 2016. <http://postcardsgods.blogspot.co.uk/2016/04/x-royal-court-london.html> accessed 6 February 2018.
Hayes, Kevin J., ed., *The Cambridge Companion to Edgar Allan Poe* (Cambridge: Cambridge University Press, 2002).
Hayles, N. Katherine. *How We Became Posthuman: Virtual Bodies in Cybernetics, Literature, and Informatics* (Chicago: University of Chicago Press, 1999).
Heinlein, Robert A., *Orphans of the Sky* (London: Victor Gollancz Ltd, 1963). Previously published in two parts in *Astounding Science Fiction* as 'Universe' (May 1941, 9–42) and 'Common Sense' (October 1941, 102–155).
Helford, Elyce Rae (2000) 'Introduction' in *Fantasy Girls: Gender in the New Universe of Science Fiction and Fantasy Television* (Lanham, MD: Rowman & Littlefield), 1–9.
Hellekson, Karen, 'Towards a Taxonomy of the Alternate History Genre', *Extrapolation* 41 (Fall 2000), 248–256.
———, *The Alternate History: Refiguring Historical Time* (Kent, OH: Kent State University Press, 2001).
Henry, Matthew S., 'Victor and the Fish', in Joey Eschrich, Manjana Milkoreit and Meredith Martinex, eds, *Everything Change: An Anthology of Climate Fiction* (Phoenix: Arizona State University, 2016), 40–59.
Herbert, Frank, 'Greenslaves', *Amazing Stories* 39/3 (1965), 6–35.
Hernandez, Mike, 'You can't change what I look like without consulting me: the shifting racial identity of the Doctor' in Lindy Orthia, ed., *Doctor Who and Race* (Bristol: Intellect, 2013), 45–60.

Herzog, Arthur, *Heat* (New York: Signet, 1977).
Herzog, Herbert, *Some We Love, Some We Hate, Some We Eat: Why It's So Hard to Think Straight About Animals* (New York: Harper Perennial, 2010).
Higgins, David M., 'Survivance in Indigenous Science Fictions: Viznor, Silko, Glancy, and the Rejection of Imperial Victimry', in Grace L. Dillon, ed., *Extrapolation* 57/1–2 (2016), 51–72.
Hoffmann, E. T. A., *Nachtstücke* (Wiesbaden: Marix Verlag, 2013).
Hopkins, Pauline, *Of One Blood; Or, The Hidden Self* (New York: Washington Square Press, 2004 [1903]).
Houghton, J. T., G. J. Jenkins and J. J. Ephraums (eds), 'Policy Makers Summary'. *Climate Change: The IPCC Scientific Assessment. A Report Prepared for the IPCC by Working Group 1* (Cambridge: Cambridge University Press, 1990).
Hoverboard, dir. Sydney Freeland (Producers Charlene Agabao, Blackhorse Lowe and Sydney Freeland, 2012).
Hughes, William, 'The Gothic', in Rob Lathan, ed., *The Oxford Handbook of Science Fiction* (Oxford: Oxford University Press, 2014), 463–474.
Humans, created by Sam Vincent and Jonathan Brackley (Channel 4, 2015–2018). Based on *Äkta människor* [Real Humans], created by Lars Lundström (Sveriges Television, 2012).
Hunt, Herbert J., *The Epic in Nineteenth-Century France: A Study in Heroic and Humanitarian Poetry from* Les Martyrs *to* Les Siècles morts (Oxford: Basil Blackwell, 1941).
Hyginus, Gaius Julius, *De Astronomica* (San Bernardino, CA: Ulan Press, 2012).
Indigenous Comic Con <https://www.indigenouscomiccon.com/> accessed 29 July 2018.
Ingold, Timothy, ed., *What is an Animal?* (London: Routledge, 1988).
Invasion of the Body Snatchers, dir. Don Siegel (Allied Artists Pictures, 1956).
Jackson, Sandra, and Julie E. Moody-Freeman, eds, *The Black Imagination: Science Fiction, Futurism, and the Speculative* (New York: Peter Lang, 2011).
Jacobs, Naomi, 'The Frozen Landscape in Women's Utopian and Science Fiction', in Jane L. Donawerth and Carol A. Kolmerten, eds, *Utopian and Science Fiction by Women: Worlds of Difference* (Liverpool: Liverpool University Press, 1994), 190–202.
Jaeger, Stephan, 'Erzählen im historiographischen Diskurs', in Christian Klein and Matías Martínez, eds, *Wirklichketiserzählingen. Felder, Formen und Funktionen nicht-literarischen Erzählens* (Stuttgart – Weimar: J. B. Metzler, 2009), 110–135.
Jakubowski, Maxim, 'Lines of White on a Sullen Sea', in Michael Moorcock and Langdon Jones, eds, *The Nature of the Catastrophe* (London: Hutchinson & Co., 1971), 173–179.
James, Edward, *Science Fiction in the 20th Century* (Oxford: Opus, 1994).
——, '*Per Ardua ad Astra*: Authorial Choice and the Narrative of Interstellar Travel', in Jas Elsner and Joan-Pau Rubies, eds, *Voyages and Visions: Towards a cultural history of Travel* (London: Reaktion, 1999), 252–271.

——, and Farah Mendlesohn, eds, *The Cambridge Companion to Science Fiction* (Cambridge: Cambridge University Press, 2007).
Jameson, Fredric, 'Generic Discontinuities in SF: Brian Aldiss' Starship'. *Science Fiction Studies*. 1:2 (Autumn 1973).
——, *Archaeologies of the Future: The Desire Called Utopia and Other Science Fictions* (London: Verso, 2007).
Jefferies, Richard, *After London or Wild England* (Cirencester: The Echo Library, 2007 [1895]).
Jemisin, N. K., *The Fifth Season* (New York: Orbit, 2015).
——, *The Obelisk Gate* (New York: Orbit, 2016).
——, *The Stone Sky* (New York: Orbit, 2017).
Jiménez González, María Isabel, *Fantasía y realidad en la literatura de ciencia ficción de Edgar Allan Poe* (PhD Dissertation presented at the Universidad de Castilla – La Mancha – Spain – in 2013).
Jimerson, Randall, 'Archives for All: Professional Responsibility and Social Justice'. *The American Archivist* 70 (Fall/Winter 2007), 254.
Jones, Gwyneth, 'Feminist SF', in Mark Bould, Andrew M. Butler, Adam Roberts and Sherryl Vint, eds, *The Routledge Companion to Science Fiction* (London: Routledge, 2009), 484–488.
Jones, Langdon, 'Lead In'. *New Worlds Magazine* 192 (July 1969), 2–3.
Jowett, Lorna, 'The girls who waited? Female companions and gender in *Doctor Who*' in *Critical Studies in Television* 9/1 (2014), 77–94.
Joyce, Steven, 'Playing for Virtually Real: Cyberpunk Aesthetics and Ethics in Deus Ex: Human Revolution', in Graham J. Murphy and Lars Schmeink, eds, *Cyberpunk and Visual Culture* (New York: Routledge, 2018), 155–173.
Jung, Carl Gustav, *Man and His Symbols* (London: Doubleday, 1964).
Justice, Daniel Heath, *Why Indigenous Literatures Matter* (Waterloo: Wilfrid Laurier University Press, 2018).
Kafka, Franz, 'A Report to an Academy'. *The Kafka Project* (2018) <http://www.kafka.org/index.php?aid=161> accessed 31 January 2018.
Kelly, Frank K., 'Star Ship *Invincible*', *Astounding Stories*, January 1935, 10–42.
Kenward, Michael, 'The New SF, *The Final Programme, Barefoot in the Head*'. *The New Scientist*, 6 November 1969, 303–304.
Khatun, Samia, 'Beyond Blank Spaces: Five Tracks to Late Nineteenth-Century Beltana'. *Transfers* 5/3 (2015), 68–86.
Kilgore, De Witt D., 'Afrofuturism', in Rob Latham, ed., *The Oxford Handbook of Science Fiction* (New York: Oxford University Press, 2014), 561–572.
Killeen, Jarlath, *Gothic Literature 1825–1914* (Cardiff: University of Wales Press, 2009).

——, *The Emergence of Irish Gothic Fiction: History, Origins, Theories* (Edinburgh: Edinburgh University Press, 2013).
King, Stephen, *Night Shift* (New York: Anchor Books, 2011 [1978]).
——, *It* (London: Hodder and Stoughton, 2017 [1986]).
——, *The Dark Tower* (London: Hodder and Stoughton, 2017 [2004]).
Klein, Christian, and Matías Martínez, 'Wirklichkeitserzählungen. Felder, Formen und Funktionen nicht-literarischen Erzählens', in Christian Klein, and Matías Martínez, eds, *Wirklichkeitserzählungen. Felder, Formen und Funktionen nicht-literarischen Erzählens* (Stuttgart – Weimar: J. B. Metzler, 2009), 1–13.
Kolbert, Elizabeth, *The Sixth Extinction: An Unnatural History* (New York: Henry Holt, 2014).
Krobb, Florian, 'Imaginary Conquest and Epistemology in Nineteenth-Century Adventure Literature: Africa in Jules Verne, Burmann, May, and Twain'. *Children's Literature* 44/1 (2016), 1–20.
Krol, Debra, 'Nebula Award-Winning Rebecca Roanhorse is Indigenizing the Future of Science Fiction and Fantasy', *SyFyWire.com*, 27 June 2018 <http://www.syfy.com/syfywire/nebula-award-winning-author-rebecca-roanhorse-is-indigenizing-the-future-of-science-fiction> accessed 30 June 2018.
Kurtzman, Harvey, *From Aargh! To Zap: Harvey Kurtzman's Visual History of Comics* (New York: Prentice Hall Press, 1991).
LaBaff, Stephanie, *Draw Aliens and Space Objects in 4 Easy Steps: Then Write a Story* (Berkeley Heights, NJ: Enslow Publishers, 2012).
Landon, Brooks, *Science Fiction After 1900* (London: Routledge, 1995).
Langton, M., 'Whitefella Jump Up: Correspondence'. *Quarterly Essay* 12 (2003), 77–83.
Larbalestier, Justine, *The Battle of the Sexes in Science Fiction* (Middletown, CT: Wesleyan University Press, 2002).
Latham, Rob, 'The New Wave', in David Seed, ed., *A Companion to Science Fiction* (Oxford: Blackwell, 2005), 202–216.
——, 'Sextrapolation in New Wave Science Fiction'. *Science Fiction Studies*, 33/2 (2006), 251–274.
——, 'Introduction', in *The Oxford Handbook of Science Fiction* (Oxford: Oxford University Press, 2014), 1–19.
——, ed., *The Oxford Handbook of Science Fiction* (Oxford: Oxford University Press, 2014).
Lavender, Isiah, III, *Race in in American Science Fiction* (Bloomington: Indiana University Press, 2011).
——, *Afrofuturism Rising: The Literary Prehistory of a Movement* (Columbus: Ohio State University Press, forthcoming).
——, ed., *Black and Brown Planets: The Politics of Race in Science Fiction* (Jackson: University Press of Mississippi, 2014).

Lavigne, Carlen, *Cyberpunk Women, Feminism and Science Fiction* (Jefferson, NC: McFarland & Company, 2013).
Lea, Richard, 'Science fiction: the realism of the 21st century'. *Guardian*, 7 August 2015. <https://www.theguardian.com/books/2015/aug/07/science-fiction-realism-kim-stanley-robinson-alistair-reynolds-ann-leckie-interview> accessed 23 February 2018.
Leakey, Richard, and Roger Lewin, *The Sixth Extinction: Patterns of Life and the Future of Humankind* (New York: Random House, 1996).
Lefanu, Sarah, *In the Chinks of the World Machine: Feminism and Science Fiction* (London: The Women's Press, 1988).
Leinster, Murray, 'Proxima Centauri', *Astounding Stories*, March 1935, 10–44.
Lewin, Ralph A, 'Humor in Scientific Literature', *BioScience* 33/4 (1983), 266–268.
Lewis, David, 'The Paradoxes of Time Travel', *American Philosophical Quarterly* 13/2 (1976), 145–152.
Ligny, Jean-Marc, *AquaTM* (Nantes: L'Atalante, 2006).
——, *Exodes* (Nantes: L'Atalante, 2012).
——, *Sémences* (Nantes: L'Atalante, 2015).
Lindsay, David, *A Voyage to Arcturus* (London: Methuen, 1920).
Lorde, Audre, 'The Master's Tools Will Never Dismantle the Master's House', in *Sister Outsider* (Trumansburg: Crossing P, 1984), 110–113.
Lovecraft, Howard Phillips, 'The Shadow Over Innsmouth' [1936], in Lovecraft, *The Call of Cthulhu and Other Weird Stories* (London: Penguin, 1999), 268–335.
Lovelock, James, *Gaia: A New Look at Life on Earth* (Oxford: Oxford University Press, 1979).
Luckhurst, Roger, *Science Fiction* (Cambridge: Polity Press, 2005).
Lukowski, Andrzej, 'X review'. *Time Out*, 6 April 2016. <https://www.timeout.com/london/theatre/x> accessed 15 February 2018.
Lynas, Mark, *The God Species: How the Planet Can Survive the Age of Humans* (London: Fourth Estate, 2011).
McCaffrey, Anne, *Freedom's Landing* (London: Corgi, 1996).
McCarthy, Helen, *A Brief History of Manga*. Lewes: Ilex, 2014).
McDougall, Sophia, '*X* by Alistair McDowall, directed by Vicky Featherstone'. *Strange Horizons* 25 April 2016 <http://strangehorizons.com/non-fiction/reviews/x-by-alistair-mcdowall-directed-by-vicky-featherstone/> accessed 9 February 2018.
McDowall, Alistair, *X* (London: Methuen Drama, 2016).
McEwan, Ian, *Solar* (London: Jonathan Cape, 2010).
McHale, Brian, *Constructing Postmodernism* (London: Routledge, 1992).
Mafe, Diana A., *Where No Black Woman Has Gone Before: Subversive Portrayals in Speculative Film and TV* (Austin: University of Texas Press, 2018).

Malaby, Thomas, 'Beyond Play: A New Approach to Games', *Games and Culture* 2/2 (2007), 95–113.

Malm, Andreas, *Fossil Capital: The Rise of Steam Power and the Roots of Global Warming* (London: Verso, 2016).

Martín Rodríguez, Mariano, 'La fictohistoria o historiografía imaginaria en las literaturas románicas desde el siglo XIX: Ensayo de tipología y panorama de un género formal insospechado (I)'. *Revista de Filología Románica* 30/2 (2013), 285–308.

——, 'La fictohistoria o historiografía imaginaria en las literaturas románicas desde el siglo XIX: Ensayo de tipología y panorama de un género formal insospechado (II)'. *Revista de Filología Románica* 31/2 (2014), 227–244.

——, 'Discurso prescriptivo, ficción literaria y cacotopía: *La hora de la verdad*, de Santiago Eximeno, en su contexto genérico'. *Signa* 24 (2015), 425–441.

——, 'Heterotopías fictopublicitarias: "La islaTM", de Javier Fernández, y el género literario de los folletos publicitarios ficcionales'. *Pasavento. Revista de Estudios Hispánicos* IV/2 (2016), 367–387.

——, 'Terror y Filología: Rafael Llopis y los apócrifos lovecraftianos españoles (1974–1980)'. *Lovecraft 2* (Madrid: La biblioteca del laberinto, 2018a), 318–340.

——, 'The Literary Spoof Paper: An Overview'. *Journal of the Fantastic in the Arts* 28/2 (2018b), 253–270.

Matheson, Richard, *I am Legend* (New York: Orb Books, 1997).

The Matrix, dir. the Wachowskis (Warner Bros and Village Roadshow Pictures, 1999).

Menadue, Christopher B., 'Trysts tropiques: the torrid jungles of science fiction'. *eTropic* 16/1 (2017), 125–140.

——, and K. D. Cheer (2017), 'Human culture and science fiction: a review of the literature, 1980–2016'. *SAGE Open* 7/3 (2017).

Merchant, Brian, 'Behold the Rise of Dystopian "Cli-Fi"'. *Vice: Motherboard*, 1 June 2013 <http://motherboard.vice.com/blog/behold-the-rise-of-cli-fi> accessed 29 November 2016.

Metropolis, dir. Fritz Lang (UFA, 1927).

Miller, George, *40,000 Years of Dreaming: A Century of Australian Cinema* (British Film Institute, 1997).

Mitchell, David T., and Sharon Snyder, *Narrative Prosthesis: disability and the dependencies of discourse* (Ann Arbor: University of Michigan Press, 2000).

Moffitt, John F., *Picturing Extraterrestrials: Alien Images in Modern Culture* (Amherst, NY: Prometheus Press, 2003).

Moody, Nickianne, 'Displacements of gender and race in Space: Above and Beyond' in Ziauddin Sardar and Sean Cubitt, eds, *Aliens R Us: The Other in Science Fiction Cinema* (London: Pluto Press, 2002), 51–73.

Moorcock, Michael, 'A New Literature for the Space Age', *New Worlds Magazine* 48/142 (May/June 1964), 2–3.
——, 'An Effective Use of Space', *New Worlds Magazine* 49/153 (August 1965), 2–3.
——, 'Behold the Man', *New Worlds Magazine* 50/166 (September 1966), 4–58.
——, 'The Ice Schooner', in *Sailing to Utopia* (London: Millennium, 1993 [1966]).
——, 'Michael Moorcock' in Paul Welker, *Speaking of Science Fiction: The Paul Welker Interviews* (Oradell, NJ: LUNA Publications, 1978), 213–228.
——, 'The Nature of the Catastrophe', in Michael Moorcock and Langdon Jones, eds, *The Nature of the Catastrophe* (London: Hutchinson & Co., 1971), 1–8.
——, M. John Harrison, Mal Dean, and Richard Glyn Jones, 'The Adventures of Jerry Cornelius', in Michael Moorcock and Langdon Jones, eds, *The Nature of the Catastrophe* (London: Hutchinson & Co., 1971), 123–137.
——, and Langdon Jones, eds, 'Chronology', in *The Nature of the Catastrophe* (London: Hutchinson & Co., 1971), 198–213.
——, and Langdon Jones, eds, *The Nature of the Catastrophe* (London: Hutchinson & Co., 1971).
Moore, Jason W., *Capitalism in the Web of Life: Ecology and the Accumulation of Capital* (London: Verso, 2015).
Morin, Christina, *The Gothic Novel in Ireland, c. 1760–1829* (Manchester: Manchester University Press, 2018).
Morley, David, and Kevin Robins, 'Techno-Orientalism: Japan Panic', in David Morley and Kevin Robins, eds, *Global Media, Electronic Landscapes, and Cultural Boundaries* (New York: Routledge, 1995), 147–173.
Morton, Timothy, *Hyperobjects: Philosophy and Ecology after the End of the World* (Minneapolis: Minnesota University Press, 2013).
Moses, Wilson J., *Afrotopia: The Roots of African American Popular History* (Cambridge: Cambridge University Press, 1998).
Moylan, Tom, *Demand the Impossible: Science Fiction and the Utopian Imagination*. Ed. Raffaella Baccolini (Oxford: Peter Lang, 2014).
Nama, Adilifu, *Super Black: American Pop Culture and Black Superheroes* (Austin: University of Texas Press, 2011).
Nancy, Jean-Luc, *The Inoperative Community*, trans. Peter Connor et al. (Minneapolis: University of Minnesota Press, 1991).
Nelson, Alondra, 'AfroFuturism: Past-Future Visions'. *Color Lines* (Spring 2000), 34–37.
Neuhaus, Nele, *Wer Wind sät (Berlin*: Ullstein, 2011).
Nicholls, Peter, and David Langford. 'Generation Starships', in John Clute, David Langford, Peter Nicholls and Graham Sleight, eds, *The Encyclopaedia of Science Fiction* (London: Gollancz, updated 19 April 2018) <http://www.sf-encyclopedia.com/entry/generation_starships> accessed 1 May 2018.

Nicholson, Hope, ed., *Moonshot: The Indigenous Comics Collection* Volume 1 (Toronto: Alternate History Comics Inc., 2015).

——, ed., *Love Beyond Body, Space & Time: An Indigenous LBGT Anthology* (Winnipeg: Bedside Press, 2016).

——, ed., *Moonshot: The Indigenous Comics Collection* Volume 2 (Toronto: Alternate History Comics Inc., 2017).

Nicholson, Rebecca 'The 50 best TV shows of 2017: No 1 *The Handmaid's Tale*' in *The Guardian*, 19 December 2017 <https://www.theguardian.com/tv-and-radio/2017/dec/19/the-handmaids-tale-50-best-tv-shows-of-2017-no-1> accessed 2 February 2018.

Night of the Living Dead, dir. George A. Romero (Image Ten, 1968).

Orgill, Douglas, and John Gribbin, *The Sixth Winter* (London: Futura, 1980 [1979]).

Ostrowski, Witold, 'Imaginary History', *Zagadnienia Rodzajów Literackich* III/2 (1960), 27–38.

Palmer, Christopher, 'Galactic Empires and the Contemporary Extravaganza: Dan Simmons and Iain M. Banks', *Science Fiction Studies* 26/1 (March 1999), 73–90.

Patai, Daphne, 'When Women Rule: Defamiliarization in the Sex-Role Reversal Utopia', *Extrapolation* 23/1 (1982), 56–69.

Poe, Edgar Allan, *The Narrative of Arthur Gordon Pym of Nantucket* (Oxford: Oxford University Press, 1994 [1837/1838]).

——, *Complete Poems* (Chicago: University of Illinois Press, 2000).

——, *Tales and Sketches* (Chicago: University of Illinois Press, 2000).

——, *Eureka* (Chicago: University of Illinois Press, 2004 [1848]).

Pohl, Frederik, *Slave Ship* (London: Four Square, 1963).

Priest, Christopher, 'New Wave', in Robert Holdstock, ed., *Encyclopedia of Science Fiction* (London: Octopus Books, 1978), 162–173.

Pringle, Stewart. 'The play *X* will have you clock-watching – but in a good way'. *New Scientist*, 7 April 2016 <https://www.newscientist.com/article/2083397-the-play-x-will-have-you-clock-watching-but-in-a-good-way/> accessed 11 February 2018.

Prometheus, dir. Ridley Scott (Brandywine Productions, 2012).

Quinn, Karl, 'Cleverman review: Yes, it's adventurous, but don't believe the hype'. *Sydney Morning Herald*, 15 June 2016 <https://www.smh.com.au/entertainment/tv-and-radio/cleverman-review-bit-of-a-muddle-but-indigenous-drama-still-worth-celebrating-20160614-gpiu5t.html> accessed 15 June 2016.

Rabkin, Eric S., 'Conflation of Genres and Myths in David Lindsay's *A Voyage to Arcturus*'. *The Journal of Narrative Technique*, 7/2 (Spring 1977). 149.

Ratcliffe, Rebecca, 'Nobel scientist Tim Hunt: female scientists cause trouble for men in labs' in *The Guardian*, 10 June 2015 <https://www.theguardian.com/uk-news/2015/jun/10/nobel-scientist-tim-hunt-female-scientists-cause-trouble-for-men-in-labs> accessed 2 February 2018.

Red Hand, dir. Rodrick Pocowatchit (producers: Bryon Burkhead, Deanie Eaton, Claudia LittleAxe and Troy LittleAxe, 2017).

Ritter, David, 'The Judgement of the World: The Yorta Yorta Case'. *Australian Historical Studies* 35/123 (2004), 106.

Rigal Aragón, Margarita, and Ricardo Marín Ruiz, 'Poe y la anticipación científica', *Signa* 23 (2014), 91–117.

Roanhorse, Rebecca, Elizabeth LaPensee, Johnnie Jae, and Darcie Little Badger, 'Decolonizing Science Fiction and Imagining Futures: An Indigenous Futurisms Roundtable', *Strange Horizons*, Issue 30 (January 2017) <http://strangehorizons.com/non-fiction/articles/decolonizing-science-fiction-and-imagining-futures-an-indigenous-futurisms-roundtable/> accessed 22 July 2018.

——, 'Postcards from the Apocalypse', *Uncanny Magazine*, Issue 20 (January/February 2018) <https://uncannymagazine.com/article/postcards-from-the-apocalypse/> accessed 22 July 2018.

——, *Trail of Lightning* (The Sixth World: Book 1) (New York: Saga Press, 2018).

——, Twitter Account <https://twitter.com/RoanhorseBex> accessed 30 July 2018.

Roberts, Adam, *The History of Science Fiction* (London: Palgrave Macmillan, 2005).

——, *Science Fiction,* New Critical Idiom series (London: Routledge, 2005).

——, 'The Enlightenment', in Rob Lathan, ed., *The Oxford Handbook of Science Fiction* (Oxford: Oxford University Press, 2014), 451–462.

Robinson, Kim Stanley, *Pacific Edge* (London: HarperCollins, 1995 [1990]).

——, *Forty Signs of Rain* (London: HarperCollins, 2004).

——, *Fifty Degrees Below* (London: HarperCollins, 2005).

——, *Sixty Days and Counting* (London: HarperCollins, 2007).

——, *2312* (London: Orbit, 2012).

——, *Green Earth* (London: HarperCollins, 2015).

——, 'Remarks on Utopia in the Age of Climate Change'. *Utopian Studies* 27/1 (2016), 1–15.

——, *New York 2140* (New York: Orbit, 2017).

Robson, Justina, 'Aliens: Ourselves and Others', in Keith Brooke, ed., *Strange Divisions and Alien Territories: The Sub-Genres of Science Fiction* (Basingstoke: Palgrave Macmillan, 2012), 26–37.

Rochette, Jean-Marc, and Jacques Lob. *Le Transperceneige* (Tournai: Casterman, 1984).

Ruddick, Graham, 'Sun and Mail Online under fire over nude Jodie Whittaker pictures' in *The Guardian*, 17 July 2017 <https://www.theguardian.com/tv-and-radio/2017/jul/17/sun-and-mail-online-irresponsible-for-publishing-nude-new-doctor-pictures-jodie-whittaker> accessed 2 February 2018.

Russ, Joanna, 'The Image of Women in Science Fiction', in Susan Koppelman Cornillon, ed., *Images of Women in Fiction* (Bowling Green, CT: Bowling Green University Press, 1972), 79–94.

——, '*Amor Vincit Foeminan*: The Battle of the Sexes in Science Fiction'. *Science-Fiction Studies* 7 (1980), 2–15.
——, *To Write Like a Woman: Essays in Feminism and Science Fiction* (Bloomington: Indiana University Press, 1995).
——, 'The image of women in science fiction', in Rob Latham, ed., *Science Fiction Criticism* (London: Bloomsbury, 2017), 200–210.
Sallis, James, 'Jeremiad', in Michael Moorcock and Langdon Jones, eds, *The Nature of the Catastrophe* (London: Hutchinson & Co., 1971), 43–58.
Sandner, David, 'Shooting for the moon: Méliès, Verne, Wells, and the imperial satire'. *Extrapolation* 39.1 (1998).
Saunders, Emma, and Turner, Lauren, 'Jodie Whittaker and the other sci-fi women breaking the glass ceiling' in *BBC News*, 17 July 2017 <http://www.bbc.co.uk/news/entertainment-arts-40626596> accessed 2 February 2018.
Sawyer, Andy, 'Space Opera', in Mark Bould, Andrew M. Butler, Adam Roberts and Sherryl Vint, eds, *The Routledge Companion to Science Fiction* (London: Routledge, 2009), 505–509.
Schalk, Sami, *Bodyminds Reimagined: (Dis)ability, Race, and Gender in Black Women's Speculative Fiction* (Durham, NC: Duke University Press, 2018).
Schätzing, Frank, *Der Schwarm* (Frankfurt: S. Fischer Verlag 2005 [2004]).
Scheckley, Robert, 'Specialist', *Galaxy*, May 1953, 69–83.
Scholes, Robert, and Eric S. Rabkin, *Science Fiction. History. Science. Vision* (New York: Oxford University Press, 1977).
Schuyler, George S., *Black No More* (Boston, MA: Northeastern University Press, 1989 [1931]).
——, *Black Empire* (Boston, MA: Northeastern University Press, 1991 [1936–1938]).
Seed, David, *Science Fiction: A Very Short Introduction* (Oxford University Press, 2011).
Seolgungnyeolcha, dir. Joon-Ho Bong (Moho Films, 2013).
Shakespeare, Tom, *Disability Rights and Wrongs* (Abingdon-on-Thames: Routledge, 2006).
Shelley, Mary, *Frankenstein* (New York: Norton, 1996 [1818]).
——, *The Last Man* (San Bernadino, CA: CreateSpace Independent Publishing Platform, 2013 [1826]).
Shenton, Mark, '*X* review: Alistair McDowall's new play at the Royal Court theatre'. *London Theatre*, 6 April 2016 <https://www.londontheatre.co.uk/reviews/x-review-alistair-mcdowalls-new-play-at-the-royal-court-theatre> accessed 10 February 2018.
Shephard, Jack, 'Doctor Who: Peter Capaldi shares the advice he's given to Jodie Whittaker' in *The Independent*, 25 July 2017 <http://www.independent.co.uk/arts-entertainment/tv/news/doctor-who-peter-capaldi-jodie-whittaker-christmas-special-comic-con-a7858676.html> accessed 2 February 2018.
Sicart, Miguel, *The Ethics of Computer Games* (Cambridge, MA: MIT Press, 2009).

Silverberg, Robert, *Time of the Great Freeze* (San Diego, CA: Holt, Rinehart and Winston, 1964).
Silverman, Riley, 'How I regenerated along with Doctor Who' in *SyFy Wire*, 22 August 2017. <http://www.syfy.com/syfywire/how-i-regenerated-along-with-doctor-who> accessed 2 February 2018
Skyline, dir. Brothers Strause (Universal Pictures, 2010).
Slonczewski, Joan, *A Door Into Ocean* (London: Women's Press, 1987).
Smith, Cordwainer, and Genevieve Linebarger, 'The Lady Who Sailed the Soul', *Galaxy*, April 1960, 58–81.
——, *Norstrilia*. 1975 (New York: Ballantine, 1988).
Sneve, Virginia Driving Hawk, 'The Indians Are Alive', in MariJo Moore, ed., *Genocide of the Mind: New Native American Writing* (New York: Thunder's Mouth Press/ Nation Books, 2003), 297–304.
Sollée, Kristen J., *Witches, Sluts and Feminists. Conjuring the Sex Positive* (ThreeL Media, 2017).
Spinrad, Norman, *The Iron Dream* (Golden, CO: ReAnimus Press, 2013 [1972]).
Stableford, Brian M. 'Science Fiction before the Genre', in Edward James and Farah Mendlesohn, eds, *The Cambridge Companion to Science Fiction* (Cambridge: Cambridge University Press, 2007), 15–31.
——, and David Langford. 'Faster Than Light', in John Clute, David Langford, Peter Nicholls and Graham Sleight, eds, *The Encyclopedia of Science Fiction* (London: Gollancz, updated 19 May 2017), <http://www.sf-encyclopedia.com/entry/faster_than_light> accessed 30 April 2018.
Stapledon, Olaf, *Sirius: A Fantasy of Love and Discord* (London: Victor Gollancz, 2000 [1944]).
Starr, Arigon, ed., *Tales of the Mighty Code Talkers*, Volume 1 (Albuquerue, NM: Native Realities Press, 2016).
Stephens, Simon, 'Foreword', in *Alistair McDowall Plays: 1* (London: Bloomsbury, 2016), xi–xiii.
Stevenson, Robert Louis, *Strange Case of Dr. Jekyll and Mr. Hyde* (New York: Norton, 2003).
Stoker, Bram, *Dracula* (Oxford: Oxford University Press, 1998 [1897]).
Sturgis, Amy H., ed., 'A Celebration of Indigenous Fantasists' Double-Issue, *Apex Magazine*, Issue 99 (August 2017) <https://www.apex-magazine.com/issue-99-august-2017/> accessed 22 July 2018.
Suvin, Darko, *Metamorphoses of Science Fiction: On the Poetics and History of a Literary Genre* (New Haven, CT: Yale University Press, 1979).
——, *Victorian Science Fiction in the UK: the Discourses of Knowledge and of Power* (Boston, MA: G. K. Hall & Co., 1983).

Taylor, Drew Hayden, *Take Us to Your Chief and Other Stories: Classic Science-Fiction with a Contemporary First Nations Outlook* (Vancouver: Douglas & McIntyre, 2016).
Tchaikovsky, Adrian, *Children of Time* (London: Tor, 2015).
Terminator 3: Rise of the Machines, dir. Jonathan Mostow (Warner Bros Pictures, 2003).
Thaler, Ingrid, *Black Atlantic Speculative Fictions: Octavia E. Butler, Jewelle Gomez, and Nalo Hopkinson* (New York: Routledge, 2010).
Thomas, Sheree R., *Dark Matter: Reading the Bones* (New York: Warner Books, 2004).
——, ed. *Dark Matter: A Century of Speculative Fiction from the African Diaspora* (New York: Warner Books, 2000).
Thomas, Susan, 'Between the Boys and Their Toys: the Science Fiction Film', in Lucie Armitt, ed., *Where No Man Has Gone Before: Women and Science Fiction* (London: Routledge, 1991), 109–122.
Tiptree, James, Jr, 'The Women Men Don't See'. *The Magazine of Fantasy and Science Fiction* 45/6 (1973), 4–29.
——, *Her Smoke Rose Up Forever* (London: Gollancz, 2014 [1990]).
Townsend, Tess, 'Most engineers are white – and so are the faces they use to train software', *recode.net* 18 January 2017 <https://www.recode.net/2017/1/18/14304964/data-facial-recognition-trouble-recognizing-black-white-faces-diversity> accessed 21 March 2018.
Tresch, John, 'Extra! Extra! Poe Invents Science Fiction!', in Kevin J. Hayes, ed., *The Cambridge Companion to Edgar Allan Poe* (Cambridge: Cambridge University Press, 2002), 113–132.
A Tribe Called Geek <http://atribecalledgeek.com/> accessed 29 July 2018.
Tulloch, John, and Henry Jenkins, *Science Fiction Audiences: Watching Doctor Who and Star Trek* (London: Routledge, 1995).
Turner, George, *The Sea and Summer* (London: Faber and Faber, 1987).
Valerian and the City of a Thousand Planets, dir. Luc Besson (EuropaCorp, 2017).
Veracini, Lorenzo, '*District 9* and *Avatar*: Science Fiction and Settler Colonialism', *Journal of Intercultural Studies* 32/4 (2011), 355–367.
Verne, Jules, 'The Purchase of the North Pole', Part 1. *Amazing Stories* 1/6 (September 1926), 510–527.
——, 'The Purchase of the North Pole', Part 2. *Amazing Stories* 1/7 (October 1926), 616–634.
——, *Sans dessus dessous* (Paris: Union Générale d'Éditions, 1978 [1889]).
——, *Voyages et aventures du capitaine Hatteras* (Paris: Editions Gallimard, 2016 [1864]).
Vint, Sherryl, *Animal Alterity: Science Fiction and the Question of the Animal* (Liverpool: Liverpool University Press, 2010).
Wakening, dir. Danis Goulet (Producers: Glen Wool and Jordana Aarons, 2013).
Walpole, Horace, *The Castle of Otranto* (Oxford: Oxford University Press, 2014).

War of the Worlds, dir. Byron Haskin (Paramount Pictures, 1953).
War of the Worlds, dir. Steven Spielberg (Paramount Pictures, 2005).
Watercutter, Angela, '*Star Wars: The Last Jedi* will bother some people' in *Wired*, 15 December 2017 <https://www.wired.com/story/star-wars-last-jedi-inclusion/> accessed 2 February 2018.
Weick, Karl, *Sensemaking in Organizations* (London: SAGE publications, 1995).
Wells, H. G., *The Island of Doctor Moreau*. 1896. Project Gutenberg (2004) <http://www.gutenberg.org/files/159/159-h/159-h.htm> accessed 31 January 2018.
——, *The Invisible Man* (Oxford: Oxford University Press, 2017 [1897]).
——, *The Time Machine* (Oxford: Oxford University Press, 2017 [1895]).
——, *The War of the Worlds* (Oxford: Oxford University Press, 2017 [1898]).
Wharton, Edith, *The Ghost Stories of Edith Wharton* (Ware: Wordsworth Editions Ltd, 2009).
White, Richard, *Inventing Australia: images and identity, 1688–1980*, Vol. 3 (Winchester, Mass: Allen & Unwin Australia, 1981).
Whitehead, Joshua, ed., *Love After the End: Two-Spirit Utopias and Dystopias* (Winnipeg: Bedside Press, 2019).
Wierzbicka, Anna, and Cliff Goddard, 'What does "Jukurrpa" ("dreamtime", "the dreaming") mean?: A semantic and conceptual journey of discovery'. *Australian Aboriginal Studies 1* (2015), 43–65.
Wilcox, Don, 'The Voyage That Lasted 600 Years', *Amazing Stories*, October 1940, 82–104.
Wilde, Oscar, *The Soul of Man Under Socialism and Selected Critical Prose* (London: Penguin, 2001).
——, *The Picture of Dorian Gray* (New York: Norton, 2006 [1891]).
Williams, Holly, 'Alistair McDowall: the pioneering young playwright on setting a play on Pluto and sympathising with his critics', *Telegraph*, 20 March 2016 <http://www.independent.co.uk/arts-entertainment/theatre-dance/features/alistair-mcdowall-the-future-of-british-theatre-on-setting-a-play-on-pluto-and-sympathising-with-his-a6939136.html> accessed 9 February 2018.
Williams, Zoe, 'A female Doctor? She's the revolutionary feminist we need right now' in *The Guardian*, 17 July 2017 <https://www.theguardian.com/tv-and-radio/2017/jul/17/female-doctor-revolutionary-feminist-ideal-we-need-doctor-who> accessed 2 February 2018.
Willingham, Ralph, *Science Fiction and the Theatre* (Westport, CT: Greenwood Press, 1994).
Willis, Ika, 'Philology, or the Art of Befriending the Text'. *Postmedieval: A Journal of Medieval Cultural Studies* 5 (2014), 486–501.
Wilson, Daniel H., *Robopocalypse* (New York: Doubleday, 2011).
——, *Robogenesis* (New York: Doubleday, 2014).

Wilson, Tim, 'Vault Festival 2017: star-gazing', *Exeunt Magazine* 23 January 2017. <http://exeuntmagazine.com/features/vault-festival-2017-star-gazing/> accessed 4 January 2018.
Wilt, Judith, *Ghosts of the Gothic. Austen, Eliot, & Lawrence* (Princeton, NJ: Princeton University Press, 1980).
Winterson, Jeanette, *The Stone Gods* (London: Hamish Hamilton, 2007).
Wolfe, Gary K., 'Frontiers in Space', in David Mogen, Mark Busby and Paul Bryant, eds, *The Frontier Experience and the American Dream: Essays on American Literature* (College Station: Texas A&M University Press, 1989), 248–263.
Wollheim, Donald, *The Universe Makers* (New York and London: Harper & Row, 1971).
Womack, Ytasha L., *Afrofuturism: The World of Black Sci-Fi and Fantasy Culture* (Chicago: Lawrence Hill, 2013).
Wright, Alexis, *The Swan Book* (Sydney: Giramondo, 2013).
Wyndham, John, *The Kraken Wakes* (London: Michael Joseph, 1978 [1953]).
Yaszek, Lisa, 'An Afrofuturist Reading of Ralph Ellison's *Invisible Man*', *Rethinking History* 9/2–3 (2005), 297–313.
Youngquist, Paul, *A Pure Solar World: Sun Ra and the Birth of Afrofuturism* (Austin: University of Texas Press, 2016).
Zipfel, Frank, *Fiktion, Fiktivität, Fiktionalität: Analysen zur Fiktion in der Literatur und zum Fiktionsbegriff in der Literaturwissenschaft* (Berlin: Erich Schmidt, 2001).
Zoline, Pamela, 'The Heat Death of the Universe', *New Worlds Magazine* 51/173 (July 1967), 32–39.
Zumas, Leni, *Red Clocks* (New York: Little, Brown, 2018).

Notes on Contributors

RAFFAELLA BACCOLINI teaches Gender Studies and American Literature at the University of Bologna, Forlì. She has published several articles on dystopia and science fiction, trauma literature, women's writing, memory, and modernist literature. She is the author of *Tradition, Identity, Desire: Revisionist Strategies in H. D.'s Late Poetry* (Patron, 1995) and has edited several volumes, among which are *Dark Horizons: Science Fiction and the Dystopian Imagination* (with T. Moylan, Routledge, 2003), *Le prospettive di genere: discipline, soglie, confini* (BUP, 2005), *Utopia, Method, Vision: The Use Value of Social Dreaming* (also with T. Moylan, Peter Lang, 2007), *Humor and Gender: Interdisciplinary and International Perspectives* (with D. Chiaro, Routledge, 2014), and Tom Moylan's new edition of *Demand the Impossible* (Peter Lang, 2014). She is currently working on kindness, solidarity, and feminist education as utopian, political acts.

SIMON BACON has co-edited books on various subjects, including *Undead Memory: Vampires and Human Memory in Popular Culture* (2014), *Little Horrors: Interdisciplinary Perspectives on Anomalous Children and the Construction of Monstrosity* (2016), *Growing Up with Vampires: Essays on the Undead in Children's Media* (2018), *The Gothic: A Reader* (2018) and *Horror: A Companion* (2019). His monograph *Becoming Vampire: Difference and the Vampire in Popular Culture* came out in 2016. He is currently editing *Growing Up with Vampires: Essays on the Undead in Children's Media*, whilst writing his second book, *Dracula and Identity: The Absolute Otherness of Count Dracula on Screen*, due out in 2019.

MATTEO BARBAGALLO is a PhD candidate and current President of the Martin Studies International Network, the first scholarly association focused on the works of George R. R. Martin. His research focuses on a comparison between *A Song of Ice and Fire* and literary works of other linguistic backgrounds. Matteo has recently written articles for collections published by Palgrave and McFarland, and he is preparing to publish a larger volume on comparative approaches to Martin's works.

MARK BOULD is Reader in Film and Literature at UWE, Bristol. Founding editor of *Science Fiction Film and Television* journal, he now co-edits the monograph series *Studies in Global Science Fiction*. His most recent books are *The Anthropocene Unconscious* (2020), *M. John Harrison: Critical Essays* (2019), *Solaris* (2014), *SF Now* (2014) and *Africa SF* (2013).

JEREMY BRETT is Associate Professor at Texas A&M University, where he serves as the Curator of the Science Fiction & Fantasy Research Collection at Cushing Memorial Library & Archives. He has worked as an archivist for the Wisconsin Historical Society, the National Archives and Records Administration – Pacific Region, the University of Wisconsin-Milwaukee, and the University of Iowa. He is a co-founder of the Concerned Archivists Alliance, a loose collective of archivists and information professionals formed in the wake of the election of Donald Trump (<https://concernedarchivists.wordpress.com/>). His research interests include science fiction, fan history, popular culture, and archives and social justice.

DAN BYRNE-SMITH is Senior Lecturer in Fine Art Theory at Chelsea College of Arts, University of the Arts London, and is the author of *Traces of Modernity* (2012). At the time of writing, he is the Horniman Museum Art, Design and Natural History Fellow, exploring links between the museum's Natural History Collections and science fiction.

ALEC CHARLES is Dean of the Faculty of Arts at the University of Winchester. He has published in such journals as *Utopian Studies*, *Science Fiction Studies*, *Science Fiction Film & Television*, *British Politics* and the *Journal of Popular Television*; has contributed to such collections as *The Routledge International Handbook of Jungian Film Studies* and the *Directory of World Cinema: Britain*; and is the author of *Interactivity: New Media, Politics & Society*, *Out of Time: The Deaths & Resurrections of Doctor Who*, *Political Animals: News of the Natural World* and *Underwords: Re-reading the Subtexts of Modernity*.

Notes on Contributors

THOMAS CONNOLLY is a researcher currently based in Maynooth University. His research interests include theories of the posthuman and representations of disability in literature, with a particular interest in science fiction, and he has published articles on various SF authors, including Arthur C. Clarke and H. G. Wells. He served as the book reviews editor for the *Journal of Science Fiction* from 2016 to 2018, and is also a member of the Science Fiction Research Association (SFRA), serving as the current chair of the Mary Kay Bray Award, which recognises the best review or feature to be published in the *SFRA Review* each year.

JOSÉ MANUEL CORREOSO-RODENAS holds a PhD in English and American Studies from the University of Castilla-La Mancha, Spain and he is currently a post-doctoral researcher at that same institution. Among his recent publications are 'The Haunting of the Spanish Empire. (Proto-) Gothic Elements in Cabeza de Vaca's *Naufragios* and Garcilaso de la Vega's *La Florida del Inca*' (*Studia Neophilologica*) and 'A Quasi-Aesthetic Approach to the Gothic Elements in *The Picture of Dorian Gray*' (*Anglo Saxonica*). Currently, he is also a member of the research project 'Edgar A. Poe on-line. Texto e imagen' [Edgar A. Poe On-line. Texts and Images], sponsored by the Spanish Ministry of Science, Innovation, and Universities (Ref. HAR2015–64580-P) and the research group 'Estudios interdisciplinares de Literatura y Arte' [Multidisciplinary Studies in Literature and Art], sponsored by the Vicerrectorado de Investigación y Política Científica de la Universidad de Castilla-La Mancha.

TOM DILLON is a PhD candidate at Birkbeck University, researching the links between the science fiction ‚New Wave' in the UK during the 1960s and the wider literary and artistic culture. His essay,"Jerry was oscillating badly": Gender and Sexuality in New Worlds Magazine' was published in *Science Fiction Studies* in 2018.

NATHAN EMMERICH is Research Fellow in Bioethics in the Australian National University's Medical School. Having a background in Philosophy and Social Theory, his recent work has focused on end-of-life issues and the politics of (bio)ethical expertise. His contribution to this collection offers definitive proof that reading too much science fiction as a teenager can no longer be considered part of his misspent youth.

IAN FARNELL was awarded the degree of MPhil after completing his MRes in science fiction and British theatre at Warwick University. His PhD expands on this subject and is funded by the Wolfson Foundation. His article on McDowall's wider work will be published in *Contemporary Theatre Review*, and he has written for both *Foundation* and *Fantastika* journals.

MARTA MARÍA GUTIÉRREZ RODRÍGUEZ is Lecturer in English in the Department of English Studies at the University of Valladolid, in Spain. She has a BA and a Doctorate in English. Her field of research is the representation of history in literature, with a special emphasis on how the Salem Witch Trials of 1692 have been adapted and altered according to different trends that have appeared in the literature of the United States since the nineteenth century.

ISIAH LAVENDER III is Associate Professor of English at Louisiana State University, where he researches and teaches courses in African American literature and science fiction. His books include *Race in American Science Fiction* (2011), *Black and Brown Planets: The Politics of Race in Science Fiction* (2014), and *Dis-Orienting Planets: Racial Representations of Asia in Science Fiction* (2017). His latest book, *Afrofuturism Rising: The Literary Prehistory of a Movement*, is forthcoming from Ohio State University Press. Most recently, he has been named a co-editor of the oldest science fiction journal, *Extrapolation*.

SARA MARTÍN is Senior Lecturer in English Literature and Cultural Studies at the Universitat Autònoma de Barcelona, Spain. She specialises in Gender Studies, particularly Masculinities Studies, which she applies to the study of popular fictions in English, with an emphasis on science fiction and, secondarily, horror and fantasy. Among her books are *Monstruos al Final del Milenio* (2002), *Expediente X: En Honor a la Verdad* (2006), *Recycling Cultures* (ed., 2006), *La Literatura* (2008), *Desafíos a la Heterosexualidad Obligatoria* (2011) and *Persistence and Resistance in English Studies* (co-ed., 2018). She co-edited, with Fernando Ángel Moreno, a monographic issue on Spanish science fiction for *Science Fiction Studies* (2017).

CHRISTOPHER B. MENADUE is a researcher who focuses on how science fiction provides a lens through which to examine social and cultural values. He is Postgraduate Fellow of the Cairns Institute and recipient of a Commonwealth of Australia Research Training Scholarship for his PhD studies.

ANDREW MILNER is Professor Emeritus of English and Comparative Literature at Monash University in Melbourne. His publications include *John Milton and the English Revolution* (1981), *The Road to St Kilda Pier* (1984), *Cultural Materialism* (1993), *Class* (1999), *Re-Imagining Cultural Studies* (2002), *Contemporary Cultural Theory* (2002), *Literature, Culture and Society* (2005), *Tenses of Imagination: Raymond Williams on Utopia, Dystopia and Science Fiction* (2010), *Locating Science Fiction* (2012) and *Again, Dangerous Visions: Essays in Cultural Materialism* (2018).

VAL NOLAN lectures on Creative Writing and Literature at Aberystwyth University in Wales. His academic work has appeared in *Science Fiction Studies*, *Journal of Comic Books and Graphic Novels*, *Review of Contemporary Fiction*, and *Irish Studies Review*. His own fiction has appeared in *Interzone*, *Unidentified Funny Objects*, the 'Futures' page of *Nature*, and the *Year's Best Science Fiction*. His story 'The Irish Astronaut' was shortlisted for the Theodore Sturgeon Award.

CHRIS PAK is Lecturer in Contemporary Writing and Digital Cultures at Swansea University and the author of *Terraforming: Ecopolitical Transformations and Environmentalism in Science Fiction* (Liverpool University Press, 2016). More information and links to articles can be found on his website at <http://chrispak.wix.com/chrispak>.

JUAN L. PÉREZ-DE-LUQUE earned his degree in English Studies at the University of Cordoba, and a MA on English as Tool for Intercultural Communication at the University of Jaen. His PhD dissertation (2013) focused on a Žižekian approach to the ideological background found behind H.P. Lovecraft's narrative work. He currently works at the University of Cordoba as interim lecturer at the Department of English and German Studies. His main fields of interest are ideological and communitarian readings of horror fiction, witchcraft and fantasy literature in general, and he is currently involved in a collective research project that deals with the connections between secrecy and contemporary fiction, where he is focusing his attention on the narrative oeuvre of Jeanette Winterson.

MARIANO MARTÍN RODRÍGUEZ is a translator and independent scholar living in Brussels (Belgium). He obtained his PhD in Philology at the University

Complutense (Madrid) in 1994. Since then, he has published numerous studies in different languages related to modern drama, scientific romance, science fiction and speculative fiction, in Spain and in Europe, as well as several critical editions of translations from different Romance languages and English into Spanish, and several critical editions of Spanish works of fantastic, speculative and science fiction. He is currently co-editor of the online journal *Hélice* (<http://www.revistahelice.com>) and a member of the research group on utopias and future history HISTOPIA (Universidad Autónoma de Madrid).

LARS SCHMEINK is Professor of Media Studies at the Institut für Kultur- und Medienmanagement in Hamburg. He is President of the Gesellschaft für Fantastikforschung and is currently co-editing *The Routledge Companion to Cyberpunk Culture* (to be published in 2019). His other publications include *Cyberpunk and Visual Culture* (co-ed., New York: Routledge, 2017) and *Biopunk Dystopias: Genetic Engineering, Society and Science Fiction* (Liverpool: Liverpool University Press, 2016).

AMY H. STURGIS holds a PhD in Intellectual History and specializes in Science Fiction/Fantasy and Indigenous American Studies. She teaches at Lenoir-Rhyne University, serves as Editor-in-Chief of Hocus Pocus Comics, and is one of the team behind the Hugo Award-winning podcast *StarShipSofa*. She has received awards for her scholarship (from the Northeast Tolkien Society) and journalism (from the Los Angeles Press Club); learn more about her work at her official website, <http://amyhsturgis.com>.

Index

2000AD 183
2001: A Space Odyssey (1968 film) 27, 155, 199
2012 (2008 film) 151

Abe, Kobo 151
ableism 143–8
Adams, Douglas 31
Adeyemi, Tomi 105
Aeschylus 64
African diaspora 98, 102
Afrofuturism 5, 97–106, 107
    alien abduction metaphor 99, 101
Agamben, Giorgio 164
Akira 180
Alderman, Naomi 126, 129–31
Aldiss, Brian W. 26, 28, 33, 35, 43, 67, 165
Aldrich, Robert 157–8
Alien franchise 15, 28, 136, 199
aliens 3–4, 10, 43–8, 89n1, 178
    cultural origins of, 46
    as stand-ins for racial Others 45
alterity 21, 78, 80, 144
    see also Otherness
alternate histories 3, 81–88, 188–9
Ancient Greece 49, 61, 64,
Anderson, Gerry and Sylvia 181
Anderson, Poul 29
Anet, Claude 156
animals 45, 46–7, 53, 156, 161–6, 188
    domestication 156
    human use 161
    vivisection 163–4
Antarctica 17

Anthropocene 3, 155–9
anti-imperialism 118
antimatter 31
apocalypse 157
Applegate, K. A. 28
archives
    bias 169–70
    limitations and subjectivity 167
Arctic 13, 13n10
Arrival (2016 film) 159
Arseneault, Claudie 157
artificial intelligence (AI) 4, 27, 44, 45, 49–58, 59–66, 89–94
    see also robots
Asimov, Isaac 26, 29, 49–53, 68, 78, 169, 188
    Three Laws 50–51
Astro Boy 179–80
Atwood, Margaret 125–31, 133, 136, 153, 158
Australia 118, 150, 152
    Aboriginal culture 109, 117
    Dreamtime/Dreaming 117, 120
    Mabo case (1992) 120
avant-garde 33–40

Babylon 5 29
Bachelard, Gaston 91
Bacigalupi, Paolo 153, 158
Back to the Future franchise 84
Bacon, Francis 163
Bailey, Hilary 39
Bakie, Jim 183
Ballard, J. G. 33, 36, 36n4, 39
Banks, Iain M. 27, 29, 43–8

Barbarella 137, 180
Barlow, George 25
Barnes, John 158
Barnes, Steven 97
Battlestar Galactica 29, 49
Bava, Mario 89
Baxter, Stephen 151, 155
Beckett, Samuel 199
Belgium 180–81
Besson, Bernard 153
biology 3, 29, 127, 131, 188, 190
Black Panther (2018 film) 102–6
Blade Runner (1979 film) 91n2
bodies 30–31, 45, 67–70, 90, 92, 101, 120, 126, 127, 139, 143–8, 163, 199
    autonomy 147
    being versus possessing 146
Bonaparte, Napoleon 82, 189
Bong Joon-ho 152
Borges, Jorge Luis 36, 167, 190
Böttcher, Sven 153
Brackenridge, Hugh Henry 10
Brackett, Leigh 169
Bradbury, Ray 127, 157, 169, 177
Bradley, James 153
Bradley, Marion Zimmer 169
Brin, David 164–5
Brissett, Jennifer Marie 105
Bruchac, Joseph 112–13
Buck Rogers 175–6
Buckell, Tobias 105
Burdekin, Katharine 127
Burden of Being, The (2014 film) 108n6
Burroughs, William S. 38
Butler, Octavia E. 97, 104–5, 127, 155, 158, 169

Campbell, Bill 105
Campbell, Ken 193
Čapek, Karel 49, 158, 193
    see also robots; theatre
capitalism 159, 200

Captain Marvel (2019 film) 136, 137–8
Cervantes 10
Chakraborty, S. A. 2
Chalkins, Dick 175–6
Chambers, Becky 30
Charnas, Suzy McKee 127
Chiang, Ted 53–6
Christopher, John 151
Churchill, Caryl 193
Clark, P. Djèlí 105
Clarke, Arthur C. 26, 27, 169, 195
Clarkesworld (online magazine) 31
classism 36–8, 82, 145, 157, 195
Cleverman 121–3
climate change 3, 149–54, 155, 158–9, 161, 163, 165, 200
    greenhouse effect 158
    responses 152–3
climate fiction 149–54
climate refugees 159
Cold War 81, 136
Collins, Suzanne 125–6
colonialism 44–5, 102, 107, 111, 112, 118, 119, 143, 156
    Americas 111
    Australia 117–19
    colonial discourse 102, 111, 123, 159
    Manifest Destiny 107
    'Terra Nullius' 118–9, 120
comics 1, 31, 108, 108n5, 109, 175–83
Comics Code Authority 177–8
community 19–22, 98–9, 102, 126, 155–6, 163
contingency 83, 86–7
Coogler, Ryan 102–6
counterfactual history 81–2
Crichton, Michael 59, 153
crime fiction 10, 70–1, 176, 194
Crosby, Alfred W. 155
cryogenics 28
cultural appropriation 117, 120
cultural survival 112–13

cyberpunk 43, 68–73, 143, 180
cyborg 68, 94, 162–3, 178, 180
    see also robots

Dan Dare 181
DC Comics 178–9
del Rey, Lester 43
Delany, Martin R. 103
Delany, Samuel R. 26, 33, 97, 104, 169
Deloria, Vine (Jr) 107
Derrida, Jacques 20
Dick, Philip K. 143
Dillon, Grace L. 107–8, 108n7
Dimaline, Cherie 109
dinosaurs 84, 113, 156
disability 143–8
Disch, Thomas M. 33, 36n3
Divergent franchise 136
Doctor Who 49, 133–42
Donawerth, Jane 138
Dos Passos, John 38
Doyle, Arthur Conan 15
Dracula 14, 86, 89, 90, 91, 92, 93, 94
Drayden, Nicky 105
Driving Hawk Sneve, Virginia 112–3
Druillet, Philip 181n12
Due, Tananarive 105
Dunsany, Lord 189
Dwoskin, Stephen 40
dystopia 5, 73, 77–8, 108n3, 117, 125–32, 137, 153–4, 194

EC Comics 177
Elgin, Suzette Haden 127
Ellison, Harlan 33, 127
Ellison, Ralph 104
Enlightenment 9, 10, 146
entropy 33, 35, 39, 83
environmental catastrophe 77, 118, 180, 195
    see also Anthropocene; Holocene
Epic of Gilgamesh 149
Erdrich, Louise 108n4, 131

espionage 38, 44
ethics 14, 29, 49, 50–56, 68–71, 73, 77, 119, 126, 161
Eve of Destruction (1991 film) 93n3
Event Horizon (1997 film) 199
evolution 46, 68, 78, 89, 152, 155, 156, 161, 163–4, 187n3

Faber, Michael 165
Fairbairn, Zoe 127
fandom 171–2
    fanworks 171
    Indigenous Comic Con 109
    A Tribe called Geek 109
fantastic voyage myths 25
fantasy 169
Farmer, Philip José 33
Farscape 27
fascism 128, 136
faster-than-light (FTL) travel 3, 27, 28, 29, 29n2, 30
Faucette, John M. 105
feminist SF 170
First World War 84
Flash Gordon 176
Fleck, Dirk C. 153
Fleming, Ian 38
Forest, Jean-Claude 180
Foucault, Michel 141
Fowler, Karen Joy 165
France 175, 180–81
Frankenstein 2, 9, 11–12, 13, 14, 49, 67, 143
Frankenstein (1931 film) 143
Franklin, Sir John 13n10
free will 59, 62, 64, 86–7, 128
Freeland, Sydney 108n6
Fukuyama, Francis 61
fundamentalism 128

Gaia Hypothesis 153
Galvani, Luigi 67

gaming 109
Garland, Alex 89–94
Gearhart, Sandy Miller 126
Gee, Maggie 158
gender 5, 38, 45, 47, 59, 80, 90, 91–4, 100, 104, 125–31, 143, 145, 147, 165, 170, 180
    and genre 125, 133–42, 169
generation starship 27–29
genre blurring 3, 4, 77–80, 86
Geoffroy, Louis 189
Gernsback, Hugo 2, 26, 30, 151, 176n3
Get Out (2017) 97–102
Ghostbusters franchise 140
Gibson, Ian 183
Gibson, William 143
Gloss, Molly 27
Godwin, William 11
Gomez, Jewelle 105
gothic and horror 9–16, 93, 100
    see also vampires; zombies
Goulet, Danis 108n6
Gribbin, John 151
Griffen, Ryan 117, 121, 123
Griffiths, Linda Marshall 193
Griggs, Sutton E. 103

Haggard, H. Rider 14–15, 44–5
Hairston, Andrea 105
Haley, Jennifer 193
Hamilton, Virginia 105
Handmaid's Tale, The (TV series) 126, 127–9, 130, 136
Haraway, Donna 40, 68, 162–3, 165
Harrison, M. John 35, 39
Hawthorne, Nathaniel 12
Heinlein, Robert 26, 28, 29, 169
Herbert, Frank 164
heroism 44, 119, 140, 165, 190–91
Herzog, Arthur 152, 153
Herzog, Werner 90

historical fiction 82
historiography 75, 81–2, 84, 98, 99, 185, 186n2, 188–9
Hitler, Adolf 84
hoaxes 13, 187
Hobbes, Thomas 62
Hoffmann, E. T. A. 11
Holocene 151, 156
Hooper, Tobe 89
Hopkins, Pauline 103
Hopkinson, Nalo 97
Hoverboard (2012 film) 108n6
Howard, Robert E. 188
Hugo Awards 29, 105, 109, 125, 151, 169
humanity 67, 113–4, 125, 161, 163, 164
    extinction 12, 77, 161
    migration 121, 128
    urban/rural population 161
Humans (TV series) 56
Hunger Games, The 112, 125–6, 136
Hurley, Kameron 30–31
Huxley, Aldous 127
hyperobjects 159
hyperspace 29–30

identity 37–8, 45, 59, 60, 61, 62, 91, 92, 93, 104, 121, 127, 128, 131, 136, 140
    see also community
imperialism 44–5, 112, 118
    'masochism' 112
    see also colonialism
indigeneity 112, 113
Indigenous Futurisms 99, 107–116
    see also Afrofuturism; *Cleverman*
indigenous scientific knowledge 113
instinct 59, 61, 78
interventionism 44, 45, 119
Invasion of the Body Snatchers (1956 film) 91n2, 101
Ireland, Justina 105
Isayama, Hajime 180

Index

Image Comics 179
Industrial Revolution 9, 156, 162, 175n1
Island of Dr Moreau, The 2, 14, 68, 163–4

Jae, Johnnie 108–9n7, 113
Jakubowski, Maxim 39
Jama-Everett, Ayize 105
Jameson, Fredric 28, 136
Jameson, Storm 158
Japan 175, 179–80
    US occupation 179
Jefferies, Richard 150
Jemisin, N. K. 105
John W. Campbell Award 109
Johnson, Alaya Dawn 105
Jones, Gwyneth 157
Judge Dredd 183
Jung, Carl 36, 39
Justice, Daniel Heath 108–9n7, 110, 111, 114

Kafka, Franz 165
Kelly, Frank K. 26
Kennedy, John F. 81
Kim Jong-un 136
King, Stephen 13
Kirby, Jack 178
Kiss Me Deadly (1955 film) 157–8
Knight, Damon 33
Kubrick, Stanley 27, 155
Kurisato, Mari 110
Kurtzman, Harvey 177

labour 157
Lang, Andrew 190
language 120, 185
LaPensee, Elizabeth 108–9n7, 113
Larbalestier, Justine 125n1, 129n3
LatinX futurism 99
Le Guin, Ursula K. 27, 126, 133, 169, 190–91
Leckie, Ann 27, 29, 30
Lee, Stan 178

Lee, Tanith 133
Lee, Yoon Ha 30
Leiber, Fritz 33
Leinster, Murray 26
Lesser, Milton 27
Lightspeed (website) 31
Ligny, Jean-Marc 153
Lindsay, David 25
Little Badger, Darcie 108–9n7, 113
live performance 193–200
Lloyd, Saci 158
Lob, Jacques 152
London, Jack 155, 189
Lord, Karen 105
Lorde, Audre 131
lost world stories 14, 15
    see also colonialism; imperialism
Lovecraft, H. P. 13, 15, 17–24, 169, 190
Lovelock, James 153
Lucas, George 43
Lynas, Mark 155

Macaulay, Thomas Babington 190
McCaffery, Anne 26, 165
McCay, Winsor 175n1
McEwan, Ian 153
McIntyre, Vonda 126
MacLeod, Iain R. 156–7
Mad Max franchise 116–21, 123, 136, 158
mad science 12, 14, 89–94
'Many Worlds Interpretation' 85
Marvel Comics 178–9
Marvell, Andrew 157
Matheson, Richard 12, 89
Matrix, The (1999) 50, 93, 93n4
Maturin, Charles Robert 9n3
medieval imagery 25, 46
memory 19, 98, 99, 102, 167, 200
mental health 200
Merril, Judith 33
Métal Hurlant 181

#MeToo movement 136
Metropolis (1927 film) 93n3, 179
Miéville, China 157, 159
Miller, Frank 179
Miller, George 116–21, 123, 158
Mills, Allison 110
Mills, Pat 183
Miner, Horace Mitchell 190
Minister Faust 105
misogyny 82, 133, 136
Mitchell, J. Leslie 156
Miyazaki, Hayao 180
modernity 36, 98, 175n1
Moebius (Jean Giraud) 181n12
monstrosity 17–24, 78
Montesquieu 10
Moorcock, Michael 33, 35–40
    Behold the Man 39, 83
Moore, Alan 183
Moore, Ward 84
More, Thomas 25
Morris, Marcus 181
Mosley, Walter 105
Munro, Rona 133
Murnau, F. W. 90
music 97, 109
mutation 68, 78, 89, 104
    see also biology; evolution

nationalism 200
Native American activism 107
Native Hawaiians 109
Navajo Nation 114
Nebula Awards 109
Neuhaus, Nele 153
New Wave 33–40, 43, 170
Newbrough, John Ballou 25
Nicholson, Hope 108n3,n5
Niven, Larry 27, 29
normalcy 144–5
Nosferatu (1922 film) 90

Nosferatu the Vampire (1979 film) 90
Nowlan, Philip 175–6
nuclear war 12, 77, 78, 81, 93, 155, 157, 158

oil economy 156
Okorafor, Nnedi 31, 97, 105, 159
Oppenheimer, Robert 93
Orgill, Douglas 151
Orwell, George 127, 188
Otherness 22, 43–8, 75, 78, 79, 89, 90, 139, 144, 162, 163, 165, 170
    see also alterity
Otomo, Katsuhiro 180

Pacific Rim (2013 film) 159
Parks, Rosa 140
Passengers (2016 film) 28
patriarchy 127
Peele, Jordan 97–102
performance 22, 64, 91, 92, 94, 136, 198
    see also community; identity
petroculture 157–8
Piercy, Marge 126
Pierson, Brenda J. 157
Pocowatchit, Rodrick 108n6
Poe, Edgar Allen 2, 10, 12–13, 13n9
Pohl, Frederick 164
political rhetoric 75, 81
pollution 156, 180
post-apocalypse 12, 15, 105, 111, 118, 119, 125, 180, 193, 199n2
postcolonial SF 4–5, 117, 121
    decolonization 112
    'victimry' 112
    see also colonialism; imperialism
Pournelle, Jerry 27
power 44, 64, 68, 73, 93, 105, 106, 127, 128, 129–30, 131, 137, 141, 167, 169, 189
Prague Spring 39
prehistoric fiction 155–6
probability 31

Proyas, Alex 89
psychology 29, 51, 59–65, 112, 133, 144, 158
pulp fiction 2, 25, 28, 31, 36, 46, 84, 151, 152, 162, 171
Putin, Vladimir 136

Quiex, Raymond 25

race 4–5, 80, 97–106, 118–20, 130, 143, 147, 169, 170
    difference 98
    stereotypes 121–3
racism 4–5, 5n1, 82, 101, 103, 105, 121, 123, 128 145
radiation 78, 157
Raymond, Alex 176
Red Hand (2017 film) 108n6
relativity 29
religion 4, 20, 25, 47, 80, 83–4, 149, 170
    Bhagavad Gita 93
    Genesis 149, 151
Renaissance 10
Rentz, Pamela 110
Repo Man (1984 film) 158
reproductive rights 126–8
Reynolds, Alastair 26–7, 29
Rich, Nathaniel 158
Roanhorse, Rebecca 107, 107n1, 108n4, 108n7, 109, 110, 111–12, 113, 113n12, 114
Roberts, Adam 10, 29, 35n2, 48, 118
Roberts, Keith 84
Robinson, Kim Stanley 27, 28–9, 153–4, 158–9, 165, 193
robots 2, 4, 11, 49–58, 59–66, 68, 89–94, 100, 139, 144, 179–180, 193
    automata 2, 11–12, 11n6, 12n7, 13n9
    golem 49
    see also cyborg
Robson, Justina 46, 48
Rochette, Jean-Marc 152

Romero, George A. 12
Rose, Tricia 97
Rosny, J. H. 155
Ross, Gayle 113
Rowling, J. K. 188
Russ, Joanna 125, 126, 129n3, 133, 137

Salem Witch Hunts 75–80
    see also fundamentalism; religion
Sallis, James 33, 35, 39,
Samatar, Sofia 105
Sanders, William 108n2
Sargent, Pamela 126
Saunders, Charles 105
Schatzing, Frank 153
Schrödinger, Erwin 85
Schuyler, George S. 103–4
science fiction
    definitions 1–5
    'hard' and 'soft' 3, 4, 26, 185–6, 188
    history 2–3, 9–10, 15, 25–31, 33–40, 43–8, 125, 149, 170
    as 'lens' 99, 113, 118, 123, 137, 143, 146, 148, 161, 193
scientific discourse 186–91
Scotland 14, 43
Scott, Ridley 91n2, 199
Scott, Walter 11
Second World War 26, 81, 157
secrecy 14, 17–24
semantics 185
sensemaking 59–60, 61
sexism 130, 133–42, 139, 145
sex-role reversal 129–30
sexuality 56, 61–2, 126–7, 170, 172, 180
    and rebellion 127
Shakespeare, William 199
Shawl, Nisi 105
Sheckley, Robert 27
Shelley, Mary 2, 9, 11, 49, 67, 143, 150
Shirow, Masamune 180

Shuster, Joe 176
Siegel, Jerry 176
Silverberg, Robert 151
Sixth Extinction 161
Skyline (2010 film) 89n1
slavery 98, 99, 100
Slonczewski, Joan 126, 165
Sloterdijk, Peter 61
Smith, Cordwainer 27, 164
Smith, E. E. 'Doc' 25–6, 29
Snowpiercer (2013 film) 152
socialization 59
   see also community
solarpunk 157
Solomon, Rivers 105
Southland Tales (2006 film) 158
space, scale and distance of 27–28, 44
   see also time
space opera 25–32, 43–8
Spain 183
speciesism 145
Spinrad, Norman 35, 84, 158
Stableford, Brian 10n5
Stapledon, Olaf 164, 189
Staples, Fiona 179
Star Trek franchise 2, 30, 133, 136, 137, 140
Star Wars franchise 2, 30, 43, 112, 133, 134, 136, 138, 143–4, 183
Stargate SG-1 29
Starr, Arigon 108n5
steampunk 84, 156, 157
Sterling, Bruce 158
Stevenson, Robert Louis 12, 14
Stoker, Bram 14–15, 89, 90
storytelling 27, 73, 111, 114, 199n2
   see also community; historiography; identity
Strange Horizons 31, 108–9n7, 113
Stross, Charles 86
superheroes 176, 178–9
Suvin, Darko 14n11, 78, 149, 187

Swift, Jonathan 25
SyFyWire 112

Tarde, Gabriel 189
Tate, Greg 97
Taylor, Drew Hayden 108n3
Tchaikovsky, Adrian 165
technology 126, 145–8
technology vs nature 163
techno-orientalism 99
   see also Afrofuturism, Indigenous Futurisms
Tempest, John 156
Tepper, Sherri 126
Terminator franchise 49, 50, 93, 93n3, 136
Tezuka, Osamu 179–80
theatre 1, 64, 193–200
Theodore Sturgeon Memorial Award 109
Third Reich 81
Thompson, Tade 159
time 195–200
   prehistoric fiction 155–6
time travel 3, 14, 38–9, 75–80, 83–5, 133, 139, 155, 194
   paradox 79–80, 84–5
   'time police' 84
Tiptree, James (Jr) 143–4, 146–7, 165
Tolkien, J. R. R. 169
Tomb Raider (2018 film) 136, 137
Tor.com 31
transhumanism and posthumanism 45, 67–74 126–8, 180
   definitions 67–8
translation 36, 120, 151, 189
Trump, Donald 128, 136
Turing Test 52, 90
Turner, George 152, 153, 158

UK 175, 181–3
   Brexit 128
   UKIP 136

Index

Uncanny (website) 31
uncanny valley 90
US 12, 84, 107, 111, 128, 152, 175–9, 180
    Civil War 84
    political assassinations 39, 81
    Vietnam War 39, 164
utopia 10, 20, 25, 44, 45, 48, 99, 100, 108n3, 125, 126, 130, 137, 153–4, 163
    vs hope 99, 102

Valérian and Laureline 181
vampires 4, 12, 15, 86, 89–94, 100
    see also gothic and horror; zombies
Vaughn, Brian K. 179
Verne, Jules 2, 13n10, 25, 118, 169
video games 31, 59, 67–74
    design 72, 73
violence 28, 37, 39, 91, 127, 129, 130, 159, 177n6, 183
virtual reality 4, 53, 193
Vizenor, Gerald 108n2
Voltaire 10

Wagner, Pheobe 157
Wakening (2013 film) 108n6
Walpole, Horace 10n4, 11
Weird fiction 4, 17–24, 159, 177
Wells, H. G. 2, 9, 14, 25, 68, 89, 89n1, 155, 163, 164, 169, 189
    War of the Worlds, The 2, 9, 14, 89, 89n1
Wertham, Fredric 177–8n6
Westworld (TV series) 59–66
Whale, James 143

Wharton, Edith 9
Whitehead, Joshua 108n3
Wieland, Brontë Christopher 157
Wilcox, Don 28
Wilde, Oscar 14–15, 15n12
Williams, Heathcote 158
Wilson, Daniel H. 108n4
Wilson, Kai Ashanti 105
Wilson, Robert Charles 157
Winterson, Jeanette 153
witchcraft 75–88
Wolfe, Gene 28
Wolverton, Basil 176n4
women in science 138–9
Wonder Woman (2017 film) 136, 137
World Fantasy Award 109
World War Three 180
    see also post-apocalypse
world-building 19, 113, 158, 190
Wright, Alexis 153
Wright, Sydney Fowler 158
Wyndham, John 143, 151, 158

Xena: Warrior Princess 137, 172
X-Men 68, 143
    see also comics

Young, Michael 189

Zelazny, Roger 86
Zoline, Pamela 33, 39
zombies 89, 159
    see also gothic and horror; vampires
Zumas, Leni 131

www.ingramcontent.com/pod-product-compliance
Ingram Content Group UK Ltd.
Pitfield, Milton Keynes, MK11 3LW, UK
UKHW021256180426
11947UKWH00011B/809